POTSHOTS AND SNAPSHOTS II
things that made us

By many hands
Edited by Peter Morton

Cover by John White photographer.
Port Lincoln

Copyright: Peter Morton 2021

All Rights Reserved
ISBN: 978-0-6450901-3-0

CONTENTS

Part I: Animals

A Covid-19 Story of a Wombat
Peter Morton – with help! 1

Man and Wild Animals – Some Unusual Tales – Or Are They?
Peter Morton and a shy mate 4

Wolves, Dogs, Genes and the Distant Past
Peter Morton 11

My Passion for Horses
Laila Morton 18

The Kiama Dugong
Colin Gamble 22

Part II: Overseas

An American Odyssey
Jackson Croser 26

My Affair with the White Lady
Dick Matson 32

Friends in High Places
Dick Matson 48

Part III: Army

Robe 2 Recovery Story
Jacqui Bateman 62

From Farm to the Army
Terry Holden..66

Part IV: People

My Writing Life
Bill Marsh 71

George Northeast
Henning 'Chook' Kath..75

Uncle Fred Scott – The Bushman
Michael Sullivan..80

The Man Who Sings The Court of King Caractacus
Ian Bishop 87

The Day I Met Sir Robert Menzies
Gavin Stevens..97

The XVI Olympics – The Friendly Games
Aileen Pluker... 101

Dr James Murray Cotton
Robert Cotton 105

Part V: Careers

An Interesting and Adventurous Career on Eyre Peninsula
Malcolm Schluter 114

R M Williams First Boots
Peter Morton 121

Silence
Jayde Shields 127

The Stationary Wibberleys of Tumby Bay
Peter Morton 137

The Amazing Robert Bedford From Kyancutta
Peter Morton 148

Introduction AKA Blind Faith
Peter Kennedy 149

A Missed Chance
Brian Mills 162

Part VI: Adventurers

The Lady who Loves a Challenge
Sue Bishop 174

Sling Your Hook – Home is the Sailor
Capt. Rob Cobban 188

Part VII: Travel

Leaving England

Lisa Morton 203

A Motor Home Adventure

Chris and Ann Watts 210

A Nauruan Funeral

Aileen Pluker 220

Locating the Centre of Mainland Australia

Neville Gregory, Terry Hill, Rod McLeod, Ron Potter 224

Adulting is Hard

Mary Gudzenovs 231

Part VIII: Philosophy

Musings on the Year 2020

Dr Stephen Ballard 238

A Window into the Cabra Sisters' Dominican Story

Sister Angela Moloney OP 259

Part IX: Courage

Not the Good Towels

Sarah Holden 266

The Mettle of the Man

Graham Fleming 271

A Tale of Two Mates

Peter Hawke 277

Part X: Olden Days

Port Hedland – 50 Years Ago

Peter Morton & Ian Phippard 294

My Mate Oscar, Our Dads' Cars, A Stolen Car and a Gun

Peter Morton 306

Part XI: Unique Tales

John Versteeg's Compendium

John Versteeg 310

The Health of Seamen in the Royal Navy – 1762

Capt. Rob Cobban 339

The Contributors 341

INTRODUCTION

Two years ago I produced a book of 60 yarns or tales by 17 writers including myself. It was about and written by people who have lived, worked and achieved success in mainly rural South Australia, particularly Eyre Peninsula but further afield as well. It is an eclectic selection of writers and tales, mostly light hearted, some informative, some funny and some about as serious as life can be.

This second edition is addressed to a similar readership but has new writers, from 10 to 90 years old, far fewer stories by me, different settings, subjects and locations with in Australia and overseas. I hope it is successful as its predecessor.

Thanks Leonore, Mary G, Brian Mills, my modest, secret squirrel, helper and the raft of writers. Particular thanks to the Wibberley and Cotton families for allowing me to use obituaries read at their loved ones' funerals.

Last but not least of course are the 30 plus people who contributed these stories.

PM

Part I

ANIMALS

A COVID-19 STORY OF A WOMBAT

By Peter Morton – with help!

We live in Port Lincoln and suffered little in the Covid troubles of 2020 except being unable to visit our son and family in Victoria. Instead, in the spring of 2020, we decided to visit the Glendambo pub on the Stuart Highway half way between Coober Pedy and Port Augusta.

We meandered our way for four days through the Gawler Ranges, looking more like the South East than station country after good rains, to Glendambo. It is a nice pub with saddles, cowhides, shearing paraphernalia, wool bales with stencilled brands and other memorabilia from some of the biggest sheep stations in the world. They get it right, it is the real outback, not kitsch.

We set up our camper and meandered over to the bar for sundowners past three blokes lighting a barbecue. They looked familiar so I said 'G'day' to one of them who looked at me and sort of smiled as we wandered into the bar. I had a couple of schooners and Leonore two butchers of West End draught and ordered a bottle of red and perused the menu to choose the cut of steak we would have for dinner.

Next thing the bloke that looked at me came into the eating area and straight over to our table looking pretty anxious and said, 'You're Doc Morton from Lincoln aren't ya?' It was not a time to discuss the fact that I had retired and was no longer registered so I asked, 'What's up?' 'Come quick

Blackie has dislocated shoulder lifting a drum of fuel off the Cruiser.'

Blackie had suffered previous dislocations of his left shoulder and could usually reduce them but not this time. We helped him lay on the ground on his back. I removed my left boot and put my foot into his left armpit and pushed gently while pulling his arm parallel with his body and it popped back. I found a sling somewhere and put it on so he did not have to move his arm. Oh, by the way, that was the Hippocratic method of reducing dislocated shoulders and 'stockinged feet' were de riguer back in his day and still are!

When that was all fixed, as blokes do at these times, we were offered a beer and they introduced themselves. 'Blackie' and 'Linso' were fencers who I had come across years ago in Port Lincoln in their late 50s and 40s respectively and both well over 100kg and strong to go with it. The other bloke, in the fencing team was 'Wombat', in his early 20s, slim and quiet.

We were asked to share their meal. It was nice meat and with spuds and onions and the bottle of red I had remembered, made a top meal. 'Linso,' asked Leonore and me how we liked the meat and we both gave it a great wrap. He added, 'Do ya know what it is?' 'Pork?' I said and Leonore offered 'Lamb?' He replied 'Na, wombat.'

It certainly was nice and I asked how they got it. 'Linso,' answered. 'We had a job south of here and one night we went spotlighting for a feed of rabbits and shot a couple on the other side of a fence. Blackie, climbed over the fence to get them and I got out of the truck to have a pee. Next thing I know Wombat goes, "EEEHHHH a wombat, I'll get 'im" and I hear a bloody great crash, grunting and yelling. I found a torch and shone it towards the noise and dust coming from a bloody big wombat hole. When I got over there all I could were the soles of a pair of boots in the dust.'

I yelled for Blackie and dived onto the boots and held on as tight as I could. I am a big bloke and stronger than most but I was being pulled down the hole and yelled again for Blackie again but a lot bloody louder. While he was getting over the fence I got pulled down further into the hole and was really scared. Then my shoulders jammed in the hole where it went between two rocks. I thought that was good but then I realised my arms were being stretched. I couldn't believe Wombat was so heavy. Fortunately Blackie was able to sit down with his feet jammed against rocks for purchase and reach my boots between his feet. He pulled me out still holding Wombat. When I could I stood up and with Blackie pulled out Wombat and ya wouldn't want to bloody well know; he still had hold of the freakin' wombat, all 25-30kg of it and he was laughin' hit tits off and then we all were. It was not really fun and very dangerous for Wombat but geez I am enjoying eating the bastard.'

MAN AND WILD ANIMALS – SOME UNUSUAL TALES – OR ARE THEY?

By Peter Morton and a shy mate.

The Australian dingo is an apex predator in Australia and presumably arrived as a genetic variant of canines in New Guinea and other land masses north of Australia when the land bridges existed from about 37,000 to 6000 years ago when the sea reached current levels.

The link with the arrivals of Aboriginal people in Australia is tenuous. Cave paintings suggest the Thylacine or Tasmanian Tiger was here long before the dingo.

Whatever the origin the dingo killed thousands of the white man's sheep particularly in the pastoral areas of Queensland and South Australia. In an attempt to halt or at least reduce these losses a fence was built in in 1880-1885 meandering from Jimbour, near Dalby in Queensland to the west of Eyre Peninsula on the Nullarbor Cliffs near Nundroo a distance of 5614 km. It is known as the dingo fence in Queensland and dog fence in South Australia.

It is patrolled by various bodies particularly station staff and has suffered much damage over the 140 years from kangaroos, wombats, cattle, brumbies, pigs, camels and the ravages of time. The fence is to keep dingos away from the sheep on land known as the inside country.

A friend of ours was a manager of a sheep station in the north of South Australia with the dog fence as its northern boundary. It was impossible to keep dingos out indefinitely, e.g., puppies could sneak through small holes. Not only do dingos kill sheep for food they also kill in a blood lust perhaps to train their puppies. Sheep may also be killed as part of a mating ritual if they are nearby when a dog is attracted to the plaintive, begging, howling of the bitch in heat. Dogs have been seen to quickly slaughter many sheep with great efficiency and then gorge themselves with the bitch before consummating the mating. It was a constant war for him to keep the fence up to scratch and poisoning or shooting dingos on the property often from a Cessna 150 aeroplane, for many years.

In the 1980s there were suggestions that other means of control should be tried and one well publicised method advocated was to castrate the dingos to stop them breeding. My friend sat through a meeting in Port Augusta where a fellow from the green heart of Adelaide proposed this rather stupid idea to a bunch of hard-bitten station people sick of their sheep being killed immediately or suffering slow and painful deaths. People on stations care passionately about their animals. If they don't they will not be there for long.

The meeting was heated. The station people were gob smacked by the futility and impracticability of this but my mate ended the meeting when he stood up and addressed the speaker and said, 'Mate you don't seem to understand. The bloody dingos are eating our sheep not f---ing, em' and sat down. The meeting ended in an uproar.

Not long ago we discussed this meeting and dingos and he told me the following story.

'I had been at the station a few years and saw some

terrible suffering by our sheep from dingos particularly when they were in a killing frenzy. They usually lived as a family with a male, female puppies and sometimes a male from a previous litter and they could do a lot of damage. Mostly though they were solitary hunters as we did look after the fence and controlled those that did get through.

One day I found a hole in the fence and a dead sheep, the victim of a dingo. I repaired the fence and a few weeks later I found another dead sheep, killed but not savaged by a dingo.

I reckon I knew where the dog came from so I set up a 'hide' in a cane grass swamp when the wind was blowing in the right direction and the second night I was there in the morning I saw him. I had a .223 rifle with a scope, an ideal weapon for this job, so I set the cross hairs on the dog and started to squeeze the trigger. What I saw was an emaciated tired old dog. All he wanted to do was to get a feed.

Something happened to me. All I could think of were the words from the song *Old Shep*. "I just couldn't do it, I wanted to run." I did not shoot him and was glad I did not.'

My friend went on to tell me and extraordinary tale. He had recently read two stories in *Great short stories of the English-speaking world* Volume 2 published by *Readers' Digest* in 1977 he found in a trunk. One was *The Sentinel Rock* by Stuart Cloete set in South Africa and the other *Bush Boy, Poor Boy* by James Aldridge set on the River Murray four miles outside the town of St .Helen in Victoria. He started reading *The Sentinel Rock on* page 1 and read the next three stories and then *Bush Boy, Poor Boy* on page 59.

'Peter, *The Sentinel Rock* was set in South Africa before the Boer War and it was about a family's desperate struggle against drought and that is something I understand. "The inexorable drying of the ground and waterholes, the dead stinking animals, the sun sucking the water out of the ground and grass and the blood of men and beasts."

The central character is an eleven-year-old boy, Jappie Van Breda, who has to look after his six-year-old sister, his mother and the farm as his father had left two weeks before with their remaining cattle looking for food and water. His sister was an athletic, mischievous, independent and disobedient free-spirited girl who, in their world, should have obeyed Jappie, but didn't. "God had given her the energy and strength of a wild mountain buck and made her very pretty with big brown eyes and devoid of fear."

As if the drought itself was not enough trouble the farm was beset by an ever-increasing number of marauding baboons under the leadership of *Old Chaka* named by his father after the Zulu King.

The baboons ate anything that moved from scorpions to bush bucks; chickens to baby goats who they ripped open for the milk they had drunk. It was a frightening and dangerous time.

Jappie did his best to hunt the big baboon leader but he never could get a shot at him on the skyline or closer than 400 yards, too far for his .22 rifle. His father promised him a .303 rifle, every Afrikaans boy's dream, to go with the Buckskin horse he had broken in, if he killed *Chaka*. He rode far and wide bringing home game for his mother and sister but never was close to *Chaka*.

No drought lasts forever and soon a storm hit that was cold enough to kill the weakened sheep and goats but Jappie drove them into a "cup in the hills in the lee of the wind where they huddled close and warm."

He went home to find his sister missing and somehow he knew where she was and found her climbing up the huge Sentinel Rock, the guardian of the farm. There was *Chaka* 100 yards away and on the skyline. He had a clear shot but he stopped because 10 feet from him was his sister and they were communicating somehow. "An old man baboon and a girl child watching the storm-one of the great mysteries of God" He thought how *Chaka* would know the rain would end the drought. He had led them to safety. Jappie wondered whether he had prayed for rain.

Jappie decided there and then to never shoot another baboon, put down his rifle and went towards them and Chaka slipped away. The last lines in the story are "His pa was not alone any more. They were two men. He did not now need a rifle to prove it. He was a man. He knew".

'The second story took place on the Murray River as mentioned and was eerily familiar although it was written in 1951 but set some years earlier, say 1920, as a T model Ford is featured, perhaps 20 years after *The Sentinel Rock.* It was about Edgar, like Jappie, eleven years old. The family was poor and a belting from his father with a harness strap for misbehaviour common place. Like Jappie, Edgar had a rite of passage and that was to catch a twenty-pound Murray Cod and to shoot a fox. He was very capable in the bush compared to his school mates but was devastated when Tom Woodley, a rich boy from school entered his world in his father's T model Ford, shot a fox with a .22 and caught a fifteen-pound Murray cod on a line eclipsing his ten-pound catch. After this he becomes quite depressed and stops going to school concentrating on his mission in life to shoot a fox and catch the elusive cod.'

There are some funny characters Peter, as we both know, living as hermits in the Riverland, where they have water, fish, yabbies, mussels, rabbits, wombats, kangaroos and birds to eat and wood for fuel. Edgar knew one of these men and one day when he cannot find a bullet for his .22 he pinched his fathers .303 and ran back to a spot where he had seen a big fox that had long gone. All he achieved was getting a belting from his dad for pinching the .303. He weeps at night for missing the fox and decides he will try harder for the twenty-pound cod.

He enlists the help of Roy Carmichael, a fifty-two-year-old hermit, who lives nearby and is an excellent fisherman. He had owned a small paddle steamer that sunk when he was operating it when quite young through misadventure of some sort. He salvaged the steel boiler that he converted to a dwelling of sorts. He is crooked on Edgar for not working hard at school as he understands the importance of being able to read and write. Somehow Edgar talks him into letting him fish at his favourite spot and off they go. Edgar soon gets a big bite with his rod and reel despite Roy repeatedly tossing his handline over Edgar's line. But there is worse to come. Roy wrestled the Rod from Edgar and lands the fish claiming it was on his handling first, despite Edgar's weeping and begging. And it was 20 pounds.

Edgar was in a bad way for months after losing that fish, with nightmares, not eating, crying and finally giving up on the dream of a twenty-pound cod but compensates by dreaming of shooting a fox. One day he ran into Roy on Pental Island, where he had lost the other fox and describes the encounter, "After he had boxed my ears for taking a revenge shot at his fox-terrier, he began to laugh at me for bawling and howling about the fish".

All was sort of forgiven and Roy took Edgar to a place where he knows a fox comes out to hunt at dawn every day. Predictably, considering my reason for writing this, he lines the fox up, doesn't shoot, and puts the rifle down. The final lines in the story are: "I had hoped to solve the puzzle of life by killing a fox for the loss of the cod. I knew I was wrong. Life for a life. The fish didn't matter. The fox didn't matter. Tom Woodley and the town boys didn't matter. Though I had spared one life to learn so much, I had killed five or six rabbits by the time we went home. "Yes life was life; but I had it licked."

"I am not entirely sure I understand this psycho–babble mate, that is more in your line, but I did feel guilty about being too piss weak to shoot that bloody dingo but stumbling onto those yarns made me take a big breath, stick my chest out and think to myself, It was ok cobber."

WOLVES, DOGS, GENES AND THE DISTANT PAST

By Peter Morton

I owned a black Labrador for a few years before marrying Leonore in 1969 and six since including our current middle-aged lady.

They are loyal, affectionate and gentle with children and excellent watchdogs who bark but rarely bite. I had always assumed that they protected our property but a friend told us that one of our dogs only barked when we were home, not while we were out—interesting.

I had to learn with my first dog. We had been alerted by his breeder to the insatiable appetites of these dogs and fat Labs were part of the landscape. One used to visit the local butcher when the meat was delivered and of course his cuteness was well rewarded by the drivers. He became so fat his owner put a sign around his neck, 'Please don't feed me.' His face was a sad sight to see when his good mates no longer fed him.

I was keen to learn about the breed. They were named after the Canadian province as were Newfoundlands from next door. Trivia of the week is that the two provinces are now one called Labrador-Newfoundland. Both breeds were and still are used on fishing boats to retrieve net ropes or items of gear that fell overboard and for land and sea rescues in these cold and foreboding waters and landscapes. They are close relatives genetically and geographically but Newfoundlands had a Mastiff get into the gene pool somewhere hence their huge size.

When I was first aware of their appetite I thought it was a great thing biologically considering the icy world they lived in. Woodcutters in Canada are said to eat 10,000 calories a day in the winter whereas an out-door worker in temperate Australia needs 2-3000 calories. The dogs 'appetites matched their environment, a win-win situation for man and dog assuming that food was available.

That appetite satiated in Australia suburbia would certainly result in a fat and unhealthy dog unless it had a huge amount of exercise. I am pleased to say that it is not a lack of will power and moral fibre in our beloved Labradors. It is genes.

In the USA a year or so ago 300 Labradors' genetics were screened. Over 80% lacked what they called the 'satiation' gene. This is a gene that essentially told the stomach to tell the brain 'Hey I am full now. Tell me to stop eating.' So, the owner must take the places of that gene. That is hard because they look so pitiful when they want something.

They just will not listen to a rational discussion about diet and their health. It gets no traction whatsoever! Not much different to smokers I suppose.

Recently I saw a TV show, *Dog Tales* about the relationship between man and dog that was described as the most successful cross species relationships in the animal kingdom. I had a piece of cheese while writing this. My Lab's nose was a foot from my typing elbow. I turned to look at her and she wagged her tail. As soon as she saw there was no cheese left she shot off to see if Mum was a better shot.

Back to *Dog Tales*. All dogs have evolved from the grey wolf. There were three types of data presented. From archaeological digs 10,000 years old were wolf skulls identical to today. There were also other canine skulls but not wolves and not like each other.

Then there was an experiment in Russia on a farm where there were hundreds of wild foxes bred for furs I assume. Foxes' genetics are closest to wolves. They selected the most aggressive males and females and mated them for ten generations and similarly the least aggressive. They did not show the savage group but the gentle ones turned out to be as cute and cuddly as a pet puppy.

So, at this stage we know that wolves lived with humans, but so did different canines. So, with time there were physical changes and the last examples shows that breeding for certain traits can change behaviour and that should surprise no one.

Wolves are smarter than dogs but are difficult to train if they don't want to do something. Someone, somewhere asked the brilliant question. 'We assume dogs cohabited with man for food but is it possible that they like being with man, as a friend.'

They then showed an experiment with two groups (A and B) of dogs they had trained to go into a MRI chamber, an amazing feat in itself. Further training was to show group A dogs a red, non- descript soft toy and feed at 5-00pm.

Group B dogs at the same time where shown a yellow toy and loved, patted, cuddled, tickled and talked to.

The brain response was measured by MRI of one dog from

each group. The dog that was fed had a response in the feeding section of the brain that looked to be maybe 1.5 x 1cm. The dogs that were NOT fed but loved had a response throughout the whole cerebral cortex. This was caused by the release of oxytocin, serotonin and vasopressin hormones the loving, feel good, chemicals released in pleasant experiences such as orgasm in humans.

Finally, there was a discussion about a genetic condition that makes some people literally love everyone one. It was suggested that a mutation to this gene in dogs, but not wolves, occurred about 10,000 years ago.

Actually, people who have dogs know their dogs love them. We just didn't know why!

Soon after I wrote this I read the book *Sapiens A Brief History of Humankind* by Yuval Noah Harari perhaps the most extraordinary book I have read and maybe relevant to this tale about Caninekind. The first page reads in part, *About 13.5 billion years ago matter, energy, time and space came into being with the Big Bang. This is called physics.*

About 300,000 years later matter and energy made atoms and this is chemistry. About 3.8 billion years ago on Earth certain molecules formed organisms. This is biology.

About 70,000 years ago organisms belonging to the species Homo Sapiens formed elaborate cultures. This is called history.

He goes on to mention the three great revolutions that produced what humankind is today. They were the Cognitive Revolution that kick stated history about 70,000 years ago, the Agricultural Revolution 12,000 years ago and the Scientific Revolution 500 years ago that 'may well end history and start something completely different.'

How this man can get all that into 200 words that are so clear, comprehensive and understandable is extraordinary.

I wonder whether our Humankind and Caninekind species somehow formed the close relationship that we now know much more about, as part of that Cognitive Revolution.

There is fossil evidence of about six human species, the most successful and long lived were *Homo Neanderthalenis* or 'Neanderthals' who populated the cold Ice Age western Eurasia. *Homo Erectus* occupied eastern Asia and did so for two million years and last was *Homo Sapiens* that evolved in Africa 150,000 years ago and 'Drove the other humans to extinction' so that by 70,000 years ago they owned the planet and 45,000 years ago they arrived in an empty Australia. This is a complicated story but they had interbred with Neanderthals as shown by 1-4% of our DNA being from that source. Harari mentions the taming of fire for cooking and making food safer to eat, to scare predators and to burn grasslands to encourage growth. The development of a culture to allow women to cooperate with each other to forage for food and look after children was important. Harari states that , 'From 70,000 to 30,000 years ago boats, oil lamps, bows and arrows and needles (essential for sewing warm clothes together) were invented' and ' the first objects that could be called art date from this era, as does the first clear evidence of religion, commerce and social stratification.'

Other animal can cooperate with each other such as ants carting food back to their nests and lions combining to ran down prey. Chimpanzees can and do communicate but only with their family or 'tribe' who they know. It is not the size of the *Homo Sapiens* brain in fact it is significantly smaller than

Homo Erectus. 'Sapiens can cooperate in extremely flexible ways with countless numbers of strangers. That's why Sapiens rule the world, whereas ants eat our leftovers and chimps are locked up in zoos and research laboratories.'

Not all the experts agree with Harari but the idea of a mutation seems logical in that Sapiens overcame all other human kind or found out ways to live where others could not e.g., the Ice Age was fatal for the Neanderthals. Harari does describe a world that would still be nomadic, but cooked food was safer than rotten carcasses, there was more cooperation perhaps, the males had weapons to provide food and to protect their families from wild animals and other humans.

We know that there is substantial evidence of non-wolf canines in archaeological digs from 10-13,000 years ago but it is not hard to find other expeditions successful as far back as 25,000 years ago so maybe it was part of or followed from the Cognitive Revolution. Why this association between man and dog started no one seems to know but it happened a long while ago. Is it just opportunism by dogs? Surely there had to be a human benefit.

Were dogs encouraged around the camps for warning and protection maybe from Wolves? Dogs bark to scare off or warn of danger to this day. Eye contact from human to dog and vice versa is said to be unusual in animals. Perhaps our eyes with their pupil, iris and conjunctiva shared between humans and dogs is unusual. One animal staring at another is often a challenge or a threat by some animals (and some humans). The physical warmth between people and dogs may be relevant. A two or three dog night is well understood in the Australian bush.

And of course, feeding would attract and keep dogs around. Interesting fossil studies have found cracks and chips on the teeth of dogs found amongst human debris and that was considered as evidence of being in contact with humans in that the damage over time suggested their diet was bones, hooves, horns i.e., human left overs. Wolf fossils found away from camps were in great shape with the nice little comment. 'They ate Mammoth steak.'

I cannot prove why the relationship between dogs and humans is so close but I certainly think it is more than just the provision of food. A normal pet dog loves his/her mum and dad. I believe that implicitly and I do not know how a guide and assistance dogs that have an extra year of training could begin to do their work without some sort of a person to dog bond and vice versa. Maybe the good old MRI will have more to say in time to come.

MY PASSION FOR HORSES

By Laila Morton

The first time I rode a horse I was about 3 years old on holiday in New Zealand. You might think that if I started at 3 and now, I am 10 I could almost be a professional at horse riding but no I am not. I have been riding on and off. When I was 3 the first horse, I rode was a palomino and its name was Paddington.

Later on, when I might have still been 3 or 4 years old, I went on a blackish brownish coloured horse called Dangermouse. I went on my first trail ride, someone was holding the lead rope and guided me across. The ride felt so long then but if I went back now it would have been really a short ride.

When the holiday was over my family and I went back to the Northern Territory, we then moved to Chinchilla, Queensland. I still didn't show much interest in horses. We stayed there or about 9 months then we moved to Shepparton, Victoria.

I was about 5 years old then when I started school, then my brother got cancer. Which was very sad. We went to some Camp Quality family camps to help families have fun with cancer. The last one we went to was a country one. On the last day we went horse riding and I really enjoyed that. I went on a trail ride by myself on a big black horse called Mr T.

I think this is when I fell in love with horses, it might have been because it was in my blood, or when I saw my mum go horse riding it looked like fun and I thought I would enjoy it too.

One day Harry (my brother) got a care package that was sent by Red Kite, another Cancer charity for families, with lots of toys and sport equipment. It was pretty unfair that most of that stuff was for Harry but I did get to share it too. Then I received a voucher for horse riding with my horse instructor in Shepparton and she told me I could have 6 free horse lessons which was very nice.

It went really quick, so Mum said if I enjoyed it that much, I could have more horse riding lessons just not for free this time. So we did. I was riding on a horse called Pepper. He was a very calm old nice horse (I think he was in love with me because he would cuddle me and let me kiss his nose.)

I had 1 or 2 horse lessons with another horse called Oakey. Oakey was a sweet horse, he was taller, he was younger, he was way cheekier, he also would not listen as much. He was a Palomino. So that is pretty much everything you need to know about him. He is still nice, sweet and as cuddly as Pepper.

When I am better at horse riding, I would like to be a horse jumper. I would like to jump on horses and maybe do dressage if that isn't too hard. I was about a week away before I could start jumping, but then we had to go into lockdown because of the Coronavirus so I have not ridden since January 2020.

Since then, I have been dreaming of getting my own horse over and over again. When I fall asleep, I want to dream about horses but the strange thing is that I need to look at horse pictures first to get a good-looking horse in my mind otherwise I might picture a donkey, or a camel. So, looking through my horse books before I fall asleep helps.

Most nights I have been reading factual horse books and horse encyclopedias. They are very interesting, and in the horse encyclopedia I found my favourite horses in it. It's an Appaloosa and a Tersk, the Tersk is my favourite and the Appaloosa is my second but they are really good horses.

The Tersk and Appaloosa are great jumping horses, they are bred to jump. The Appaloosa is a great horse with a great posture [according to the picture] so that means that it will be a good jumping horse like the Tersk.

Here are some facts or things you should know about the Appaloosa and the Tersk.

1. Tersk: stands at about 15hh, the colour of the Tersk is mostly grey but very occasionally chestnut and was bred in the USSR.

2. Appaloosa: Stands at about 14-15.2hh the colour of the Appaloosa is spotted and was made in the United States.

The Appaloosa and Tersk are both warm blooded horses which is a good balance between cold blooded, who are bred for heavy work and hot blooded who are bred for speed. Both these breeds temperament is easy going and they are sociable which makes them a great horse all round.

Finally, I got to go horse riding again on Saturday 19th September 1920, that was a long wait. I rode a chestnut-coloured horse called Bonnie, she was 20 years old and 15 hands high which is a name for the height and is called a Galloway. She was still fast at trotting even at 20 years of age, I enjoyed doing rising trot and steering her in and out of the cones as it was quite challenging for me.

So that was the story of how my passion for horses started.

Sorry one more thing, yes silly me. Ok, I've moved to Whyalla, South Australia now and I had to have my last horse-riding lesson in Shepparton which really sucked. I love horses and horse riding which you probably already know so, I'm going to tell you what my last day of horse riding was like.

It was Friday the 26th of February 2021, I was really nervous because it was my last day of horse riding at Sally's place and let me just say Sally, the horse-riding instructor, she was great, she really was. The last day was probably one of the best days. I cantered by myself, I trotted by myself and I guided Ollie (the horse I rode) across the paddock with poles on the ground and barrels to ride around.

So that's pretty much it. I had a great time and hopefully I will find a person to do horse stuff with in my new home town Whyalla (don't tell my mum but if I can't I might get a horse instead yay).

And that's the story of how my passion for horses started. Now I'm finished bye, thanks for reading.

THE KIAMA DUGONG

By Colin Gamble

When I was a boy in the 1950s I often went to cattle sales on Saturday with my father. It was great but after the sales I had to wait in the Ute while Dad was in the pub.

One Saturday the sale was at the Showgrounds in Kiama, a lovely coastal town about 25 km South of Wollongong. The cattle came from Buderoo National Park situated on top of Jamberoo Mountain. In those days many cattlemen used national parks as stock runs. These cattle were born on the mountain and not handled like cattle on flat country so some were wild when mustered now and then to go to a sale. For some reason this sale was held at the show cattle judging yards which were very poor yards indeed.

Almost at the end of the sale in came a big red cow breathing fire and brimstone. She was so wild and agitated the yardman luckily escaped the yard. Just as she was knocked down to my old man she jumped over the fence, luckily where no one was sitting.

From the yards the cow ran towards the oval where a cricket match was recessed for lunch. She ran thru a gate, across the pitch and exited out a gate on the far side. When she first escaped from the sale yard, Dad, myself and a few of his mates ran to a car and followed her. We drove around the oval and saw her leave the oval and run towards the edge of the showground. From there she ascended a steep incline onto a rock platform next to a calm ocean and incredibly we saw her plunge into the water and strike out for somewhere East. Someone in the car suggested we go to the nearby harbour and see if there was a boat. Sure enough there was a man in a long boat with no cabin powered by an big old inboard motor near the water's edge and after a quick conversation he agreed to try to rescue the cow. We chugged out the harbour and after a while saw her swimming just behind the entrance to the Kiama "blow hole". We came up beside her spent, due to a swim of about 400 metres. We put a rope around her horns to keep her head up and another bloke held her tail to stop her drowning. We turned the boat around and chugged back into the harbour with the cow tucked in beside the boat. As we neared the beach the boys let her go and she staggered near the water's edge where she collapsed completely buggered. While she lay there the boys were hatching a plan on how to get her back to the show ground. After about 15 minutes she got up on all fours, glared at us with us glaring back at her. Both sides were pondering this latest development when suddenly from down the beach came yapping little dog. This dog was the catalyst for her to turn around and leave the beach and take off towards the town.

Crossing the street between curious onlookers the cow headed for the Brighton Hotel. The Brighton was built in 1835 and had about 70 accommodation rooms, a dining room, saloon bar, public bar and lounge bar. Most notably, the Brighton Pub was where Don Bradman spent his honeymoon. Unfortunately, the Brighton was demolished some 20 years ago.

Back at the pub someone had left the door to the public bar open and that is where this mad cow entered. We arrived just after she went in and could hear the noise of people screaming, table, chairs and glasses hitting the floor. As luck would have it the cow somehow got into the back yard passing thru the kitchen where she was subdued. Later a truck reversed into the yard and our wild cow meekly climbed the ramp onto the truck. What a day and this was my first ride in a boat!

Years later, before he died, my Dad and I were reminiscing over a whiskey and he stated that this cow was the wildest thing he had ever seen but there was no way she broke so many glasses as the pub made Dad pay for 50 broken glasses.

Part II

OVERSEAS

AN AMERICAN ODYSSEY

By Jackson Croser

So, America... let's just stay it's kicked off a lot differently to what I expected. Who would have thought a global pandemic would be under way during the once in lifetime event. We have coped as well as possible with whatever restrictions are in place.

When Dad was offered the job to work in the USA, the decision to accept depended heavily on me as Mum and Dad knew that University, work and study might take priority. Of course, I took the opportunity as how many 19-year-old Aussies would get to live, travel and experience the USA for two years? Of course, this meant leaving my closest mates and girlfriend at the time when we had shared the hardest years of school. That was one of the toughest, hardest experiences I've had to go through but in the end I knew that an opportunity like this would not come again. I am a firm believer that whatever happens and however long it takes, if something is meant to be, then it will be. Any sadness and regrets I may have are softened via modern technology. It's great to be able to keep in contact with everyone back in Australia with video chats and social media. I am so jealous about their trips to the pub... damn it, the drinking age over here are 21 and over.

We have been incredibly fortunate and this is the icing on

the cake. We lived in England when I was 12 to 13, and I wasn't old enough to appreciate the different cultures, landscapes, cities, food, people, countries and the cost of travelling. We travelled through a large part of Europe when I was 13. I didn't appreciate it as much as the USA as I am older with a different mind-set Don't get me wrong though, I sure thought it was pretty crazy good at that age. At 19, I've travelled to almost 20 countries in the world, from Fiji, to Japan, Indonesia, most of Europe and now the US. There's no doubt how fortunate and grateful I am for the opportunities I have had.

High School in the States was an unforgettable experience. I'm now lucky enough to have graduation certificates in both Australia and the USA and the pictures of me all kitted out to go with them. I imagine it must be relatively rare to have done that and I certainly do not know anyone who has. The common question from my mates is: "What is school like over there?" and generally I give a simple answer of: "It's like the movies. Lockers lining the hallways with a herd of students rolling through them without school uniforms to make their way to the classic joint table and chair that was not designed for 6'3"people. Graduation was also the movie style cap and gown with the presentation of diplomas with Covid-friendly practices in place.

The sport opportunities were quite different to what I expected. With my past years of playing Rugby League I was eager to have a crack at some American Football but when I moved over, the football season didn't line up so I had an attempt at baseball. It was great to get amongst it and have a go but going up against guys who have played since being in nappies, sorry diapers, in the baseball capital of the world more than beyond outshined a foreign bloke who's never played. Let's just say that foreign bloke didn't make the team but I still had a fun experience though. I did get introduced to the local Rugby Union team in my area, the Southern Pines Jokers, by some mates at school. In comparison to baseball, I can say I had an upper edge with experience and knowledge on how to play compared to the Americans. Here I met my Welsh Coach whom I now work for, fulltime as a landscaper at Colonial Landscapes. Who would have predicted I'd play a non-American sport with a Welsh coach and become a landscaper? This has opened many doors for the near future, one of course having cash to travel and experience America as planned. The job type essentially being in the construction industry also provides experience for when I get back home and get into carpentry and building management.

With the U.S being such an enormous country with so many different things to see it's impossible to experience them all. In our living room, we have a large map with all the places the family wants to visit, including New York City, the Grand Canyon and Disneyland. The luxury we have is we can chip away as we please in comparison to flying from Australia to have maybe a month to see as much as possible. Unfortunately, Mr. Covid has heavily impacted what we're able to do. Our snowboarding trip to Park City, Utah was cancelled, a real let down but there was nothing we could do. In situations like that, it helps to be positive and I well remember and am grateful for what we have. I've already travelled to Los Angeles, Tennessee, the Outer Banks, some amazing Lakes and some gorgeous mountain ranges. North

Carolina and its neighbouring states have got some of the most stunning landscapes imaginable. My plan for traveling more distant states is currently underway as I now have a mountain bike to ride and camp in the state parks. I've wanted to get into mountain biking since living in England. How humorous I had to move to another country to finally commit to actually getting a bike.

I can't stress how much of a crazy opportunity it has been so far and I thank Dad and Mum for the opportunity. Even being here for 9 months when writing this, it still gets to me that I am actually living in the United States of America. No wife, no kids, it's the time in my life where it's the best for me to have these experiences and I'm going to take as many opportunities thrown at me. I have to say though, I do miss Australia.

It is now 2021, my second year living in The States, the short future is looking significantly better than 2020. The year finished in Colorado, celebrating only my second white Christmas with the family snowboarding some of the world's most renowned ski resorts, Breckenridge and Keystone. To be able to fly halfway across the country seems quite absurd considering how strict Covid restrictions were when we wanted to snowboard in Utah at the beginning of 2020. Now's the time to take those opportunities before anything changes. The shared experience we had together was just simply amazing for the fact we're not used to the scale and beauty of the mountains in Colorado in comparison to Australia. Australia just doesn't have anything of that scale which makes sense Aussies travel to Colorado for skiing. Colorado was unforgettable but the solo trip I took shortly after was quite significant for me.

Early in the New Year, I had a snowboarding trip to Washington State at a resort called Steven's Pass. This trip was a milestone as I've never travelled to that extent completely by myself. With a rented Jeep Wrangler I drove through breathtaking landscapes on the snow-covered roads. The highlight of the trip was the sheer quantity of snow that mother- nature decided to turn on. I couldn't have gotten any luckier with my timing of this trip. The first two days I was snowboarding, Stevens Pass received 86cm of snow. To put that into perspective, Perisher in Australia receives an average annual snowfall of approximately 200cm. Stevens Pass almost got that in one week.....For everyone that has skied or snowboarded through powder, you know the indescribable feeling it is. It's just something that brings a smile that can't be wiped. Even writing this, I'm grinning. With the snowboarding completed and a few drives through the back roads on Washington, I took the scenic route back to Seattle for my departure which included a few stops plus a day's worth of sightseeing of what Seattle had to offer. I'm immensely grateful that I was able to have the opportunity to experience that part of the globe.

I will say solo traveling and traveling with family both have their pros and cons. The beauty of travelling by yourself is that you do everything and only the things that you want to do at your own pace. Feel like sleeping in a little longer? No problem. Having the shared experiences together though is still important, especially with family. Even though the trip to Washington was amazing, I'm glad I got to celebrate a white Christmas with my family somewhere different. Solo traveling doesn't involve irritating siblings but at the same time traveling with your siblings can be pretty special.

As mentioned earlier with 2021 looking brighter, the family and I are keen for trips we have planned in the coming months. Some of the trips include, Miami, Texas, the Grand Canyon and more.

My next trip is a Mother/Son trip to Texas. With a road trip planned to the major cities and stops along some small Western towns, I'm just excited to see another part of America whilst having the experience with Mum. Shortly after Texas, the family and I are again off to Colorado to snowboard Vail. Our goal was to snowboard quite often whilst in the States as you can't beat the snow quality. No better time than now. I'm also excited for a solo trip planned across northern Arizona and southern Utah for approximately 11 days. The planned trip involves mountain biking some of the best destinations in the world and exploring some of the most stunning national parks that America has to offer such as the Grand Canyon and Zion National Park. The trip is most likely to have a shared experience at the Grand Canyon with the family over the weekend then solo traveling for the rest. I'm looking forward to experiencing another part of America which is entirely different to what I've travelled to and experienced in my lifetime.

So far traveling across the country has provided the most enjoyable, unforgettable experiences whilst over here and I can't wait to see where the rest of 2021 is going to take me.

MY AFFAIR WITH THE WHITE LADY

By Dick Matson

I slung on my backpack and bent over to pick up my trekking poles after a mid afternoon break on our way down from the mountain pass which marks the international border between Italy and France. The guide and the rest of our party were still in sight but having stretched the break out longer than the rest, they were nearly 100 meters down the trail from me. As I straightened up I was suddenly overwhelmed by a violent stabbing and tearing sensation in my lower back. It was as if someone drove a white-hot ice pick handle-deep into my lumbar spine. I had never experienced anything like this. The pain was so intense my knees immediately buckled and I gasped involuntarily as I dropped to the ground. I remained there on all fours trying to regain my breath, fight through the pain, and understand what had just happened. I worried that I might not be able to make it to the hamlet of Ville des Glaciers still a 5-6 km descent, where we were going to be picked up and driven to Beaufort, France where we were planning to spend the night.

It was day 5 of our 7-day Tour de Mont Blanc (TMB), a trek around Mont Blanc, the highest mountain in the Alps, located in eastern France where the borders of Italy and Switzerland intersect. The 170 km TMB is one of the top alpine treks in the world and takes about 11 days if you walk the entire route.

For me it was the trip of a lifetime. I was used to multi day backpacking trips where you schlepped a 40-pound pack, pitched your own tent, slept on the ground, and cooked your own meals, but this was a proper "gentleman's" trip. Most days we were given a choice of a hard or easy hike. Each morning after breakfast we were driven to a predetermined trailhead and released for the day with our guide and a daypack. After 5-7 hours of trekking including a leisurely lunch stop – often a hot one at one of the rustic alpine refuges along the way – we would be met at a different trailhead late in the afternoon and whisked away to our hand-picked hotel for a warm shower, hot dinner, and a comfortable bed. While we were hiking, our luggage would be transported for us between hotels. After a hot breakfast the next morning we'd do it all over again each day for seven days until we'd circumnavigated the entire mountain beginning and ending in Chamonix, France.

This particular trip started in late August, 2012. The idea was conceived earlier that year when Ken Hartung, one of my former partners from our days together in the insurance business, suggested it. I was 65 then and he was 77 but we were both in good physical condition. I had been running regularly for cardio vascular fitness since I was 30 with a goal of 1,000 miles a year. Over 35 years I can count on one hand the number of years I didn't make that goal and then it was usually because of a running injury. Ken and I were also backpacking mates. In the years prior we typically did one multi day round-the-mountain trek each summer somewhere in the Pacific Northwest of the USA. A year or two prior we had even hiked down into the bowels of the Grand Canyon from the south rim to Phantom Ranch where we spent the night and then climbed back out. These were all challenging trips. Ken and his wife Anne had gone on a number of guided walking trips throughout Europe with a Portland, Oregon based tour operator called Walking Softly Adventures. The company was owned and operated by John and Amy Osaki. They had recently formed a sister company called Mountain Hiking Holidays and John was considering a TMB trip that summer that he was going to lead so he could recon the route, scout the hotels, and sample the local cuisine. It didn't take long for us to agree to make that our summer 2012 backpacking trip.

Some years earlier my wife Sheri and I had befriended an Italian couple, Marco and Chicca Micheli. Their primary home is in Genoa, Italy but they have a chalet in Les Houches, France on the flanks of Mont Blanc about 8 km southwest of Chamonix. We had visited and travelled before with them in Italy and they had visited and travelled with us in Oregon and Washington. When they learned of our TMB plans they invited us to stay with them in Les Houches for a few days before and after our trek.

Sheri, Ken, and I flew to Geneva, Switzerland and were picked up by Marco and Chicca at the airport mid-day on Sunday, August 26th. It was a sunny day and the Mont Blanc Massif, a collection of 11 major peaks along a granite mass each exceeding 4,000 m, came into view on the drive to Les Houches. It was absolutely spectacular. The massif is draped in snow the entire year and covered with dozens of glaciers. Mont Blanc itself is sometimes referred to as "the White Lady" or in French, "La Dame Blanche." Many of the other major peaks in the massif are steep and sharp as needles and some are, in fact, named after the French word for needle (aiguille"), such as Aiguille d'Argentière, Aiguille du Chardonnet, Aiguille du Tour, etc. The Micheli's were excellent hosts and introduced us to the area while we recovered from jet lag and prepared for the TMB. Their chalet is perched above the village and has dramatic unobstructed views of the mountain out of all of the windows that face it. The exquisite meals and conversations we enjoyed together on their back deck while watching the constantly changing colours and shifting shadows on the towering white mountain as the sun set in the west were unforgettable.

Late in the afternoon on Wednesday, August 29th, we left Chicca and Sheri in Les Houches and Marco drove Ken and I to Chamonix to the hotel where we were to meet the rest of our group for the TMB. Chamonix is a picturesque mountain town, a year around international tourist destination, and the home of the first Winter Olympics in 1924. John Osaki greeted us at the hotel. We had dinner there during which John introduced us to our local guide, Matthew, and gave us an overview of the days ahead. As it turned out, only one other couple, Randy and Cheryl, from Colorado had signed up so we had the good fortune to get a lot of personal attention from John and Matthew over the days to come.

Our itinerary called for us to spend Days 1 and 2 hiking two areas not far from our hotel in Chamonix. Then we would begin leap-frogging around the mountain in a clockwise fashion stopping for the evenings at hotels in Champex, Switzerland (Day 3), Courmayeur, Italy (Day 4), Beaufort, France (Day 5), and Contamines-Montjoie, France (Day 6) before returning back to Chamonix (Day 7).

The first few days were overcast and cool with rain at times. On Day 1 we rode the cable car from Chamonix up to La Flegere, a high meadow-covered bench at 1,877 m elevation which serves as a departure point for a network of trails and spent the day hiking to several alpine lakes.

On Day 2 we took the cable car from the nearby village of Le Tour to the Col de la Balme (2,195 m) which marks the border between France and Switzerland and then hiked down on the Swiss side through the Triente Valley finishing up in the post-card village of Triente.

On Day 3 we hiked from the Col de la Forclaz (1,527 m) up to a saddle called Fenêtre d'Arpette (2,665 m) ("Fenêtre" is French for window). This is one of the highest points on the entire TMB where we were to be rewarded with some spectacular views, however, upon arrival it was snowing and clouds swirled all around us limiting our visibility to a few hundred meters in any direction. Disappointed, we descended to our hotel in Champex.

Our route on Day 4 took us from the hamlet of Ferret up to the Grand Col Ferret (2,537 m) where we crossed from Switzerland into Italy and then descended to Arp Nouvaz for transport to our hotel in Courmayeur. This day's views of the Italian side of Mont Blanc were some of the best because of the elevation we were hiking, the closeness of some of the nearby peaks and the long deep verdant valleys that separated them, and the fact that this was our first mostly sunny day.

Day 5 began at the hamlet of La Visaille. We hiked up the long gradual upslope that was Val Veni ("Val" is French for valley) passing several glacial lakes before stopping for lunch. After lunch we hiked up to the Col de la Seigne, crossed into France, and began our descent to Ville des Glaciers. It was on that descent at about 3:00 in the afternoon that my accident happened. While still on the ground recovering my breath, I could see the rest of our group. They were oriented downhill and out of voice range so no one saw me drop to the ground or heard me cry out. I struggled to regain my feet supported by my trekking poles and slowly put one foot in front of the other to see if I could walk. The pain in my lower back changed in character to an aching, burning, and throbbing sensation but remained no less intense. Although it was an effort, I determined that I could still walk aided by my trekking poles and began plodding downhill in a futile attempt to re-join the others.

Matthew was in the rear of the group ahead when he turned to look back in my direction. He saw that I was having trouble and came back to see what the problem was. After I explained, we continued slowly downhill. We had a long unobstructed sight line ahead of us all the way down to the Ville des Glaciers at the bottom of the valley now perhaps 5 km ahead of us. With the help of his binoculars Matthew reported he could see John's vehicle parked at the trailhead. Using one of the walkie-talkies he and John used to communicate, he raised John and explained what had happened. At one point as we continued to make our way downhill, they talked about calling for a helicopter to bring me down but when I got wind of that I waived them off telling them I thought I could make it to the vehicle which I could now see with my unaided vision. As we continued I could feel my back slowly stiffening up adding to the pain and impairing my already limited mobility. Realizing that Matthew and I were missing, the rest of the group had stopped and waited until we caught up. As we resumed the descent together the level of pain slowly increased almost to the point where I couldn't tolerate it. I began to regret declining the helicopter assist but didn't say anything.

Eventually, we got to the trailhead and I was shoe-horned into the front right side passenger seat of John's vehicle and we began the drive to Beaufort. The road was narrow, steep, and winding. During the hour it took us to get there I squirmed constantly shifting from side to side trying to find a position where the pain might subside a bit but was never successful. Arriving at our hotel in the early evening, John parked immediately in front of it while everyone unloaded. Someone opened my door. Matthew and Ken came over to help me get out but after putting my feet on the ground and raising up from the seat I collapsed in the street like a falling-down drunk. My legs could not bear my weight without giving way underneath me. With one arm draped over each of their shoulders Matthew and Ken carried me into the hotel and up to my room where I flopped down on the bed. While there, Matthew established that one of the local doctors was still in his office. He and Ken got me back in the vehicle and off we went.

The doctor was cordial and spoke good English. After taking a history, hearing my complaints, and doing a brief exam he suspected I had herniated a disc in my lower back. He recommended we drive to the nearest hospital in Albertville, France (the site for the 1992 Winter Olympics) where they had imaging equipment and could make a more definitive diagnosis. Albertville is only about 20km southwest of Beaufort but it got dark and seemed like an eternity before Matthew arrived at the emergency room entrance. I was helped into a wheel chair and after being admitted and getting a CT scan the ER doctor also suspected an injured disc in my lower back. They apparently didn't have a neurosurgeon on staff as he explained that he was going to send the images to one in Grenoble, a little more than 80 km southwest of Albertville, for an opinion. It was now about midnight and he said I would have to spend the night to be monitored and in the morning after hearing back from the neurosurgeon they would have a better handle on a treatment recommendation. Matthew had the good sense to stop by the hotel on our way out of Beaufort to grab my luggage so he left everything with me before saying good bye and driving back to the hotel.

When I awoke in my hospital room Tuesday morning, September 4th, the pain had subsided in response to some medication I had been given but I had almost no feeling in my left leg and lying on my back I could not raise either of my legs off the surface of the bed. I had my cell phone among my personal items so I called Sheri and gave her an update. The doctor on call stopped by later in the day to tell me he had heard from the neurosurgeon and he said I had herniated a disc in my lumbar spine. The doctor got my attention when he said my progress over the next few days was going to be critical and depending upon how things unfolded, I may need surgery in the next few days although they were not yet ready to make that recommendation. He explained that in a worst-case scenario, I may never be able to walk again and added that it was highly unlikely I'd be able to return home that Friday, as we had originally planned. I had enjoyed excellent health all my life and never before spent a day in the hospital so this was quite a sobering turn of events. I was now immobile, over 5,000 miles from home, and in a hospital in a country where I didn't speak the language. That afternoon, I emailed Carrie, my legal assistant, at my office in Vancouver, Washington requesting she fax a copy of my health insurance policy to the hospital (as they had requested a copy) and chase down some information for me on the extent of coverage I might have for an accident on foreign soil.

When I awoke on Wednesday, I could see immediately that there had been some improvement as I was able to move my legs a bit. I was further cheered up with a visit in the afternoon from Sheri, Marco, and Chicca. Thursday arrived with more good news. With the help of a walker, I was able to make it to the bathroom under my own power and even took a much-needed shower that afternoon. More good news came when I heard from Carrie that my health insurance provided coverage for this accident subject to a deductible and co-payment. Sometime that day, the attending physician said that as long as I continued to show improvement they were encouraged by my progress and that a decision on surgery could wait until I returned home. He said that with three conditions, he would be agreeable to discharging me on Saturday, September 8th. The conditions were that I would have to be taken by an ambulance from the hospital to the airport so that I could lay flat on my back during the trip, that I would have to upgrade to a business class seat so I could do the same on the plane during the 9-hour flight home, and that upon returning home I consult with a neurosurgeon to discuss further treatment.

I had an uneasy feeling that things were going too well and that I was overdue for some bad news. It arrived late that afternoon from an imperious and cold-hearted discharge nurse who stopped by to tell me that before I could be released on Saturday, I would have to pay my bill in full in cash. When I asked how much it would be, she said she wouldn't be able to tell me until Saturday. She refused to even give me an estimate. I am a trained negotiator but could not get her to cut me an inch of slack. She refused to take my insurance arguing that I could submit my own claim for reimbursement when I returned home. Measuring the anticipated bill in my own mind using an American yardstick I was expecting it to be in the neighborhood of mid five figures (in U.S. dollars) because that's what it would have been at home for a comparable stay. I simply did not have that amount of cash immediately available nor could I raise it in two days. I was at wit's end in short order.

After she left the room, I thought to myself that this nurse reminded me of someone and then it came to me. It was Nurse Ratched from the 1975 movie, *One Flew Over the Cuckoo's Nest* based on a novel written by Oregon author Ken Kesey. According to Wikipedia:

"Nurse Ratched [was] the head administrative nurse at the Salem State Hospital, a mental institution where she exercise[d] near-absolute power over the patients' access to medications, privileges, and basic necessities such as food and

toiletries. She capriciously revoke[d] these privileges whenever a patient displease[d] her. Her superiors turn[ed] a blind eye because she maintain[ed] order, keeping the patients from acting out, either through antipsychotic and anticonvulsant drugs or her own brand of psychotherapy, which consist[ed] mostly of humiliating patients into doing her bidding."

Friday arrived with more progress. A physical therapist I had seen earlier in the week left a pair of forearm crutches in my room for me to experiment with. They are designed to take some weight off your legs while you ambulate. I gave them a try and found I could walk short distances in the hallway outside my room without too much difficulty. That afternoon I had another visit from Sheri, Marco, and Chicca. After explaining my dilemma, we discussed our limited options and hatched an escape plan. Hearing that I would likely be discharged on Saturday, Sheri had managed to change our flight home to early Sunday morning. Marco and Sheri would come back to the hospital on Saturday at 1:00pm and park immediately outside the main entrance. Before they arrived, I would get myself fully dressed and use the forearm crutches to walk out as if I owned the place timing my arrival at the main entry for Marco's arrival. Hopefully, Nurse Ratched would be busy tyrannizing some other hapless patient and the rest of the staff would not notice or if they did, they wouldn't fully appreciate that an escape was in progress. I would take only my wallet and my cell phone and leave the rest of my luggage in my room so as not to arouse more suspicion than necessary. Upon reaching Marco's car, I'd get in and he'd drive us straight to the airport where Sheri had reserved a room at an adjacent hotel to make it easier to catch the early morning flight on Sunday. After we got home, I would submit a claim to my health insurance carrier and pay any difference to the hospital.

My good fortune returned on Saturday morning. Nurse Ratched stopped by to give me my bill and while it was in Euros, I knew what the exchange rate was, and I was astonished to see that it was only about a tenth of what I had expected. I knew I was on a roll when she agreed to take my credit card for payment. A bit later, the attending doctor that I'd been working with stopped by to give me some pain medication for the trip home and copies of my medical records so that I could convey them to the neurosurgeon I had agreed to consult when I got back. Given the progress I had made that week, he even agreed to forego the requirement that I be transported to the airport by ambulance when I explained that Marco was prepared to drive me there and that his front passenger seat could be reclined. I called Sheri to convey the good news. She, Marco, and Chicca arrived at the hospital a few hours later. I was transported with my luggage by wheelchair to their vehicle and by late afternoon we arrived at the airport hotel in Geneva where we said good bye to our friends and checked in.

Early the following morning we were shuttled from the hotel to the departure area of the airport. Sheri had arranged for a wheel chair transport to the departure gate and it was not long before it arrived. After checking in we were whisked to the gate by-passing normal security and utilizing the abbreviated lines typically limited to the flight crews. A short time later we were comfortably ensconced in our business class seats. Mrs. Matson wasted no time ordering some French champagne while I reclined and let my pain medications do their work.

Epilogue

After arriving home, I continued to make good progress although for the first few weeks I needed the help of a strong medication to keep the pain manageable. Within a few days, I consulted a neurosurgeon by the name of Dr Rokas. He took a history, examined me, took the French medical records I brought for him, ordered an MRI scan, and told me he'd contact me after he could get the records translated and reviewed along with the MRI scan he ordered. I got the MRI scan done and waited for his call. By then, I was able to walk short distances without crutches and I returned to work. A few days later, I received a voice mail at work stating, "Mr Matson, this is Dr Rokas. You need surgery. Call me."

Now, I hope this doesn't sound arrogant because I certainly don't mean it to be. While I am not a medical professional, for a layman I have a better than average understanding of back injuries and treatment modalities. For the first 10-15 years of my litigation practice I cut my teeth defending personal injury cases and have defended dozens of traumatically induced back injury cases (car crashes, slip and falls, products liability, etc.) all the way from minor soft tissue injuries to quadriplegics. I have attended classes taught by medical professionals on the anatomy of the spine, mechanisms of injury, treatment options, and how to read medical records. I have reviewed thousands of pages of medical records, examined many doctors including orthopaedic surgeons, neurosurgeons, and physiatrists in depositions and at trial, and even retained my own such medical professionals to consult with and assist in the defence of these cases. Based on my experiences, I had formed the opinion that conservative treatment (rest, medication, physical therapy) was about as effective as surgery in treating cases like mine where I was still making physical progress and the pain was manageable. And, of course, there's no guarantee that further harm won't occur as result of surgery even in cases where an excellent surgeon has met the standard of care.

I went back to see Dr Rokas. He confirmed that with the aid of the MRI, I had herniated a disc at L3-4 in my lumbar spine and that it was impinging on a nerve root that was causing radiating symptoms down my left leg. The symptoms I was experiencing could go on indefinitely and it might be as long as a year or more before I became medically stationary (reached a point where I could not expect to get better with further treatment or the passage of time). We had a good discussion of how my condition might progress over time and the treatment modalities available. I decided to forego surgery, at least for the time being.

Although some lower back pain continued, within a few weeks I was able to wean myself off the prescription medication and after a few months I noticed I no longer had constant pain. I had a variety of intermittent neuromuscular symptoms in my left leg the most significant being a tendency for my left knee to buckle without warning. Sometimes, I could catch myself before falling. Other times, I went down like a sack of potatoes. A few months after the incident, I stepped off a curb coming out of a restaurant and fell into a busy street. A few months after that, I fell at home and broke four ribs and bruised two others. I have paraesthesia (pins and needles) in my left leg from above my knee to above my ankle. Occasionally, I experience spasms in the muscles of my left thigh, sharp stinging sensations around my left knee, and aching and throbbing in my left hip and knee.

About a year passed before I sensed I was close to being medically stationary. My left quadriceps muscles had atrophied visibly by that point. Today the circumference around my left thigh is nearly an inch and a half less than my right thigh. I have a modest loss of strength and control in my left leg. It's challenging for me to balance on my left foot. All of the neuromuscular symptoms continue to come and go randomly except that my knee no longer buckles to the point where I fall.

In 2018 I had an episode of a few weeks duration where the symptoms were so regular they would wake me up at night and prevent me from getting back to sleep. Over-the-counter medications were of no help. My regular doctor prescribed a stronger pain medication and physical therapy. I worked with a physical therapist he referred me to for about six weeks and she prescribed a series of exercises for me to do daily. The symptoms abated significantly and then eventually went away. I now do a half hour of physical therapy nearly every morning and only occasionally have painful symptoms but not to the point of requiring medical attention or prescription medications. Several times over the years I've tried to resume running but it takes too much effort and energy to maintain a proper gait so, I gave up and began a program of regular walking. I now walk at least 20 miles per week most weeks. I also do an hour of strength training twice a week. In the last few years I've also added cycling to the mix. I've resumed hiking and have been on three multi day backpacking trips since the accident.

All things considered, I am pleased with where I am physically and I have no regrets about declining surgery. I am fortunate to be able to enjoy most of the things I used to before the accident with minimal impairment and for the most part, no significant pain. To a large degree, I can mitigate any recurring symptoms by continuing physical therapy and I am highly motivated to continue to do that. Life is good.

FRIENDS IN HIGH PLACES

By Dick Matson

It was a sunny Friday morning in late August 1975 - we had survived the Arab Oil Embargo (summer 1973), the resignation of President Nixon following the Watergate scandal (August 1974), the end of the Viet Nam War (April 1975). My wife, Sheri, and I were speeding eastbound on Interstate Highway 84 through the heart of the scenic Columbia River Gorge on our way to meet friends for an amazing horse-back adventure into the Eagle Cap Wilderness in north-eastern Oregon. This trip had been over a year in the making.

At the time, we were in our late twenties and had been married for six years and we were living and working in Portland, Oregon. It was two years before our first child would arrive and it was one of those rare times when we had the freedom and the resources to embark on an epic adult adventure. Our drive that day would take about six hours including a lunch stop. After leaving the Columbia River Gorge behind us we travelled through the high desert country of central Oregon and then crested Cabbage Hill and Deadman Pass along the original route of the Oregon Trail into the Blue Mountains. At the town of La Grande we left the interstate highway for the last leg of our drive heading northeast on State Highway 82, also known as the Wallowa Lake Highway, into the Grande Ronde Valley. Our destination was the home of Bob Chrisman, in the small farming and ranching town of Wallowa, a community of about 800 people at the time.

Before my mid-life career change to the legal profession I spent seventeen years in the insurance business and met Bob in about 1972 in the course of our work in that business. He had deep roots in Wallowa County having been born and raised there. In 1972, after a short career in education, he joined an independent insurance agency in Wallowa that had been started by his father. As an independent agency, his firm represented multiple insurance companies. It was likely the most successful such agency in the county.

I worked as a marketing representative for United States Fidelity & Guaranty Company, a Baltimore based insurance company that no longer exists, out if its Portland-based branch office. I was encouraged and expected to wine and dine my agents. I had a company car, a generous expense account, and regularly drove some of the most scenic back roads in the Pacific Northwest covering my territory.

My job was to provide technical assistance to our agents in the field in support of their efforts to develop and place commercial insurance business with my company. I loved that job. I had a portfolio of about thirty independent agents and travelled extensively throughout the northern half of Oregon and southwest Washington.

I came to understand that insurance people, were usually extroverts and often the movers and shakers in their communities. Bob Chrisman was no exception. He was big strapping gregarious guy that I immediately liked. He was a four-year letterman in basketball in college. His hobbies included fishing, hunting, sports, and camping. He passed away in 2011 and in his obituary it was accurately stated that, "He especially enjoyed conversation and spent countless hours talking to friends and family."

So, not only was he an easy guy to spend time with, but Bob held court in one of the most scenically spectacular parts of the state. The Wallowa mountain range located in his backyard is one of the smallest in the Pacific Northwest but what it gives up in size is more than made up or in scenic grandeur. Unlike the isolated volcanic peaks of western Oregon's Cascade Range, the Wallowas consist of dozens of clustered granite peaks approaching heights of 10,000 feet separated by glacier-carved valleys and high alpine meadows spotted with numerous lakes. For reasons that become obvious to visitors, the region is often called the "Alps of Oregon" or "Little Switzerland." The mountain range itself is one of the Seven Wonders of Oregon.

While Bob's agency was one of the furthest away and most geographically remote from my office in Portland, I looked forward with anticipation to each of my trips to Wallowa and frequently sought ways to extend my time there or leverage my business trips into a personal vacation. During one business trip in the summer of 1974, Bob invited Sheri and me to join his family on a back country horse packing trip they were then planning for the following summer into the Lakes Basin in the Eagle Cap Wilderness which is within the Wallowa Mountains. The plan was to hire an outfitter who would guide us to Mirror Lake, one of the larger lakes in the Lakes Basin, help us set up camp there, take all the livestock back down, and return for us a week later to take us back out.

These coveted trips were hard to come by because of their popularity and there is only a short window between mid-July when the snow melts and mid-October when it returns when you can actually get in and out of there. It turns out Bob had some shirt-tail relative who was an outfitter that specialized in taking groups of hikers, campers, and hunters up into the high country. We were able to book a trip for late August the following summer which is after the mosquito hatch dies down and in the sweet spot for what is usually the best summer weather in the mountains. We jumped on the opportunity.

The family lived in a large two-story Craftsman style home with a large and inviting covered front porch that spanned the entire width of the house. The welcoming committee included Bob, his wife Linda, and their two sons Douglas, 13 years old and Anthony, 10 or 11. After we checked in, the menu committee (Linda and Sheri) went to Wallowa's only grocery store to stock up on groceries and returned with the equivalent of two large shopping baskets brimming with items. Bob and I headed for the liquor store to be sure we were adequately provisioned in that regard.

We arose early the next morning to an overcast day. Sheri and I dressed in the dude uniforms of the day consisting of Levi's jeans, Pendleton shirts, Frye western boots and cowboy hats. We had purchased the boots about a week before we left home and the two pair together set me back more than a week's wages, however, it proved to be a good investment. After 45 years we still have those boots and they still make encore appearances whenever we get involved in some sort of activity involving horses such as, four years ago for a horseback tour through a pinot noir vineyard in Oregon's Willamette Valley hosted by a wine club we belong to. Last summer they came out again for a couple of trail rides during a multi-generational family vacation with our children, their spouses, and our grandchildren to Yellowstone and Grand Teton National Parks.

After a hearty breakfast, on Saturday morning, we loaded up and drove 25 miles south east through the town of Lostine and then south along the Lostine River Road to the Lostine Pack Station. The pack station was located at about 5,600 feet elevation along the East Lostine River on the outskirts of the Eagle Cap Wilderness ,on a grassy meadow surrounded by forest and was used by outfitters as a staging area during the summer and early fall. The only structures there were a wooden barn for storage and wooden hitch rails where the stock was tied to wait for riders or be loaded.

We were met by two wranglers with a string of horses for the riders and six or seven mules for our gear that had come from a ranch in the valley in a large trailer. We watched with interest as the wranglers laid everything out on the ground and then packed the gear they supplied along with our things into a number of identically sized rectangular plywood boxes specially designed to drape in pairs over a mule's back. The boxes had to be filled with about 60 pounds each so that each mule carried about 120 pounds. It took one mule just to carry the adult beverages which consisted of two cases of canned beer and I've forgotten how many bottles of wine and bourbon. After about an hour, we were ready to begin our trip along the East Fork Lostine River Trail to Mirror Lake.

We left the pack station mid-morning under an overcast

sky escorted by one of the wrangler's dogs, a black and brown border collie mix. There was a wrangler in the lead followed by the six of us on horses followed in turn by the second wrangler with the string of mules. The entire entourage stretched out nearly the length of a football field. The pace was leisurely and it would take us over five hours to make the 7.3-mile 2,000-foot climb to Mirror Lake. The first three miles consisted of steep switchbacks through a mixed forest of fir and pine trees. Our trail paralleled the East Lostine River - more of a large stream at this point - which remained in sight most of the way as we climbed toward the stream's high glacial valley. By the early afternoon, we left the forest and completed the steep part of our climb entering a beautiful sub-alpine meadow which formed the floor of a wide u-shaped ice-carved valley radiating down from Eagle Cap's north slope. The rest of the trail was a gradual ascent to Mirror Lake and became more scenically spectacular with each passing mile. The crystal-clear stream meandered along the lush green valley floor. There were still some wild flowers left over from the seasonal bloom. Steep jagged granite ridge lines flanked us on both sides. The one to our east was called Hurricane Divide and had peaks exceeding 9,000 feet. There was no snow on the valley floor but numerous patches still lingered on the slopes to our left and right. As we worked our way up into the high valley, Eagle Cap gradually became more and more imposing.

Eventually we reached Mirror Lake, one of dozens of glacier-carved lakes in the Lakes Basin spreading out from the base of Eagle Cap in a northerly direction at about the 7,600-foot level. At 9,595 feet in elevation Eagle Cap is not the highest peak in the Wallowas but it presides over the Lakes Basin like a judge presides over a packed courtroom during a high-profile trial. There's no mistaking who's in charge. Mirror Lake takes its name from the photogenic reflections of Eagle Cap and the surrounding peaks that can be had on its surface on clear days. For our campsite, our guide found us a level turf-covered granite bench perched above the lake a suitable distance away from it with a full view of the mountain. After a long day in the saddle, we began the process of unloading and setting up camp.

There was a frenzy of activity as the wranglers rushed to help us establish our camp so they could get all the animals back to the pack station before dark. We had brought our own canvas camping tents, a four-person dome tent for Sheri and I and a larger cabin-style tent for the Chrisman family, which Bob and I teamed up to erect. They were both nearly tall enough for the adults to stand in. Part of the luxury of packing in with a string of mules is that we were able to bring so much more gear and supplies than if we had backpacked in. We had cots to sleep on, cast iron skillets to cook in, and a well-stocked pantry and bar. Sheri and Linda began setting up the kitchen and cooking areas and the boys went off to explore the neighbourhood. The pack boxes which the wranglers left with us were designed to stack on top of each other so that they could be used as kitchen cabinets. The lake water was ideal for chilling the beer and keeping it cold. Around dinner time we began to experience a few rain showers that was a preview of things to come.

It rained on and off during the night and the following day. We stayed dry in our tents but that morning we decided we needed to erect a shelter over the kitchen area and cooking fire with some tarps the wranglers had left so that we could keep our provisions and ourselves reasonably dry while preparing and consuming our meals. We were above the timberline with only scattered clumps of stunted trees nearby. The Wilderness rules prevented us from cutting down the few live trees there so we had to range far and wide to find firewood and enough dead trees with trunks long enough to construct our shelter. Sourcing the timbers for our cross-braced corners and the limbs we needed for rafters and constructing the shelter took a large part of our day. Once completed, however, we had an overhead canopy tall enough and an area large enough for all of us to get under during the frequent showers that persisted. Someone decided that was sufficient cause to celebrate and a bottle of bourbon was soon located and began circulating among the adults.

    The rain continued on and off for several days and when it wasn't raining the cloud level lingered at the surface or low enough to obscure Eagle Cap. It was unseasonably cool and wet with temperatures reaching highs in the 50's F during the day and dipping down to below freezing at night. Most mornings there was a thin skin of ice on the lake's surface in the wind sheltered coves. We didn't have the kind of high-tech water-resistant outerwear we have today and it didn't take long for the rain to penetrate our clothing. There was typically a light wind that would chill you to the bone if you were wet and send you scurrying back to the campfire to warm up and dry your clothing. The nasty weather kept us close to camp and limited the activities to gathering firewood, camp chores, meal preparation, eating, drinking, and story-telling. The area in and immediately surrounding our campsite became soggy and muddy as the week progressed. At this rate we were sure to run out of bourbon before the trip was over.

The only activity away from the protection of our camp that got much traction during the week was trout fishing in the nearby lakes and the network of streams that connected them. The fish weren't very big, perhaps 6 to 8 inches each, but there were plenty of them, they were fun to catch and good to eat. Not only were they small but their heads were disproportionately large in relation to their bodies. According to Bob, this had something to do with the fact that they spent three-quarters of their lives in lakes frozen over with very little to eat until the ice melted. The fish were wary and difficult to catch. You had to sneak up on them and cast stealthily from behind a bush or rock because if they saw you they would immediately dart away. Nevertheless, everyone got into the act at one time or another and perfected their technique sufficiently that we were able to catch enough fish to make several good meals.

Of course, fishing inevitably leads to fish stories around the campfire at the end of the day. The prize for the best fish story, some might say a whopper, went to Bob. It seems a friend of his was bank fishing for spring Chinook Salmon in the Kalama River in southwestern Washington a few years earlier. Chinook are the royalty of Pacific Northwest salmon and are prized for their delicious flavour attributed to their high oil content. The Kalama is known for its spring run of Chinook which are generally moving up river to spawn in April, May, and June. While these magnificent fish are typically 12-15 pounds each, they can reach weights north of 20 pounds. One day in May, Bob's friend was drifting eggs when he hooked and landed a 25-pound springer deep in one of the canyons that the river cuts through. He wrapped the fish in plastic and secured it to his wooden pack frame which he secured on his back like a backpack. As he was making his way out of the canyon on his way back to his car, he was jumped from behind and knocked face-first to the ground. He quickly rolled to his side just in time to see a large cougar disappearing into the brush about 15 feet away with his fish in its mouth. The claw marks on his pack frame were the only evidence of the encounter.

    My one goal for this trip was to climb Eagle Cap and it was looking like that wasn't going to happen because of the weather. However, when we arose on Thursday morning we were surprised to see the rain had stopped and the sky was blue with only a few clouds. Skiers would call it a bluebird day, a beautiful bright sunny day usually following an overnight snowfall. A reflection of the mountain was majestically displayed on the surface of Mirror Lake. I wasn't going to risk putting off an attempt to summit until Friday and Saturday we'd be breaking camp and heading back down the valley. The Chrisman's oldest boy, Doug, was the only other member of our group that I was able to recruit to go with me. From a guide book I had read, the summit trail was a non-technical climb on a marked trail all the way to the top. It was a 2,000-foot climb over about a 2.5-mile route from our campsite at Mirror Lake. Piece of cake.

    We left mid- morning and easily made the summit by lunch. There was plenty of snow nearby but the trail was mostly clear and dry. We signed the register and lingered on the summit to enjoy our lunch admiring the 360-degree view and taking a few photos as proof of our accomplishment. Perfect glacier-carved valleys having their origins high up on the mountain radiated in every direction. For our return I was feeling like we needed more of a challenge than simply retracing our steps back to camp so I looked at my guide book and surveyed the options from the summit. Glacier Lake lay a little more than a mile to the east. While there was no trail from the summit of Eagle Cap to Glacier Lake, I could see from the guide book that there was a trail to the east of the lake that would take us back to our camp. I decided we would work our way cross-country to the east skirting Glacier Lake leaving it to our north, go around the lake counter clockwise, and then pick up the trail back to camp just northeast of the lake. In doing so, we would have to scramble cross-country through a boulder field containing a smattering of isolated patches of snow and then laterally cross the small glacier from which the lake takes its name. Doug was a good soldier and enthusiastically endorsed my plan.

It was slower going than our ascent on the summit trail but we were able to work our way downhill toward the lake and through the boulder field without much difficulty. Within about an hour we arrived at the edge of the glacier. It looked bigger and steeper than it had from the top of Eagle Cap. We accessed it at a point about midway between the ridge uphill to our south where it originated and the lake below to our north where it ended. We had about a quarter mile to cross before we would get back to dry ground on the far side. After scouting a line across it that would keep us at about the same elevation we began crossing the glacier. The first few hundred feet were fairly easy to negotiate without much risk of a fall. As we encountered the steepest part in the centre I realized Doug had on sneakers with smooth soles. The snow on the surface of the glacier was sticky and slick. We didn't have trekking poles. In the event of a fall it was several hundred feet straight down to the lake and without crampons, an ice axe, or any other way to arrest a fall you would slide straight down into the lake. If you survived the fall it would only be a short time before you became hypothermic in the frigid lake waters. I had confidence in my own ability to get across safely but it dawned on me at that point that I had put my friend's son at a higher level of risk than I probably should have. Fortunately, I had lug sole hiking boots on and was able to use the firm soles to kick out level steps into the soft mushy snow of the side slope every couple of feet so that Doug could more safely follow in my footsteps. After what seemed like an eternity of gingerly picking our way across the remainder of the glacier we safely reached the far side and dry land. Within an hour we were back in camp with stories to tell of our great adventure.

The showers returned on Friday. Some of us braved the elements to trout fish that day and we caught more than enough to have a very excellent fish fry for dinner. The showers increased overnight and by Saturday morning we had steady rain. It was the coldest morning of our trip and the wind picked up to the point where it whipped up white caps on Mirror Lake. Our campsite which had dried out on Thursday was again wet and muddy everywhere. With the wranglers and the pack string expected later that morning, we had to break camp and pack things up in preparation for their arrival. As the tents and our shelter were taken down, we had nowhere to shelter from the rain and by the time our rides home arrived, everyone was wet to the bone. The trip back to the pack station was miserable. The trail was muddy and slick with a small stream of water running down the centre in places. The livestock occasionally lost their footing on steeper sections of the trail. No one took a fall but there were several close calls as animals slipped and clawed frantically to regain their footing. The East Lostine River which had been a quiet stream on the way up was a raging torrent. The rain and even hail, at times, pelted us relentlessly all the way back to the pack station.

Because of the weather, this was not the trip we all expected but for me it was a trip I'll never forget. My guess is that that's because it was such a new and different experience from anything else we had ever done at that point in our young lives. Mrs Matson doesn't agree with me but 45 years later after a lifetime of backpacking trips in stunning mountainous terrain throughout the western United States it remains one of my top outdoor experiences. As I write this on Thanksgiving Day amidst a global pandemic, I am grateful to my late friend Bob Chrisman for arranging this memorable trip and inviting Sheri and me to join him and his family.

Part III

ARMY

ROBE 2 RECOVERY STORY

By Jacqui Bateman

It wasn't until I watched a presentation on Post Traumatic Stress Disorder (PTSD), by a veteran, at Duntroon back in 2014 that I realised I needed to do something. Somehow, out of all of the wonderful causes I could have decided to get involved with, the plight of veterans suffering PTSD from their military service, was the one I wanted to help with.

I'd planned to join the police force or the army when I left high school. But I started dating my then to be farmer husband instead, so needless to say, my career dreams were never realised but I'd always taken a keen interest in the forces and often wondered what might have been if I hadn't stepped through that particular sliding door that I did.

The Duntroon presentation struck a chord with me and it was in the front of mind as I travelled home. After being inundated by calls from various (and very well deserving) charities, I decided that, rather than dipping my hand in my pocket and donating cash to a charity and not actually knowing where the money was going , I would like to do something tangible. To directly help. Supporting veterans was what I chose.

We were fortunate enough to own a little holiday cottage at Robe, and I thought this would be the perfect option: I'd donate a couple of nights' accommodation to a veteran and their family, for a few days rest and respite, in our beautiful little seaside village.

At a chance meeting with Justin Brown, a veteran Army Combat Engineer and Co-Founder of Robe 2 Recovery, at McLaren Vale in the Adelaide Hills where my son was participating at a military obstacle event, everything fell into place. Justin, at the time, was State Coordinator for *Soldier On*. I spoke with him and pitched my idea. He was immediately on board and organised a meeting the following week and Robe 2 Recovery was born. Justin has been an integral part of the organisation since then.

Through his job at *Soldier On,* Justin found the perfect first candidates and they were scheduled for a night or two at the beach with complementary accommodation.

I live in one of the most generous and supportive communities I have ever known. Small country communities are like that. Everyone knows everyone and they're always there to lend a helping hand to those who need it.

I approached a couple of local businesses; a café, the pub, the local dairy, the ice-cream shop and a winery – explained to them what I was doing and asked if they would give a voucher or in-kind donation to the visiting veteran and family. They all immediately said yes. I asked if each voucher/donation could be accompanied by a personal note from the donor.

The local gift shop created a beautiful hamper with the donated goods and notes and, along with a box of home-made slices and goodies made by my mum, the hamper was left on the dining room table for when the veteran and his family arrived.

My mum greeted Matt, his wife and two children, showed

them around and let them settle in. She popped back with buckets and spades for the kids and found Matt and his wife, both with tears sliding down their cheeks, as they read the notes accompanying the donated goods in the hamper.

Never, in the time since leaving the military, had they been thanked for their service. The beautiful hand written and heartfelt words from members of our community, saying thank you to them was a very touching experience.

It was then I knew I was onto a winner.

I took my idea to our local Robe Tourism Association meeting and pitched my idea to them. I believe that everyone who was there at that meeting, all put their hands up to participate.

To date we have most have local businesses including the bakery, patisserie, pizza shop, cafes, pubs, restaurants, fish and chips shop, ice-cream shop, the local brewery and wineries, all on board to support veterans during their stay by way of donations of vouchers. We have donated accommodation at more than forty holiday homes and we have a small army of locals who help out with what has turned out to be a true community initiative.

Even in this Covid19 year, we are expecting to host more than twenty-five veterans and their families, ranging from those who fought in Vietnam, to contemporary veterans who represented our country during the Afghanistan conflict and all theatres of war in between.

With exposure on ABC's Back Roads Program generating huge interest, we have expanded our Veteran Respite Program to three other towns: Port Lincoln SA, Phillip Island and Cobden in Victoria and have just begun to establish a program in Albany WA.

To date, Robe alone has hosted over forty veterans and their families, using this very simple formula. We have hopes to organically expand our R2R initiative right around the country into like-minded communities who want to support our veterans.

FROM FARM TO ARMY

By Terry Holden

In 1965 I was working in Geelong with Elders Pastoral Company. I was 20 and my birth date out came out of the barrel to be conscripted for National Service. After numerous interviews and medicals, I was sent to Puckapunyal in Victoria and introduced to the rigours and discipline of Army life. There were 10 weeks of marching, fitness and weapons handling with other 20-year-olds from all walks of life.

During our recruit training we were told by our commanding officer that we had two choices as to which corps we would be assigned. I was told that inexperienced rifle shooters would be selected for the Infantry so that they could be given more training in handling rifles and those who could already handle a rifle had a choice. Because of my farm experiences I managed to shoot with great accuracy and chose Transport which is one of many divisions of the Service Corps.

From Puckapunyal I was sent to Bonegilla, in Victoria, near Albury-Wodonga, for 5 weeks of training where we learnt to drive and service many and varied forms of Army transport. Then it was Wacol in Brisbane for a further 10 months being trained to carry out the many facets of an army truck driver during warfare.

In 1967, my platoon of 88 personnel flew by commercial aircraft to Darwin where we spent the night in RAAF barracks and then the following day we flew to Vung Tau, Vietnam in an extremely noisy Hercules. I will never forget the unbearable heat and dreadful smell that washed over us when the doors of the Hercules were opened.

The operational task of our company was to support the First Australian Task Force located at Nui Dat – 32 kilometres north of Vung Tau.

The commanding officer Major N. McVilley gave us our first briefing which included the statement 'Do not concern yourselves when driving through the village of Hoa Long as you WILL be fired upon by a single villager. We have deliberately let him be because he may be replaced by someone who can shoot accurately'

Our jobs were many and varied. We drove jeeps, moved troops to and from battle zones, moved pallets of artillery and ordnance, did the ice runs, waste rubbish runs, transported rocks and gravel for road maintenance and building supplies for a new village. Once we helped move 900 refugee Vietnamese to re-settlement camps. We were in Vietnam to drive any size vehicle for any purpose.

The very first day on duty in Vung Tau a truck driver, with me as a lookout manning an F1 sub-machine gun at the ready, were doing the regular rubbish run. We drove around our camp picking up all the large kitchen bins. On our way to the tip with our putrid load, we stopped at a large wooden landing. We had unloaded two of our bins onto the landing and were immediately surrounded by scores of Vietnamese civilians. They came out of their shanties carrying receptacles of all sorts they used these as scoops to fill from the bins. It was their next meal. I felt quite ill.

The vehicles we used for moving soldiers were eight International Mark 3 1 tonne flat tray 4wheel drive trucks. Each truck could carry 16 fully equipped soldiers seated back-to-back on bench seats running the full length of the tray. My platoon could carry an infantry battalion's core fighting elements, 4 companies of some 120 soldiers in one lift.

Vehicle protection, when on the move with infantry men, was quite formidable. The M 60 machine gun carried in each infantry section meant that both sides of the road could be covered by fire from the truck. In addition to each soldier having his own weapon. We hoped the presence of such a volume of firepower would or should deter any sensible enemy from thoughts of ambush.

Apart from the official enemy, we also had to run the daily gauntlet of the, aptly named, "cowboys". These were local Vietnamese thieves who worked in pairs on motorcycles and their most lucrative targets were vehicles carrying saleable items. They would ride alongside a moving cargo-carrying truck and the pillion passenger would clamber onto the cargo tray. He would then proceed to throw as much of the load onto the side of the road before being seen. If challenged he would re-join his mate on the motorcycle and disappear. Meanwhile the jettisoned cargo had already disappeared from the roadside.

The distances we travelled in the Phuoc Tuy Province were not long by Australian standards, but the state of their roads meant vehicle movement was painfully slow They were rutted dirt tracks or very narrow pot holed bitumen roads. Planned speed for routine tasks was up to 40 kmh. However, this speed was being optimistic, and at times wildly so. More likely 25 kmh.

This added to the danger of exposure to us, let alone the troops we were carried. The possibility of mines posed a serious problem. We tried to avoid driving over buffalo droppings or unusual mounds of earth as these could be hiding a buried mine. Little could be done for protection from these as steel plates on the truck transports would grossly overload the vehicles. They could be added under the "gun jeep" seats where we had to sit directly above the Land Rover fuel tanks. However, I felt it was more a psychological benefit rather than real one.

On one very disturbing occasion we were ordered to recover a "gun jeep" that had run over a mine killing 3 soldiers. The vehicle was severely damaged by shrapnel and covered in blood splatters – mentally challenging I must say.

It is extremely disappointing to me that I have read many books on many wars we Aussies have been involved with and I have not seen stories about the troops in the backlines. Not just about transport, but about any of the other Units e.g., ordnance, supply and stores, workshops, light aid detachments, ground liaison units, petroleum platoons, signal troops, field medical and dental units, construction, field canteen unit, field hygiene company, intelligence squadron, postal division, just to name a few. All so important.

There is no joy in war. However, we did create our own fun on occasions, and we developed strong bonds of friendship and trust.

Part IV

PEOPLE

MY WRITING LIFE

By Bill Marsh

Recently my twentieth book of Great Australian Outback Stories was released. The collection took just on three years to write, during which time I clocked up something like 30,000 kilometres and interviewed over a hundred people.

The series of Great Australian Outback Stories began back in 1999 with Great Australian Flying Doctor Stories. People often ask how I can publish a book per year, yet each book takes three years to write. Basically, I work on a 'three-year cycle'. While one book is going through its editing stage, leading to publication, I'm interviewing people for – in this case – a collection of Great Australian Volunteer Fire Service Stories. This is the stage where I write up a draft of someone's story from the interview and send it to them for their okay. These stories will be presented to ABC Books-HarperCollins early in 2021, ready to go through their editing process and be published later on in the year. At the same time I'm gathering contacts for a book to come out in 2022.

The next question people ask is, 'How do you get your contacts to interview?' Over the years I've met a number of people who are as keen as I am to get these Australian stories recorded and written. They're my first port of call. I send out a group email along the lines of, 'Do you have a story to tell about a certain topic, and if not do you know anyone who may?'

Other times I try and get interviewed on a national radio program like the Summer edition of Australia All Over where I can put a call out for people to contact me if they have a story to tell on the topic I'm about to start to write. I remember when I was starting to write Great Australian Shearing Stories. I was interviewed on the radio mid-morning and, by lunch time, something like thirty-five people had got in touch. With Great Australian Trucking Stories, I was interviewed at some ungodly hour of the morning and I still received something like twenty responses. And of course, each of them knew a mate or three who also had a story to tell.

My much-preferred manner of interviewing is face-to-face. My feeling is that people are more relaxed and comfortable within their own surroundings. And, what's more, with me covering around a third of Australia each year, they're appreciative that someone would come all that way to visit them. So, when someone rings or emails me, I get their contact details. I then take out a large map of Australia and I put a pin in the place they live. Over the course of my 'contact-year' I end up with a hell of a lot of pins stuck in the map. When it's time to plan a trip, I get a piece of string and thread a possible route around as many pins as is practical to do on a two-month or so trip. I then start ringing around and organising a time they might be at home and available to be interviewed. If that doesn't work out, I'll interview them later on by phone – as I have to do with the people I'm unable to meet.

Once a trip is organised, I then start sorting out accommodation and ringing around libraries in the area to see if they'd like to host me for an author talk-performance.

During these talk-performances I tell stories from my various books and, being a songwriter, I sing some of the songs I've written and recorded about my books and my travels. To try to make each performance as entertaining as possible, I add in the three magic tricks I've been doing for the past forty years. Oh, and I also sell books and CDs at these 'shows' to help keep the wheels on the road.

For my book of outback police stories, the major part of my travels was from Adelaide to Port Augusta, Ceduna, Streaky Bay, then across the Nullarbor Plain in to Western Australia, over to the Northern Territory and back home in to South Australia. Though I'd already organised a number of people to interview along the way, there's also those who just pop up out of the blue. I remember getting to Kalgoorlie and not having anyone to interview there. I thought, surely a place like Kalgoorlie would have some great stories.

So, I rang the local ABC Radio station and, as luck would have it, the woman who answered the phone had interviewed me previously about another book I'd written. She was aware of what I write and so she put me on to the local Detective-sergeant. Having been in the police force for many years, he had heaps of stories to tell – there was a book in himself. Then, just as I was about to leave, he asked, 'So where are you heading next?'

When I said, 'Meekatharra,' he rang up his police mate in Meekatharra and told him that I'd be passing through and would like a chat.

When I'd finished interviewing the police officer in Meekatharra, they asked the same question, 'So where are you heading next?' They then rang up their police mate in that town and said that I'd be popping by. And so it went on, from Kalgoorlie to Meekatharra to Newman to Tom Price to Karratha to Port Hedland to Broome, across the Gibb River Road to Kununurra, then across into the Northern Territory, to Katherine, and back down the Stuart Highway to Tennant Creek, Alice Springs. From the Alice it back in to South Australia and home sweet home via Marla, Cooper Pedy and Port Augusta. And at each police station along the way, the receptionist would call out to whoever I was going to interview, 'Hey, Swampy's here to have a chat.'

GEORGE NORTHEAST

By Henning 'Chook' Kath

The Betoota Pub is Betoota, apart from a racetrack and an airstrip and is about a mile from Mount Leonard homestead in south west Queensland and 100 miles east of Birdsville and 140 miles west of Windorah. The pub was built in the 1880s despite strong protests by surrounding pastoralists and others.

By 1895 there was a police station, court house, customs post, Cobb and Co stables and grocer, likely a general store judging by an old picture when the so-called Rabbit Proof Fence/s were built. By the early 1900s it had declined due to the changes of Federation in the 20th century.

Everything else but the pub closed over the years but Sigmund (Ziggy) Remienko, a Polish grader driver, bought it in 1957 and operated it until 1997. He died in 2004 and it passed to others.*

A special customer and resident of the pub in the 1970s was George Northeast. He slept there, was always there when not working, had his mail addressed to him there and had his swag laid out on an old shearers' stretcher on the side veranda. I suppose that constitutes 'living' somewhere but he didn't actually have a room to himself.

*The Betoota Pub re-opened in July 2020 but is shut over the summer period 2020-21 at present.

George had worked his way around the corner country, where South Australia joins the Northern Territory, Queensland and New South Wales, all his adult life, trying to "make ends meet" and the "ends" were about as close to meeting at Betoota as anywhere else. He worked at nearby Mount Leonard Station when they needed him and stayed at the pub while the cheque still stood for his liquor and when that ran out camped down the creek until mustering time started again. Ziggy took advantage of George unquestionably. An ex-manager of Mount Leonard told me he had banished George to the creek bed where he lived in his old car. It rained and floods came. Fortunately, the manager I mentioned saw what was happening and sent riders to save George from probably another lonely grave. For a man the likes of George, in those times, there was little else one could realistically hope for in this life.

I have no idea what he looked like, as he was long gone before I landed here. I have never seen a photograph of him as photography usually petered out by the time anyone reached Betoota. From what I have heard let's just say he was of smallish build, had a lot of loose skin around his face and arms due to malnutrition and nearly always needed a shave.

A truck driver called in late one night to the Betoota Hotel to get a coke and on his way out he noticed poor old George slumped on his swag, in a rather unorthodox sleeping position. On closer inspection to see if he was even alive, he noticed that all of his uncovered skin looked like carpet with the thousands of mozzies sucking blood while he lay motionless and completely oblivious. Even the parts of his genitals peeping out from under his shorts were not spared.

Another story goes that on an annual trip to Charleville perhaps to "do some business", he was pulled over by the cops and they asked for his name.

"George Northeast" he replied.

"And where do you work"

"In the far south west" he replied quite innocently, but of course he did, of Queensland.

The policeman, thinking George was being cheeky, gave him a belt under ear and a night in the lock up. Perhaps the policeman was saving himself a job he would have to do later in the night anyway.

When George was employed at Mount Leonard it was as the camp cook during the mustering season. Camp cooking was a big and important job with collecting fire wood, making damper, hanging the salted beef in a tree at night and covering it with leaves and swags during the day to protect it from blow flies and the heat of the day. On top of these chores, the camp would have to be shifted every few days. The cook was the first one up and the last to bed. On days they were branding he would keep the fires going to keep the brands hot and so on. There was always something that needed to be done to make it better for the men to do their work and of course, forever boiling the billy.

To start a muster, the manager would assemble a team of 4 to 6 men, run the horses in from their spell in the horse paddock and assign 6 or so work horses per man. There were saddle horse for general use, broncos for bronco branding, camp horses for drafting fat bullocks, night horses for watching the mob at night and pack horses for carrying tucker, cooking equipment, swags, spare horse shoes etc. They all had to be shod. A total of 50 to 60 horses were readied and gear loaded. A process that took the best part of a week. The last thing to do was to get George Northeast on the way past the Betoota pub. They would grab him and sit him on a quiet horse and drive him along in the mob with all the other horses. There is no explaining why he never fell off, or perhaps he did every so often and would be propped back on again.

The first few days on camp would have been horrific for George and the head stockman as he dried out. He was absolutely useless when in the horrors, or DTs as some people would say. He would rant and rave, want to fight everyone, yell at imaginary things and try to bash ghosts with whatever he could grab. The axe and rifle had to be guarded at all times. A kitchen knife was regarded as a weapon back then. A ration of brandy had to be taken on camp and administered to George in ever decreasing doses and at less frequent intervals until he eventually came good. That weaning process would take a few days. You knew he was getting better when he would apologise profusely with "Sorry boss", "Stuff the grog", and "Never again". This was then followed by weeks of efficient, timely, cheerful and immaculate work. As far as camp cooks go, George Northeast was one of the best.

Eventually the muster would come to its final stages. George might ask "How long till we get home?" as if to make just a random inquiry at first, but then ask again later, as if he actually had some important business to attend. Next he would mutter "Stuff the bush" under his breath and then meals would become scant and late and his temper thin. On the final leg home he would be chirpy and singing and start slurring his words in anticipation. Even stumbling over on a rock or some fire wood as though he were drunk. As the horses came past the pub on the way over to the homestead, George would peel off like a sneaky old piker bullock and make a bee line for the pub away from the horse-tailer he travelled with who had to go round him up and drive him back into the mob with a harmless crack of the whip. "No George, not yet. Back in the mob you go. You have to unpack all the gear and put it all away first."

His seat would be empty at the homestead kitchen table that night. The cycle was complete. He was back at the Betoota pub for a spree until he would be needed again.

It could be said, and without a reasonable argument, that at least George Northeast was reliable. You could always easily find him and then you could expect unrivalled good work. There were some bad days at the beginning and maybe at the end but the days in the middle were good. That's more than can be said for most.

UNCLE FRED SCOTT – THE BUSHMAN

By Michael Sullivan

When invited to make a contribution to this book I instantly recollected my boy hood bushman fantasy of my Uncle Fred! To me he epitomized everything to do with the Outback. The iconic Aussie bushman with the Akubra Sombrero hat, dark stained bush khaki shirt, with drill trousers, wild rhino boots and stockman's oilskin jacket complete with snake skin whip hanging curled over the shoulder. The facial features had narrowed weathered and worrying eyes, leather toughened and sunburnt unshaven skin together with an iconic Aussie drawl. However, when I first encountered my Uncle Fred I was sorely disappointed and my balloon imagination popped.

Fred wore clothes left over from his days in the Air Force. Blue regulation issue overalls covered in grease, dust-soaked kaki shirts & air force shorts with a double buckle in front and very baggy legs. His rugged & weathered unshaven face was topped with a mat of jet-black curls. These matched the forest of hairs covering his sunburnt and solid arms, right down to his nicotine-stained fingers forming extensions to his huge hands. His bandied legs extended from baggy shorts displaying wear and tear scars encountered from a lifetime of labour.

I have never forgotten the reality compared to the dream I had about Fred and a visit to Mount Leonard Station, my grandmother's home, with my sisters Leonore and Jacqueline and Leonore's husband Peter in 2018 rekindled my interest in Uncle Fred.

Frederick Albert Scott was born in Longreach, Queensland on December 9th 1920. As was the trend of that time his Mother, Alberta Jessamine Scott (nee Tucker), had travelled some 550 kilometres from Mt Leonard Station by Model T on a dirt track road, to give birth at the hospital and to then convalesce. This made Fred a grandson to Susannah Josephine Tucker and son to John James Scott. Tragically, Fred's birth coincided with the drowning of his Father ('Jack') during a cattle drive in the Diamantina River near Mt Leonard. The subsequent outcome saw Fred travel with his mother and four siblings (my mother Jean amongst them) down the Birdsville track to Adelaide, some 1700 kilometres in 1920! A combination of car on dirt roads to Maree then Ghan train south. Can we even start to imagine what that journey would have been like?

They took up residence in Rose Park and Fred attended Christian Brothers College in Wakefield St. On completion it was decided to send Fred back to Mt Leonard to allow him a glimpse of his absent Fathers legacy. So, at 16 years of age and fresh from the comforts of home and private boys' school, he left the leafy suburbs of Adelaide for the rugged ways of the bush as a station hand. His experiences would have included riding, stock muster, fixing fences, general upkeep of out buildings, saddlery and some animal husbandry; a boyhood dream perhaps. More to the point Fred would have experienced a challenging metamorphosis from boy to man amongst the rough and ready life of a station hand.

The outbreak of World War 2 gave Fred an opportunity to

follow in his older brother's footsteps and join the Air Force. Squadron Leader John Leonard Scott would have presented an awesome mentor for Fred. He enlisted in Adelaide on April Fool's day 1940, 21 days after his brother Len. He saw service at various locations around Australia concluding as a mechanic Leading Aircraftman No.2 Squadron Flying Boat Repair Depot at Rathmines NSW, near Catalina Bay on Lake Macquarie. The Squadron made a successful national tour in RAAF Short Sunderland Aircraft in support of the 3RD Victory Loan during the period April May 1945.

Tragically, his brother Len was executed by the Japanese in August of 1944 as a prisoner of War on Ambon Island in the Dutch East Indies (now Indonesia). This life changing experience and the fact that Len would have been Fred's father replacement did not serve him well in the years to follow. He discharged on the anniversary of Len's enlistment in 1946.

So commenced a transient period of jobs and locations throughout the Flinders Rangers regions. Fred took his mechanic expertise up to places like Maree, Farina & Lyndhurst. At one point he was driving talc from Mt Fitton Talc Mine to Lyndhurst and Farina to be loaded for trains south to Port Adelaide. It would have been a very hot, dirty & unhealthy task. Fred was to find this out with a bout of hepatitis that laid him low in Lyndhurst. His sister (Clare Dolores Scott) came to his aid and that of Fred's fellow workers providing much missed home care in the way of nursing & housekeeping. Clare later recalled what an exciting time it was for her and how happy an existence she and Fred shared!

Also, during this period Fred came to know a true bush character by the name of 'Possum' Kipling. They met in Lyndhurst during Fred's stint at the talc mines. Possum would go on to notoriety as a driver in the infamous 'Redex' Car Trials of 1953, 54 & 55.

Characters such as 'Gelignite' Jack Murray, who literally threw sticks of dynamite from his car during the rallies and Jack Davey, a very popular radio personality of the day; accentuated the cow boy approach to these adventures. The rallies travelled some 10-11,000 kilometres around Australia. Possum drove a 1948 Holden FX & a 1954 Holden FJ respectively. Through Fred's mechanical background he assisted Possum on the maintenance of these rally cars. In 1955 Possum opened a Shell Roadhouse in Port Wakefield where Fred became 1 of his many staff.

Now his life took a new turn as he started to 'settle down' in Port Wakefield. He met and married Valerie Sharman in March of 1960 and shared 4 children, 3 grandchildren & 2 great grandchildren with her. Fred's eldest son was respectably christened John Leonard Scott. Apart from the Shell Roadhouse, Fred continued his eccentric activities with The Highways Department and at one stage ran chickens on the nearby Australian Army Proof Range where he tended gardens as well.

Fred became a victim of the scourge of the day, lung cancer. I recall a poignant farewell visiting him with my Mother in Royal Adelaide Hospital. In a very hoarse voice he swore me to avoid smoking at all costs! He passed away with his family around him at the Balaklava hospital just shy of his 55th year.

My sister, Leonore, relays a beautiful story about Uncle Fred from our childhood days. As most of his life was in the country, Fred had the accepted habit of appearing on our door step unannounced. On one such occasion he had contacted his sister Jean, my Mother. Jean Marie Scott, Alberta's third child. had the auspicious title of 'Queen of the Diamantina' bestowed upon her as being the only child of Alberta & John to be born on Mt Leonard Station!

He wanted to offer her two turkeys for the approaching festive season. Mum gladly took up the offer anticipating two country turkeys dressed for the Xmas Oven and it would be such a welcome relief to her normal busy kitchen, especially at Christmas. However, as the days drew nearer to Santa's arrival Mum became a little anxious as to lunch's arrival! But Fred always came through and communication then was not the best with he being in the bush so often. True to his word, he arrived on Christmas Eve, walking up the driveway to the rear of our house, past the sunroom where we boys were corralled. He called out via his normal greeting "Are you their Jean?" I loved it when he called Mum Jean, his big sisters name. For me it made Mum so woman like as opposed to our matriarch. We boys always got a giggle out of it. Announcing to all and sundry his arrival accompanied a chorus of loud honking geese. There was Fred standing at our back door with two bottles of Southwark Bitter beer in one hand, his gift token and signature drink and in the other, suspended upside down and flapping at a rate that would have them half way to the next post code two *live* fully grown geese emitting a honking crescendo bordering on panic for their dear lives! Mum was aghast! What was she to do this close to the big event? Dad was nowhere to be seen, we kids were either rolling in hysterics or as was the case with baby Simon, crying for fear of attack from these monstrous eagles of death! Mum quickly had Fred dispatch the feathered intruders into the laundry clamping the door shut behind him. By now Fred had certainly earnt his 'gift' and so resigned to the kitchen to drink a Christmas toast with his older sibling. Along comes Dad home from a weary day of penny collections from his faithful Insurance family only to be accosted by the laundry occupants. Retreating to the kitchen to discover an explanation he was heard to emit "bloody Fred – it had to be you!" However, true to his nature Fred soothed the situation with another good yarn and the second bottle of Southwark. Dad was appointed chief executioner and commenced the gory task of butchering Xmas Lunch. He opted to make one a sacrifice and the other a gift to we children. Christmas came and went and 'goosy' became a family favourite around the backyard. It had the tendency to follow us to the gate as a vain attempt to join us on our excursions to various adventures. Sometimes it would escape into the neighbourhood causing Mum further grief. Finally, the day came when Dad put on the apron again and proceeded to the fowl house with carving knife in hand. Despite tumultuous tears and hysterical pleas for 'goosies' life from us all she was eventually served up as roast dinner and Mum & Dad would have drunk a toast to Uncle Fred in eternal gratitude!

    Uncle Fred Scott remains in my memories to this day. To me he was that sunburnt Aussie Bushman look alike, that rugged male archetype, that spirit of freedom and independence that I crave from time to time when the pressures of city life mount up. Then I shut my eyes and hear his call "Are you there, Jean?"

'LIFE ISN'T ALWAYS EASY BUT A GREAT ADVENTURE' SAID THE MAN WHO SINGS *THE COURT OF KING CARACTACUS*

By Ian Bishop

In 2020 our son Timothy, his wife Lisa and their two children stayed with us at our home in Port Lincoln over the Christmas period. We were joined on New Year's Eve by Chris and Erinn Bishop and a huge freshly cooked crayfish. The boys had known each other at school and played football together and when Tim and Lisa lived in Port Lincoln they were neighbours.

Lisa has described the life in Port Lincoln as 'Champagne, sausages and sport' and missed her family and home very much in this strange new world. She and Erinn became close friends and still are. Lisa is English and Erinn Canadian and they had met these young men respectively in the USA and Japan. I am sure that the psychic channels that Lisa and Erinn established during those difficult times in Port Lincoln was, albeit subconsciously, something to do with Chris and Erinn calling their children Jackson and Lexie after Leonore's and my eldest grandson and our late Labrador they knew at the time.

During the New Year's Eve celebration I mentioned writing a book of tales about interesting people I had met. Chris's ears pricked up and about a week later he sent me a list with 20 dot points about his dad's amazing life. I must confess I recalled my father telling me, 'Be careful of what you wish for son, you might get it.'

Long story short. On the 2nd February we visited Ian and Sue. Ian stood up from his chair and greeted me with a firm handshake and cheeky smile and Sue with a gentle smile, cuppa and cake. It was an easy interview as Ian and Sue are both good conversationalists, with extensive general knowledge, articulate, pleasant and intelligent. Ian showed me Obama's *Promised Land* and Bill Bryson's *1927*, two books each about 10 cm thick, he was reading to compare two political periods in America. To make things easy for me to write his story Ian gave me a copy of an article, 'Life isn't always easy but a great experience' he had written as part of an autobiographical series in our local paper.

This is Ian's story:

'I was born in Melbourne on 25/08/32 the youngest of three boys. My Dad Vivian had seven brothers and one sister. He was my best mate - a person I could confide in about anything, particularly personal worries. When I was a young kid, say 10 or 11 years of age, I was totally ignorant about the First World War and the fact that Dad had served in Egypt and France. I understand that whilst in Egypt he climbed some way up one of the pyramids, which is probably the reason that I am fascinated by them!

Whilst in France he was badly wounded by a flying piece of shrapnel that caused a bad wound in his right buttock. He apparently lay in a shell hole for many hours before being found by stretcher bearers from Australian Army Medical Corps and taken to the nearest Regimental Aid Post where he remembered a doctor and a nurse attending to him. He was eventually repatriated to the UK and while he was in hospital he was interviewed by Australian Flying Corps (AFC) personnel as a likely candidate to be trained as a pilot and that's what he became, a pilot for the Army based AFC. The AFC was disbanded in 1919 and the RAAF replaced it in 1921.

After the war, he joined the Victorian Railways in an administrative role where he remained until his retirement. His job entailed keeping track of the rolling stock as Melbourne was a major source of men, perishables, ammunition, aeroplanes, (that we built in Australia), vehicles, canned food etc. that was needed overseas and in Australia in World War 2. He had to know where all the rail trucks were coming from, what they were carrying and where they were going, a big job!'

Ian spent most of his childhood in the beach suburb of Sandringham, was active in Boy Scouts and loved the beach, cricket and football. Food was rationed at the time and Ian fondly remembers the days US Army trucks drove onto the local cricket ground and the crews invited the kids to join their picnics when 'We stuffed ourselves and drank Coke until it came out of our ears.' I believe that was called Coca Cola diplomacy.

Ian tolerated school but didn't particularly enjoy it: a lot of his teachers had been brought out of retirement to teach during the war and were old and crabby! He had inherited a sound work ethic from his father, and when he was a teenager did two paper rounds before school, sometimes falling asleep during French lessons!

In his teenage years Ian decided he wanted to work on a cattle station and as fate would have it one of his dad's workmates had a daughter who had been a governess at Mount Moffatt, 400-square-mile cattle station 470 miles from Brisbane on the same latitude as Bundaberg and told him how to go about getting a job there. And that was it. Ian was seventeen and caught a train to Brisbane and then Mitchell where he was picked up by someone from the station and sat in the back of a Ute for the 100 miles journey to the Mount Moffatt property.

Some semantics are to be introduced. Jackaroos I have seen defined as, 'impoverished colonials' but by Ian's time they had some sort of status and were defined as, 'Young inexperienced workers on sheep or cattle stations. They were generally considered to be apprentices to continue the pastoral world their forebears ('Bunyip Aristocrats' to some) had forged in the tough outback of Australia. They came from pastoral properties aka stations, farms or the like. Ian wanted to try that life. Many were treated well and trained in management of stations but others were treated as sweated labour. It was a tradition that Jackaroos sat at the dining room table with the owner or manager to learn appropriate behaviour and manners as well as how to manage a property and to move in the right circles.

The station hands, ringers and so on ate and lived in the 'quarters'. Ian had a separate cabin to himself but ate with the family, maintaining the illusion that he was being educated. Mount Moffatt was owned by a Jim Waldron, 'A difficult man.' He had a wife and four daughters, Pat, Heather, Ann and Brenda. Jim rarely spoke other than to give orders and Ian remembers one day when he was scared to go into a race to turn a wild 'mickey' bull around, he threatened to beat him with a hobble chain if he didn't. When I asked Ian about the family he thought for a while and said, 'The girls were tough. They joined in the mustering, cooked and did what they had to do. A couple of them were OK and one was a lot darker than the others. I met her father creeping around the sheds once when he came to see if she was OK before he disappeared on walkabout one of the men said. The girls, from what I remember, had unsuccessful marriages, so who would know what went on. Remember Peter I slept in my own quarters.'

Ian's day began at 04.30, when he returned the night's corned beef to the barrel of brine, collected the night horse, who often eluded him, from the horse yard, and guided eight or nine cows into the shed, milked them, separated the milk and delivered the cream to the boss's wife in the kitchen. When Ian was telling me this, quietly and seriously, but with some difficulty as he has lung problems and struggled at times, he let loose with a perfect cry of a cocky imitating the boss's wife. Most mornings she screeched, 'You been runnin' them cows again. The cream is too thin.' He later gave voice to one of the girls with a different bird's cry but just as raucous. Our 'interview' became much less formal after that. Oh! And he had to do the laundry two or three times a week, help with the gardening and chop the wood every morning before breakfast for the kitchen stove and more in the winter for other fires.

That was all before day-to-day work; he also fenced, trapped or dug up rabbits, checked the cattle and their waters and mustered when necessary and like their fellows elsewhere in the outback, they would do it tough. They would sometimes kill a beast and eat fresh meat and salt the rest or would have only salt beef they kept in saddle bags until it was shiny from rubbing back and forth with the horse's movement. 'I was also told to shoot brumbies but refused and that made me unpopular because they were beautiful animals, not the ugly in-bred creatures that are so common now.' The cattle were brought back to the yards at the homestead for any drafting, branding, castrating or drafting for sale.

A pleasant memory of Ian's was listening to Blue Hills at midday when everything stopped for the beloved serial on the ABC that ran from 1949 to 1976 surprisingly perhaps coexisting with television for 20 years. 'One other thing I didn't like, although I admit it was peaceful, was the family ticking off to the Ekka for a couple of weeks a year and leaving me on my Pat Malone. I don't know what that stood for but it was the Brisbane Show.'

He went on, 'After I had been there for a while I was sent to an out station, Havelock, to batch with a young bloke who had just started as a manager and did it ever rain; for three or four days it bucketed down. There were only the two of us: no radio, no phone, no vehicle, although we did have horses. The bread and such came by mail each Friday to a mailbox three miles from our two-room hut. Onions and apricot jam was all the food we had left by the third day. We tried to hit bronze winged pigeons with stones; we had no rifles and that was ridiculous. We tried or at least thought about swimming the flooded Maranoa River on our horses and we finally did on the third day and reached our neighbours 15 miles away to be greeted with hot scones, jam and tea with milk. They and other neighbours had feared for our lives. Slim Dusty wrote,

'When the rain tumbles down in July,' so he did OK out of it. After two years I had had enough and left. 'Many years later on one of our caravan trips we called into what was the Mount Moffatt Station, now part of the Carnarvon Gorge NP and were warmly welcomed at the dining room tables where I had supped and watered hundreds of times before.'

After the station Ian then had a bit of a spell in Melbourne and worked selling hardware, helped run a boy-scout troop for a few years and believe it or not coached square dancing at the St. Kilda town hall in the '50s and even did a bit of calling.

'I enjoyed the spell in the 'smoke' but by 1960 I was looking for something more serious and joined McPhar Geophysics, a Canadian mineral exploring outfit. They introduced electrical impulses into the ground at certain frequencies and plotted and recorded the data to get a profile of what was under the surface for geologists to examine. My first job with them was at Cockburn in South Australia about 30 miles from Broken Hill. The silver-lead-zinc ore body, known as the line of lode is boomerang shaped with the convex side pointing up and the tips deep underground. BHP removed the easiest ore and left Broken Hill to the other mines that had been established on both sides of BHP. The McPhar people thought that the line of lode may plunge south and re surface somewhere between Broken Hill and Radium Hill.

We were contracted to Broken Hill South mine and used a small American built 4x4 Jeep.

The crew was, crew leader Ted Drane, Harry Jones and me. There was barely enough room for the three of us in the front seat, there was no back seat and no seat belts. Ted and Harry rarely saw eye to eye.

Each day we travelled down the Barrier Highway past workmen who were widening the narrow highway bridge so they had made a rough cutting through the creek so that traffic could by pass the bridge.

Ted was driving this day and as he approached the cutting Harry said, 'Slow down Ted you're going too bloody fast. Ted sped up into the cutting, the Jeep hit rocks and turned end over end twice before ending up on its wheels.

The railway overseer grabbed his first aid kit and ran towards and made the comment, 'These guys are either dead or way past first aid.' Amazingly we were all ok probably because we were jammed so close together. Ted was sacked and rightly so and we lived to see another day and before we left Cockburn had a unique experience. The NSW/SA border passes through the outside toilet at the Bordergate Hotel, so one can urinate with one foot in NSW and the other in SA.

I did enjoy working for McPhars that became quite a big concern with 26 crews (a crew leader and two operators) in Australia, the Philippines and the Pacific.

In about 1968 I was appointed crew leader for Australia and they kindly let me name my own price so I bought a nice home at 70 Hill St Netherby that became party central in the era of the Beatles, Rolling Stones, CCR, Neil Diamond etc. but nothing lasts forever. In January 1975 I married my beautiful wife, teacher Susan Trott who had not long finished Teachers' College. She had won a rural scholarship which meant that she received an allowance while at College but had to teach in the country when she graduated and that was fine by me. Suzi has been my special love and dearest friend forever, patient, loving and caring. We soon moved from Netherby to a bigger house at Fairview Park. Christopher came along in late 1975 and then Matthew in 1978 and Lachlan in 1986 at Cleve.

The Whitlam Government ruined our business, as exploration had to be done by Australian companies and there were none. I did a bit more work in that declining industry and managed the honey plant at Southern Farmers for five years, then we decided on a massive change.

In 1983 we purchased the General Store and Post Office at Wharminda, a small town north of Port Lincoln. This was good for us in many ways but we, like so many in rural Australia, were hit hard by drought and the depopulation of rural areas for many reasons. We did a mail run three times a week, I delivered bulk fuel to farms, managed the local silos, ran the manual telephone exchange (for the first 2 years) and Suzi also did some teaching. We worked hard - up to 80 hours a week - but certainly enjoyed our time at Wharminda serving the local farming community. After nine years it was time to move on and we moved to Port Lincoln. I became a house-husband when Suzi was offered a permanent full-time teaching role until she retired in 2014.

Since then we have travelled extensively in Australia, particularly the outback in our caravan, but also overseas.

I became interested in the rhythm of the square dance calling and I also liked cumulative songs like Old MacDonald had a farm, 12 days of Christmas and although I lost a lot of money playing drinking games, with the Barley Mow, I liked that as well. I spent a lot of time driving alone with my work over the years and I would pick one of these songs and work on it until I got it right and then move on. The hardest cumulative song in my view was *The Court of King Caractacus* and it took ages to learn but it became a tradition at special family celebrations such as my 70th birthday when Matthew joined me. The key was to have enough drinks to lubricate my voice!

The zenith of my performing this Welsh song undoubtedly was my international debut when I performed at Chris's and Erinn's wedding in Thailand, in my shorts with no shirt or shoes. I will remember the deafening applause forever.

I do regret though that we had to leave when we did as the hotel asked me to sing at a function for the visiting Welsh Rugby team a few days later.

I read and re-read this and the story Ian wrote in the paper and thought about what he and Sue had told me. He had many hard times but he never mentions those except at Mount Moffatt.

The connection between Ian and Sue is beautifully clear. He is older and seriously ill but cheerful. Sue is aware of everything he is saying and doing. They did not complain about any single thing in their lives then or now. They just got on with it and they still are doing just that. Ian said it all. 'I still enjoy sampling good wines with a small circle of like-minded friends.'

I read a story years ago about an elderly couple who were offered broccoli by a waiter. One turned to the other and asked, 'Which one of us doesn't like broccoli?' I laughed at that thinking 'silly old buggers.' Having read and heard Ian's and Sue's story and bearing in mind Leonore's and my 51 years of marriage, I get it now!

THE DAY I MET SIR ROBERT MENZIES

By Gavin Stevens
And a tenuous link to the present by the editor!

Introduction.
Gavin Stevens was a great friend of my parents and myself and is our daughter Kirstin's Godfather. His parents both died when he was in his teens and he became very close to our family and semi seriously used to call Mum, 'mother.' He was an excellent opening batsman and played many years for South Australia and a few tests in India where he sustained life threatening hepatitis that ended his career. I suspect the innings describes is the double century he made on the SCG that catapulted him into the tour of India. He batted against fearsome bowlers who released the ball about a metre nearer than the batsman than today and at least one of them literally 'chucked' not 'bowled' the ball. And he wore no helmet and little body protection as did all batsmen in those days.

Hi Peter

I enjoyed your other book of yarns and offer this tidbit that I recall with very mixed feelings indeed but the good things outweigh the bad. You may find this interesting

I haven't watched any of John Howard's Menzies series mentioned so often in the Australian, but they all sound rather serious and doubtless rely on a lot of guesswork.

Many people may be aware that know that John Howard is a great lover of cricket but few know that Sir Robert Menzies was the model for those who became known as 'cricket tragics.'

I met John at the reunion of old Test players in Sydney in 2000, as did a lot of others. There would not be many at that function, however, who could say they met Bob Menzies.

In January 1958 at the SCG, SA v NSW, I had to resume my innings on Monday morning, being not out from Saturday night. I had a major problem though. I had eaten something on the Sunday that had given me "the trots". This resulted in about 5 visits to the toilet between 3.00am on Monday morning and the start of play. Needless to say, even armed with the "liquid cement" I had obtained from a chemist, I was in agony for the Monday's morning session. At lunch I was still not out. All I could do though, after rushing off the field straight into the toilet, was lay down on the massage bench.

I was so distressed I didn't even take the pads off I had my eyes shut when a very distinguished voice, very close to my face, said "Well played - great innings". I looked up and there was Sir Robert Menzies. I went to get up but he told me to relax. He then said "I believe you are suffering from a condition similar to that created for me by Colonel Nasser." Bob had been co-opted by The United Nations to try and negotiate with the Leader of Egypt at the time, the said Colonel who had nationalized the Suez Canal, which was totally disrupting the trade, for example 66% of Europe's oil came through the canal, between Europe and the East. Poor old Bob had the job of trying to fix it, a job nobody was rushing to get off him. It was only on reflection after I realize his wicked sense of humour and his command of our language.

It was a great privilege to have two such great leaders of Australia and the fact that they were 'cricket tragics' was 'icing on the cake'.

Regards
The 'Ox.'
Jan 2021

Ed note: Gen Nasser nationalized the Suez Canal in 1956, the height of the 'Cold' war. Israel invaded Egypt, the Second Arab -Israeli War, followed by Britain and France. The USA opposed the action of their Allies and the Russians were rattling their sabres. I will remember the fear expressed in the newspapers of World War 111. But it was not to be. A UN force was inserted and the humiliated Britain and France withdrew and everything settled down.

With the benefit of hindsight perhaps Britain's and France's diminished role in world affairs started then and continues to this day.

Israel fought with Egypt in 1948-49, 1956, 1967 and 1973. In 1974 Egypt and Israel signed effectively a peace treaty witnessed by USA President Jimmy Carter. In 1994 Jordan followed suit, witnessed by President Clinton.

For almost 30 years there was no progress in the relationships between Israel and the Arab world. In 2020 Donald Trump was able to witness similar progress between

Israel and Bahrain, the United Arab Emirates, Sudan and Morocco. Sadly, there has been a near silent response to Trump's contribution to peace in the Middle East, perhaps history will look more kindly on this achievement when the current political situation stabilises.

THE XVI OLYMPICS – THE FRIENDLY GAMES

By The Silver Fox (aka Aileen Pluker)

The year was 1956, the date November 22 and the place, just outside the Melbourne Cricket Ground. Joan and I had not been able to get tickets for the Opening Ceremony. Instead, we had a good position along the race through which the athletes would march before entering the stadium.

1956 had not been a happy year. The Cold War was raging, the two super powers trying to outdo each other in inventing bigger and better plutonium bombs, and in Australia, England was testing atomic bombs at Maralinga. World peace was being threatened everywhere.

Colonial powers were fighting a losing battle as emerging nations fought for independence and Nasser had just annexed the Suez cannel. It was a miracle that the games would even take place. Egypt, Iraq and Lebanon had withdrawn in protest at the Israeli invasion of Suez. Switzerland, Netherlands and Spain had withdrawn in protest against Russia's invasion of Hungary and the Peoples Republic of China refused to compete alongside the Republic of China (now Taiwan). The one bright spot was Germany. Athletes from East and West Germany competed as one, the last time it happened until 1992.

We waited, excited, proud but apprehensive. Would the games be without incident and how would we, ordinary

Australians, react when we saw people who had been, or were now regarded, as our enemy?

Our first confusion came when the first team to enter was a small team of very burly men, marching under a blue and white flag, but a better-informed member of the crowd explained that Greece always led the procession in honour of the original Olympics. Behind them came the Austrians and then several countries whose names began with B. Where was Australia? Once again our knowledgeable friend explained that the host nation always marched in last. With this information we settled down to enjoy the spectacle, commenting on looks and uniforms. The French easily won the fashion stakes. A special cheer went up for the Chinese. They were on our side, not like those traitors on the mainland. Germany was also well received. We wanted them to know that all was forgiven.

And then came the Hungarian team. When they had left their country they were free, having just driven out their Communist overlords. They had even managed to alter their flag and the insignia on their uniforms. By the time they had arrived in Australia the Russians had sent in tanks and the insurrection had been brutally crushed. Even worse, the western powers had done nothing to intervene. To hide our embarrassment, we cheered and cheered them as if they were our own. A number of them did become that, because it was too dangerous for them to return home.

After Hungary, there marched a young, blonde man proudly carrying the flag of his homeland, Iceland. I was surprised that he didn't look small and dark like an Eskimo. Though alone, he did his country proud, winning a bronze medal. Then we cheered for the new nation, Israel, because they had shown the rest of the world that they were here to stay.

There was a hush when we realised that the next letter would be J. That would mean Japan, Though the war had been over for ten years, feelings were still raw. Would we cheer them, politely clap or let them know our displeasure by silence? But when they entered they looked so small, so scared, so civilized that we took them to our hearts. We cheered, they smiled and soon we were waving at each other like old friends.

The teams marched on until we came to R, but no Russia? Were they too ashamed to show their faces after what they had done to Hungary? No. We learnt that they were not just Russia but the Union of Soviet Socialist Republics. They had a huge team, only slightly smaller than the United States of America who followed. Here were two mortal enemies marching peacefully, one behind the other. Perhaps World War Three would not erupt on the streets of Melbourne after all.

We were ecstatic when our team finally marched past. We even knew some of them personally or from the newspapers. They were the finest looking, best dressed and most athletic team we had seen all day and we knew they would win a swag of medals. We cheered and cheered until the last athlete had disappeared into the tunnel.

But there was still one more surprise. Who was going to carry the torch? A number of names had been bandied around but when the tall, young man carrying the torch aloft passed us we recognized him, Ron Clarke, an eighteen-year-old, up-

and-coming runner. It was as well that he was a distance runner, as he had to carry the torch from the Fitzroy oval, where the Athletes had assembled, along the race and around the circumference of the MCG before climbing several steps to the caldron.

We could not see this but when the flames shot up and white doves were released we knew that the XVI Olympics, known later as the Friendly Games, had begun.

Footnote: The Hungarian team won a violent water polo game against Russia 4-0.

In 1956 our world changed. TV was introduced in time for the Olympic Games. Ed.

DR JAMES MURRAY COTTON
STREAKY BAY DOCTOR
1928 - 1954

By Robert Cotton

James Murray Cotton, born on 19th May, 1903, was the first white child born at Murat Bay (Ceduna). He was the eldest son of James Henry and Flora Milroy Cotton. The Cottons were English Quakers and the McKenzies of Scottish decent. Both families were early settlers. Murray's brothers and sisters were Clarice, Hazel, Howard and Frank.

Murray was brought up at Streaky Bay on a farming property and then moved into the township. His father eventually took over the General Store and named it the J. H. Cotton Store. His early education was at the Streaky Bay school and he won a scholarship to study in Adelaide, attending Adelaide Boys' High School (where Sir Mark Oliphant was a student in the same class). At eleven years of age he rode his bicycle from Streaky Bay to Port Lincoln to save the bus fare, camping out on two nights along the way and then sailed on the *Wookator* to Port Adelaide.

Murray left a warm, loving and gentle family to board with his Auntie Eva Cheyne. Later he boarded with strangers at the end of Rundle Street. Although his landlords argued a lot, from there he was able to walk to school. They gave him one lettuce sandwich a day for lunch, so that he was always hungry and he spent his pocket money of one shilling a week on food. He was only able to return to Streaky Bay once a year at Christmas time. Murray did well at school, topping the State in Physics. He won a bursary, one of only two, to attend Adelaide University where he studied medicine. Graduating after six years, Murray then spent a year as a house surgeon at the Royal Adelaide Hospital.

Having gained his degree, he worked his way as a ship's doctor on a cargo ship to England, then travelled to Edinburgh to study at the Royal Infirmary where he gained his L.R.C.S (Licentiate of the Royal College of Surgeons). Three students sat for the exam but he was the only one to pass, even though he had only six months to prepare as he could not afford to stay longer. During this time he assisted in, and saw, a lot of surgery which stood him in good stead for when he later practised at Streaky Bay. Murray was then 26 years old and he worked his way back again to Australia on an Indian cargo ship.

His first appointment was in Western Australia as a locum in the country. One of his first cases was a man who had three perforations in his bowel from a shotgun accident. The wound became infected, but eventually healed. It must have been quite frightening for a young doctor just out on his own. However, the patient survived. After that he did locums all over the South Australia including Mount Gambier, Mannum and Clare, and also travelled at one time with an insurance salesman doing insurance health assessments.

While a student at Adelaide University, Murray had met up with Don Drever, who was in the same year of Medicine, and originally from Calca near Streaky Bay. Through him he met his sister, Melba, who was at that time nursing at the Royal Adelaide Hospital. They married in 1932 and went to live at Streaky Bay. Mignon was born whilst they lived there. A couple of years later they moved to 445 The Parade at Kensington. Of all the houses he owned, this was his favourite. He could still recite the telephone number 61 years later!

He set up practice on The Parade at Norwood where the old tower stands. Robert was born from Kensington. Murray also attended Glenside Hospital as a GP and Yatala Prison. Mignon well remembers sitting in the car while he was visiting there. Then along came Christobel and the family moved to Halsbury Avenue, Kingswood.

He was later divorced and married Elsie Noble, again living on The Parade, this time at Norwood, where Alan and Graham were born. He moved back to Streaky Bay, where he felt he belonged, and Juliette was born there. Murray had a profound knowledge of the West Coast and loved the area, planting many trees around the township of Streaky Bay and thoroughly enjoying finding oysters, razorfish, and catching whiting. He had a pact with the hospital – he would take time off to go fishing and if he was needed they would pull a blind down on the verandah signalling he was needed.

Murray had a busy practice at Streaky Bay and at times had to travel to surrounding towns such as Wudinna and Ceduna. It must have been horrendous during World War II as he was responsible for a large area from Ceduna to Elliston, and was also the dentist, chemist – as well as the Vet when anyone had a sick cow! Murray often had to pull a tooth and said that he lived with the worry that a tooth may break off when pulling it out – fortunately it never happened!

His family remember him driving all night, to bring a patient to the Adelaide Hospital – this man had a heavy machine dropped on him. Another time he was called to a farm where a man's arm had been ripped off at the shoulder.

On another occasion Murray had attend a patient on a farm at night. In order to find the track into the farmhouse one of the children had to hold up a sheet while another swung a tilley lamp behind it to mark the turn off.

Murray did emergency surgery and was responsible for the anaesthetic simultaneously. He would start the anaesthetic with Ethyl Chloride and then Ether, then he would hand over to the nursing sister while he performed the operation. He delivered up to 100 maternity cases a year. He used Chloroform for the anaesthetic in some maternity cases.

He could also do a range of surgery e.g., tonsillectomies, adenoids, appendicectomies and ruptured peptic ulcers. He also did a few 'Ramsted' operations under local anaesthetic on babies for Pyloric Stenosis of the stomach. Those babies all survived. Murray was proud of the fact that he never lost a mother in childbirth.

Murray even had to do an emergency tracheotomy, on the kitchen table, for his sister's son, Ross Graves, who had croup and was choking.

Another time he had to remove an injured eye from a young man.

Between such dramatic episodes, Murray spent time in the billiard saloon room at Streaky Bay and became a fine billiards player. He also loved playing Bridge. He was an avid reader and was still reading medical books into his eighties. Murray had a wide general knowledge and on cruises he often won 'Brains Trust' competitions and quizzes. He was always a very self-confident man, climbing Uluru at the age of 75, driving his car to Western Australia when 76, and from Mount Pleasant to Streaky Bay into his nineties.

One of the greatest tragedies in his life was when his brother Frank, having survived being one of the Rats of Tobruk, was killed in the Battle of Lae in New Guinea during World War II, in a sniper attack, at the age of 26. The family had dreaded receiving such a telegram. And one day it came.

Murray had a wry sense of humour. At an AMA dinner, sitting next to his son, Robert, he said, 'I guess not too many of these doctors have delivered babies in wurleys as I have.' He treated Daisy Bates as a patient – a famous woman who lived and helped the aborigines on the West Coast.

Later Murray was divorced from his second wife and he moved to Adelaide to live when Alan, Graham and Juliette were teenagers setting up practice on the North East Road, North Walkerville, and bought a house in Second Avenue, St Peters. Sadly, Juliette passed away in her thirties.

He worked as a General Practitioner for over 60 years. A 'no nonsense' doctor, his practice at North Walkerville contained a dozen odd dining-room chairs, worth about 20c each, a fan, chained to the table because someone stole the last one, a few ashtrays and some very old, tattered magazines. Murray never employed a nurse or receptionist and he typed out his accounts on Sunday nights. He later trained his patients to pay on the way out – he said it saved them, and himself, a stamp!

Patients flocked to his practice and were very fond of him. Just plain good medicine is what they went there for. In fact, his grandson, David Radloff, married one of his patients, Dianne Thurmer. People had a lot of faith in him, and many travelled from Streaky Bay to consult with him. He had a name in the district for stopping and saying to an old lady, a patient, 'Now Mrs Smith, what are you doing in the garden, I told you to rest.'

Once a week Murray visited an old lady patient in her nineties. The old soul caught a bus to the city each week to go to the market and buy crayfish or prawns to make sandwiches and strawberries to have with the scones and cream for lunch. It gave her an incentive to live as he was her only visitor.

Murray loved gardening, only growing vegetables. He dug up the tennis court to grow them! He believed the key to good health lay in eating a wide variety of foods including plenty of fish, fruit and vegetables.

Murray had a very happy relationship with his cousin Melva Redding who housekept for him for many years, and he was very close to his cousins Vena and Mack Cheyne.

Murray did not retire until he was 86 years old and later when he sold the St Peters house, the Headmaster of the East Adelaide School came over to visit him and said, 'I heard that you have sold your property Dr Cotton. The school wanted to buy it.' Murray's sense of humour answered him, 'I'm eighty-seven now, just when were you thinking of asking me?' The school bought it from the developer but had to pay an extra $40,000 to get it.

Murray built a small house on Robert's property at Mount Pleasant, where naturally he dug up a patch of ground to grow his vegetables, especially his sweet white onions. He joined a bridge club and played once a week.

Then he met Annie Drew, another West Coaster, whilst shopping at The Avenues. They formed a very happy relationship for the last seven years of his life, together travelling to Alma, Hamley Bridge, Salter Springs and around Adelaide attending 80th and 90th birthdays and Golden and Diamond wedding anniversaries.

His mother was one of eleven children and most married and had five or six children, so he had dozens of long-living McKenzie cousins. He and Annie went with Christobel on a Pacific cruise on the *Fairstar*, and later he and Annie went right around Australia on a bus tour. They also had a number of trips to the West Coast with Annie driving.

He had a long and wonderful life, he said. He enjoyed good health for most of it, in spite of being a smoker 'rolling his own' for many years. Murray had the measles when he was nine years old and then no illness to speak of until about 86 years old, when he had his first hip replacement. He certainly didn't like being on the other end of the hospital bed and he tried to pull rank. He told the staff he would look after his own medication as he was a doctor – it didn't work! He took his own salt and pepper shakers with him to hospital. Some weeks before he died he said, 'No more doctors, no more treatment.' He flatly refused to go to a nursing home or hospital and died at the age of 94 years at the home of his very dear friend, Annie Drew.

We remember him as a very loving father. When we went out with him twice a week to the Koala Farm, beach or Brownhill Creek, he just played with us and enjoyed us – we had great fun. We never heard him swear and he remained polite and a gentleman to the end. He always said most sincerely, 'Thank you for coming to see me.' He just loved little children, and little children loved him. He could really relate to them and make them laugh.

Murray was a very frugal man but could be generous to his family. Never a fancy dresser, one day he shuffled down to the Co-op with his grandson to open an account for him. The woman at the desk snapped, 'You have to have $500 to open an account ' With that he handed over a cheque for $50,000 - her attitude changed immediately, the boy reported when he returned home! He had a 30-year-old Toyota Crown car for the last part of his life and kept it in good condition. I believe he learnt to be frugal during the Great Depression.

We are all proud of this man who was our father. He loved his work and his work was his life. An old West Coaster has returned to rest in his favourite town, Streaky Bay.

Part V

CAREERS

AN INTERESTING AND ADVENTUROUS CAREER ON EYRE PENINSULA

By Malcolm Schluter

I joined the South Australia Police at 16 years of age on 1/1/63, after completing my (then) Leaving Certificate at Norwood High School. Back in those days there were many options for employment and I remember considering school teaching, the AMP or the Bank of Adelaide, but the police force seemed more to my liking – the idea of chasing villains around the countryside was appealing.

The police had acquired Fort Largs from the military a year or two before, and it became the main training facility taking over from the Thebarton Barracks. The four-year training was a wonderful experience and we were taught so much through our developing years to manhood. The 26 members of my course were all of the same age and we were sworn in as police constables on our 20th birthdays.

Graduating from a probationary constable to a patrol officer in the city, and eventually being a Motor Traffic Constable riding a motor cycle for several years, and then served in the Vice Squad for a year or two, scratching the surface of humanity. I was accepted into the Criminal Investigation Branch and eventually transferred to Elizabeth CIB, a place then in the 1970s with emerging social problems, and nonetheless I was able to look at the crimes and follies of mankind and closely observe the ugly surface of life, which I found fascinating.

In April 1974 I was selected for transfer to Ceduna, and with my then wife Fay and our two-year-old daughter Sarah, made the long haul, with a furniture truck to follow and made our home in a modern police house at Thevenard, opposite the silos.

As the sole detective for the huge area, I travelled far and wide, often accompanied by other police members, in the investigation of all manner of criminal activity, but putting the malefactors to one side, I received the education of my life interacting with the West Coasters. I found the men and women of diverse backgrounds a great source of practical wisdom and were always ready to help me navigate the problems I came across in my role. I began to learn the importance of manly courage, personal honour, patriotic duty and other traditional virtues.

On one occasion a tribal woman was murdered at a camp near the Nundroo Roadhouse and after witnessing the post-mortem examination on a kitchen table at the rear of the roadhouse, the hunt for the killer commenced.

Arriving at his camp at Yalata we found he had fled on foot a few minutes before. Three Aboriginal trackers (Tommy Gibson, Lindsay Poopidie and Maurice Queama) were co-opted and we tracked the offender Sydney Williams for the most part of the day through scrubland until arresting him late in the afternoon.

Without any food or water and being the only smoker in the police party, I had to supply cigarettes to the trackers and soon emptied my pack. Witnessing the trackers doing their great work was a wonderful experience and especially when they found a 'water tree', fossicking out suitable tree roots, ripping the bark off and holding the root vertically while lovely clean and cool water dripped out, kept us all going.

The murder trial took place in Adelaide at the Supreme Court, and as the witnesses were mostly tribal aborigines with poor English language skills, I arranged for the late George Law, a farmer from Bookabie, who was highly respected by the Yalata people, to assist the court with his interpreting. Unfortunately, George was unable to accurately interpret the Pitjantjatjara language into English precisely as was demanded. George could well describe what the witness was trying to say but Justice Wells would have none of it and required George to accurately translate the language. Eventually poor George's services were suspended and an expert from the university took his place. The accused was found guilty of manslaughter and by order of the court I was required to accompany him back to Yalata with court order, and for Sydney to be ruled and governed by the Tribal Elders. The case attracted widespread publicity with TV crews seeking to be present when Sydney was to be speared as tribal punishment.

The trial (R v Sydney Williams) was an important case inasmuch there were a number of implications in respect to the interviewing by police of tribal aborigines and the requirement to have 'a friend' present.

The tracker Tommy Gibson and I had a great friendship and I arranged for the Commissioner of Police to write to Tommy thanking him for his good work. Tommy carried the letter in his hat and whenever circumstances required it, Tommy would produce the letter and it smoothed the way through a variety of police interactions over the years.

On another occasion two men were found dead in a car just off the Eyre Highway near the WA border. They had fallen asleep on a cold night, wrapped in blankets with the engine running to keep warm. When I arrived at the scene after a five to six-hour drive from Ceduna, it was about 3.00am and it must be remembered that the Eyre Highway was unsealed from just out of Penong and all the way to the WA border. After making initial enquiries and determining what had occurred, being carbon monoxide poisoning, with the absence of the rubber grommets around the brake and clutch pedals leading to the engine compartment, some practical decisions were needed. We loaded the deceased into body bags and placed them in the boot of the police Valiant sedan, drove to Eucla and slept at the motel for a few hours and then commenced the journey back to Ceduna, towing the men's vehicle to Koonalda Station where Cyril Gurney (who always reminded me of Uncle Tom and his cabin) and his wife provided my offsider Graham Johnston and me with lunch.

We finally arrived back at Ceduna during the evening and stopped at Dr Richard Jolly's home and the good doctor certified the men as dead and I then drove to my home for a change of clothing. I remember telling my wife Fay the story of my exploits and she asked 'where are the bodies now? to which I replied 'outside in the driveway in the boot of the police car.' After being refreshed, off I set to Whyalla for the post-mortems the following morning. I stopped in a parking bay somewhere near Wudinna in the early hours of the morning, sitting in the car eating sandwiches and drinking coffee from a thermos my wife had provided, when I became aware of a not very pleasant smell emanating from the boot. I attended the post-mortem at the Whyalla Hospital later that day and I clearly remember the surgeon dolefully showing me the black lungs of one of the deceased, and explaining to me the folly of smoking. I did continue with the habit for some years despite the practical and enduring example of its dangers.

The east-west railway line in those days was still maintained by groups of fettlers stationed at the various sidings, all named after Australian Prime Ministers, and some villain I was chasing, was suspected of being at Reid, just over the border in Western Australia. So, I set off one day and drove to Eucla where I stocked up with some food and drink and then headed north towards the railway line, about 120kms away. My police vehicle was a Valiant automatic sedan.

I reached about two thirds of the distance and struck a rock and immediately lost power. I found that the car could be driven in reverse and I drove for some distance in that way until that failed as well. Fluid was leaking from the transmission of course and there was nothing I could do but wait for a passing vehicle. I remained there for a day and a half in very pleasant weather conditions thank goodness, before a railway fettler and his family came along and towed me to the siding at Reid.

The family put me up for several days until a freight train came along heading east and I was able to load the police car on the train and travelled with it to Adelaide. I walked from the Mile End railway yards to the Police Barracks at Thebarton to the transport department where I was provided with the replacement car. I thought I would be typing reports about this misadventure for weeks, but I managed to slither out of it without any repercussions whatsoever.

A colourful character 'Goog' Denton, who had a farm north of Ceduna had the foresight to build a track from his farm to the east-west railway line coming out near Tarcoola. He was able to push his grader through about 30kms before the authorities caught up with him, threatening all sorts of legal action unless he desisted. I was invited to join a party including the late Hon. Arthur Whyte MLC, and a group of Ceduna based people, to accompany Goog along the track. I felt like an early inland explorer, camping out and forging beyond the end of Goog's Track.

Smoking marijuana was really coming into vogue in the 1970s and it was a well- known feature of life in the surfing community at Cactus Beach, at Point Sinclair via Penong. On several occasions we conducted raids very late at night or in the early hours and confiscated bongs, dope and associated materials after waking the sleeping surfies and their girls who were mostly shacked up in pretty basic shelters. We would arrest them and take them to the Penong police station where they faced a couple of local Justices if the Peace, fined $50.00 and returned to the beach again.

A couple of years ago the book 'Cactus: Surfing Journals from Solitude' was published and documents the first 25 years of surfing at Cactus Beach and I got a none too flattering mention about the above-mentioned police activities.

The sealing of the Eyre Highway to the WA border was a major project and the commissioning of the highway was celebrated at Wigunda Tank near Nullarbor in 1976, completing a project which the Western Australians finished in 1969 to their side of the border. My job on the day was to drive the Commissioner of Police, the Army Commander Central Command and the general manager of the RAA from Ceduna to Wigunda Tank, and then return later in the day. Most of the officials were conveyed by special bus from Ceduna but the Police Commissioner correctly foresaw the return journey on the bus was likely to be rather a 'sloppy trip' and chose to be driven by police car. Suffice it to say that I had to be on my best behaviour all day, and from various sources the Commissioner's choice of transport was very wise.

I look back on those days with great fondness and especially the friendships I developed and the great examples of public integrity and the many who were constantly striving to eke out an existence under very difficult farming conditions. Ceduna back in those days was rightly termed a 'wild west town' with numerous personalities and a big drinking culture. It was a community which strongly supported its police and I was proud to have spent my time there.

R M WILLIAMS – HIS FIRST BOOTS

By Peter Morton

Reginald Murray Williams was a remarkable man, born in 1908 at Belalie North near Jamestown in South Australia and passed away peacefully at his property in Queensland aged 95 in 2003.

Perhaps no one could describe his life better than Paul Myers in a story "Bush Craftsman" where he writes. "But there has always been much more to RM than bush clobber. This remarkable Australian was also an explorer, pastoralist, horseman, stockman, stonemason, leather craftsman, goldminer, well sinker, author, businessman and historian - excelling at all and more".

His father was a blacksmith that made him "want to make things" and he certainly did. When he was 10 the family moved to Adelaide for the children's education. At 13 he rolled his swag and headed off in 1921. In the next few years he worked at incredibly hard jobs well sinking, tank building and even camel driving.

Somehow, he wound up in Oodnadatta and met a William Wade who, in RM's words was, "Born in London, a Cockney, spent his early life as a sailor, was converted by the Salvation Army and spent the rest of his life as a missionary to the Aborigines".

This was to be Wade's first mission and he needed

someone to look after the necessary camels. To RM, who had never seen a camel and thought of them as big horses and treated them as such. After a few lessons from an Afghan Cameleer they roamed, unarmed, in the Victorian, Gibson and Great Sandy Desert for three years from 1926-1929.

To put this into perspective these three deserts cover over 300,000 square miles, about a third the size of India. The last white men to venture there were Forrest in the 1860s and Giles in the 1870s and the next was Len Beadell in the 1950s when he surveyed the Woomera Rocket Range, built the famous Gun Barrel highway as well as many other roads and the odd atomic bomb testing site.

In 1929 RM returned to Adelaide and married. The Depression took its toll and with his wife and child he moved to the Gammon Ranges and camped in Italowie Gorge for what became two years where he did odd jobs and struggled mightily with many others.

One day a most unlikely harbinger of fame and fortune drove into his camp in a mule pulled buggy. This was one Michael George Smith aka Dollar Mick. He taught RMW to make boots from one piece of leather as well as other leather work and the rest we know.

In the early 1930s he returned to Adelaide because he and his child had 'Sandy Blight" a very painful and potentially severe eye disease we now call Trachoma.

He later borrowed money from Sidney Kidman and made pack saddles for Kidman's many stations and later boots, the first pair of which he sold in 1932 I believe to a man I knew as explained below.

In 1979 my wife and I moved to Port Lincoln to work and

live. In 1982 we bought a grazing property 60 -70 km from Port Lincoln in partnership with Brian and Pam Murray the managers of Parakylia Station, near Woomera.

A Frank Lillecrapp was the Land agent involved and met with the four of us in Port Lincoln. Frank had been a boundary rider along the Dog or Dingo fence that ran 5600 km from west of Brisbane to Fowlers Bay in South Australia and part of it was the northern boundary of Parakylia. Frank had been a bomber pilot in the RAAF during World War 2 and Brian flew light aircraft so there were many stories told.

Frank also told us that when he was 14 he was camped, on his own, with a mob of sheep he was droving near Orroroo east of the Flinders Ranges. Lo and behold, none other than RM rode into his camp on a pushbike. Over many cups of tea RM told Frank he was going to Adelaide to make boots and there and then Frank promised to buy his first pair and said he did just that.

My wife and I came to know and respect Frank and his wife Maeve and I have no doubt he was telling the truth.

About 15 years later there was an advertisement in "Outback" magazine and or other publications with a picture of RM and a caption. "I wish I knew the name of that bloke from Hiltaba Station who bought my first boots".

Our daughter's best friend worked as a clothes designer for RMW. I told her about this and she flicked it to the boss. His comment was "Couldn't he be on a horse"?

To digress: horses were expensive and needed cleaning, feeding, shoes and so on and travellers such as shearers, labourers and battlers rode bikes or walked. Horses in the early 1800s cost 18 months of a labourer's wages and that is the price of a second-hand Land Cruiser today—well they were four-wheel-drive transport animals!

The boss did not know about the Hiltaba advertisement, Frank, his wife and one daughter were dead and I did not know the name of his other daughter and RM in a personal letter to me said he could not remember but knew the Lillecrapps so it all faded away.

Another 10 years or so passed by and a chap researching the history of RW contacted me. From the information I gave him he believed Frank's story and that is why there is a sign indicating the RM WILLIAMS WAY in the main street of Ororoo.

When RM first started in Percy Street despite doing well with the pack saddles for Sidney Kidman he was in financial strife and wanted to make boots but had no customers.

In his 1986 book, "Beneath whose hand" RM writes, "It was then I made the most rewarding experiment of my whole life. I spent sixpence on a small two-line advertisement in "The Adelaide Chronicle" "Elastic side boots made to order. Twenty Shillings. Cash with order. 5 Percy St Prospect". He then writes, "Within days came a letter with a pound note enclosed and a size for the boots." He then describes making the boots and finishes "I have forgotten his name but he lives like a giant in my memory. Sufficient that he came from Hiltaba Station, ever afterwards a romantic name." So, he clearly remembered the event.

There is a logistical question. Port Augusta is 350km north of Adelaide and Hiltaba is 280 km west of Port Augusta as the crow flies but the train would go to Kingoonya 330km and then by road it is 160km to Hiltaba.

It is just not tenable that a newspaper could reach Hiltaba and RM get a reply, "within days." The only way that could happen was that the sender was in Adelaide or nearby, read the paper there and posted the letter in Adelaide giving his address as Hiltaba.

We know that Frank tended the Dog Fence and drove sheep hundreds of kilometres from there in the early 1930s so it is far from impossible that he did a stint at Hiltaba.

I suppose it all comes down to whether he was telling the truth and I believe he was.

Postscript:

In 1968, when a final year medical student, with two friends I visited Wertaloona Station, east of the Flinders Ranges. Bob Wilson was the owner and his brother Bill owned the adjoining Frome Downs. We were welcomed by Bob, and that was particularly nice as our organiser had forgotten to contact him about us visiting! It was all good. We camped in the shearers' quarters, were shown around and ate in the homestead. We met his daughter, Jane (now Benson), and the man she would later marry.

Four months later I was a brand-new Intern at the Broken Hill Hospital and on a day off was asked to go for a ride in a Flying Doctor plane to Wertaloona where we picked up a man with a broken leg.

Fast forward 30-40 years, Jane Benson is a friend of ours and has given me an introduction to several outback people who have helped very much in my literary career, such as it is. She also gave me a picture of 'Dollar Mick' working as a blacksmith at Wertaloona and told me that was where he showed RMW how to make boots. The boot last/s they used were given to the R M Williams Museum at 5 Percy Street, Prospect, and I have seen a photograph of them.

SILENCE

By Jayde Shields

Silence. Nothing but silence as the new Shearer approaches the board. The rouseys quit their chit chat and with a slight turn of the head, indicate mild interest. He looks around, alert, slightly anxious. Feeling the eyes upon him.

Takes in the smell of the shed. A peculiar mix of lanolin, ammonia and sheep dung. The hand cut railings on the wooden wool bins and above each the grades stencilled in white. The manual wool press used for the skirtings set behind the rectangular skirting table.

Admires the polished shearer's board with the shiny nail heads slightly embedded into the timber. The fine dust coating the cobwebs in every corner of the shed. The spiders long gone or baked from the heat of the corrugated iron.

'Yer stands over there', pipes up the wool classer.

A nod of the head and the silence breaks as the sheep are pushed into the pens.

'Mornin', 'mornin' from the shearers on each side. Then back to their routine of gear inspection, a diversion from conversation.

He unpacks his tools in methodical order. The comb bag hung with a wool bale clip on an old nail, bent and twisted by past shearers. The cutter run set at the precise angle for a quick change. Hangs the wash bucket and comb strap. Pulls out the smoothest handpiece. Recently rebuilt on a wet day. Places it on the rail, grabs his towel and walks over with counter in hand to inspect the sheep just penned.

Notices the size, roundness and temperament. Feels the wool for softness, openness and dirt. Parts the fleece and checks the micron. Contemplates the comb choice.

Sets the counter to zero and hangs it at the gate. Positions the towel at head height. Checks the penning gates to ensure smooth travel. *Don't want them swinging into your back pulling out a big wether.*

Glances over the pens, up the race and gives the penner a quick smile and a nod of the head. Makes a mental note to introduce himself. *Always want the penner on your side to push the rough sheep past your gate.*

He raises his head to check the time on the clock. A critical component in any shearer's day.

The Contractor strides up and makes a timely introduction, *'No sheep pulled from the pens before or after time',* his final words before walking away.

The roof is low, with no ventilation at the top. The corrugated iron windows on the opposite side are open and propped with timbers as old as the shed. No breeze, just the last of the morning freshness departing. The corrugated iron roof rusted in places allowing the sun's rays to penetrate into the shed.

He hangs the water bottle at a height to take a drink and not to delay or break the momentum during the run. Walks back. Picks up the downtube. Checks the cogs for tooth wear, checks the cone wear and gap on the drive wheel, removes the short tube and inspects the short gut. Replaces. Oils the down tube and pulls the shearing plant into gear, checking for smooth operation and breaking the silence.

He positions the back-support system and fits the back aid. Checks the height, checks the positioning and free movement. The finish position directly in line with the chute.

He picks up the handpiece. Blisters now replaced with callouses to conform to its shape. Selecting and analysing the correct comb for the sheep. Pulls a cutter and sets the lead. Taking particular notice of the cutter alignment to the comb teeth. Tightens, oils and tests the makeup. Sets in position on the down tube. Places the oil can within easy reach so he can keep the equipment cool and not delay momentum. Selects a second comb and places it on the rail. Looks up as the wool-classer bellows the rouseys into action.

Stretches his body, walks to the pen and takes a drink. Focused and complete as the clock ticks over and the shearers push into the pens.

Click, as the ropes are pulled, the cones engage with the drive wheel and all the shearers' handpieces fire into life. He grabs the closest sheep in the pen. Drags it to the stand.

Click, adjusts the handpiece tension and the run beings.

Top notch removed. A slight step back and the first full blow down along the belly, two more and the belly wool removed. A slight position change and a full blow along the front leg down over the hip to the back bone, two more along the same line and around the crutch. One blow on the underside of the tail and up the opposite side. A step forward placing one foot in between the rear legs of the sheep. Opposite upper leg and torso supporting the sheep while he makes blows along the neck and around the head. Slightly raises the front leg of the sheep and removes the wool from the front leg, as he simultaneously swings the sheep into position for the long blow. The handpiece never leaving the wool or idle in motion. The sheep positioned in a slight arc he makes blows from tail to head. The last blow on the underside of the backbone as he brings his rear foot around. His free hand and arm raising and turning the sheep while the wool is cut from around the head. The blow continuing in fluid motion down the opposite side of the neck and out along the front leg. With pure finger and upper body strength he maneuverers the front leg while stepping back and positioning the sheep in a sitting position on its inside rear end. All while the blow is completed to the top of the opposite rear leg. The sheep always calm he completes the last side and in a matter of minutes the fleece is removed and the sheep out the chute, shorn for another year.

The rousey moves in and picks up the fleece. The cycle repeats with cutter changes as required to maintain the optimum cut.

He stops to change a comb change on the hour. Checking, ensuring its precision. The equipment and planning is the edge to ensure a full tally at the end of the day. Aware of the odd glance his way. A silent recognition.

The two hour run finishes and the sheep are counted. The pens re-stocked. A nod, a smile or 'g'day mate' as the other shearers file off the board. He removes the spent comb and cutter, drops it into the wash bucket. Prepares for the next run. The wool-classer approaches. Introductions, a firm handshake with the customary idle conversation.

No rush to the smoko. Observe the pecking order, wait

your turn and wait for your time. Mutton sandwiches with cheese and pickles. The meat cut thick, no shortage of mutton in a shearing shed. Strong black tea brewed in a kettle from an era long passed. Large enough for the team with a metal thick enough to carry the weight of the water it has to hold.

Rouseys congregate on the wool bales as the shearers meander back to the board. The presser staples the last full bale from the run, always the last to smoko. He finishes the sandwich, takes a sip and with cup in hand heads back to his stand. Places it on the rail to allow it to cool. Looks out through the open wooden framed window. Gnarled timber, as hard as the shearers in the shed. He watches the grazier drenching and branding the shorn sheep. His ever obedient and loyal dog at the rear pushing the sheep into the race way.

He lay flat on the board with towel under his neck and legs slightly elevated resting on the penning board rails. Contemplating nothing, relaxing and mentally preparing for the next run.

Click, the run begins as the daily temperature starts to rise. The odd waft of breeze that comes and goes is not enough to stop the sweat running off the bridge of his nose. Long full blows, comb down on the skin. Maximizing the fleece cut and keeping the comb below the fine dirt layer. Protecting the equipment from nature's sand paper.

The sheep out the chute, simultaneously pulling the handpiece out of gear. Strides to the pen, wipes his brow on the towel, takes a drink and grabs the next sheep. Drags to the stand and continues the routine like a well-oiled synchronized machine.

The sun is now high in the sky as the team stroll to the

quarters for lunch. The birds have gone into hiding apart from the ever resilient and observant crow, peering down upon them clinging onto the wide sparse branches of the white gum. Leaves shimmering, slightly curled at the tips, hanging low like an old shearer. He re-adjusts his thoughts and proceeds to the washtub. Fills the wash bucket with water, noticing the customary yellow Sunlight soap bar.

Washes up in the luke-warm water from pipes, not buried deep enough, that run from the galvanized tanks.

'What will it be, cold meat and salad?' invites the cook? 'Mutton?' he asks. 'Of course, son.' He finds a spare seat, reserved for the Shearer and sits down to eat. In silence.

He gazes around to the older shearers. Hardened lumps on the knuckle joints, semi bent fingers in the shape of the handpiece and their taut oversized forearms. Each with slightly hollowed cheeks and deep weathered lines on their faces. *As tough as Iron bark trees.*

One breaks the silence and the conversation flows around the table. Words of advice, stories of: remember that day and the never-ending topic of, what's for dinner cook! A question that didn't ever need the answer. The wool classer, presser and penner arrive just as the shearers stride back to the shed.

The tally book has been updated and reflects the Shearer's counter. The shed has been re-stocked and a new line is penned. Smaller sheep, wool from head to toe, mouths slightly agape. Younger sheep, a little nervous as they bleat to companions in further pens.

He makes a change in comb style and thickness. Adjusts the lead, oils the handpiece and sets on the down tube. Re-oils the downtube, lowers the back aid one hole. Walks across, tilts his head and takes a big drink. Observing the underside of the tin roof shimmering in the midday day heat.

He moves across and lies flat on the board. Legs slightly elevated resting on the penning board rails. The silence resumes as he relaxes and mentally prepares.

Click, the run beings. The Shearer is in full concentration, his muscles are that of an athlete, the rising temperature is of mild concern as he focuses entirely on his technique. The smaller sheep, now settled have the rousey's working overtime as the shearers pick up the numbers. Their efficiency, agility and timing are a blur to him, like two machines working in unison. The clock ticks over and the run is finished.

He takes a drink, wipes his face on the towel and looks across to the skirting table. Fleeces stacked, the wool-classer giving orders while simultaneously checking fleece quality and placing in the allocated bin. The presser moving wool in armfuls half his weight. Building his strength, preparing for when he becomes a shearer.

Smoko is up, the black tea is loaded up with two spoonsful of sugar. A few biscuits and return to prepare the equipment for the next run.

He rests his body, lying flat on the board, legs slightly elevated resting on the penning board rails. The silence inside him resumes as he relaxes and mentally prepares.

Click, the last run beings. He steps up the pace aware that bodies will be weary. Sets his pace to half a sheep behind the Gun shearer. A mental and physical game to determine if the Gun can handle a little pressure. The other shearers sense the challenge and the numbers increase; weariness set aside the adrenaline levels rise. The penner gives orders to his dog filling the pens as fast as they are emptied. Rouseys run the board working overtime, their faces bright red hoping that the shearers drop back a gear.

He doesn't aim to beat the gun. Not today, it will unsettle the team. He remembers some wise words. *People always remember the cleanest shearers, not the fastest, speed will come in your technique. Keep the harmony and earn the respect of the team.*

The minute hand on the clock ticks over and the run is complete.

Sly smirks from the shearers, a nod of the head acknowledging the enjoyment of the game. The rouseys dawdle as they pick up the last fleeces for the day. The sheep are counted and the days tally finalized in the book.

With the spent combs and cutters from the day now cleaned. He sets up the grinder and cutting discs. New papers glued on the discs and set with the backing plate to ensure a complete bond to the disc. He finds an area out of the light and prepares to secure the grinder for levelness and to minimize vibration. He trims the paper along the edge of the disc with a short fine bladed sharp knife. Removes the cutting discs from the backing plates and installs to the grinder. "The coarser paper for combs and the finer for cutters".

Hangs the light and with a spin on the discs, fires the grinder into action. Grinds the combs and cutters. Checking each one under the light for removal of dull sections, scoring and angle of the grind. Peering closer and ensuring the lines run straight up the comb teeth. A quick buff on the backside of the combs to bring back the shine on the underside and reduce drag from grease build up.

With the sun drifting towards the horizon. The team wanders back to the shearer's quarters. He unloads his mobile washing machine and grabs his bags. Finds a spare room and unpacks his clothes. Then heads for the showers where a large Salmon gum stands proud and tall. Most likely an introduced species it would appreciate the yearly watering from the shower run off. Providing also, some shade and a roost for pink and grey galahs settling in for the night.

The ever-reliable Donkey hot water system gives out a gentle spurt from the vent line indicating the water will be hot. He washes away the dirt and grease of the day. Scrubbing out the fine wool that can get caught in skin pores and lead to wool sores. Dressed in the customary blue singlet, shorts and thongs he heads for the kitchen.

Opens the timber framed fly wire door and asks the cook the inevitable question. 'What's for dinner?' 'Lamb chops and veg.' replies the cook.

He turns to the table, all eyes upon the new Shearer. 'Anyone shear a lamb today?' Laughter breaks out, the conversation starts to flow and he takes a seat at the table.

The sun has set and the red outback glow silhouettes the surrounding shrubs. Lifting the colour out of the ancient floodplain soil and bringing to life the small ironstone rocks.

He takes a seat and a big drink on a cool beer. The penner and his dog walk up. A pat and a ruffle of the ears for the dog, before it rolls on its back waiting for further attention. The penner takes a seat.

They take a swig on their beers as the brilliant outback stars start to come to life. The galahs complete their roost, the odd sheep bleats for a companion and quiet conversation can be heard around the quarters.

A gentle breeze comes and goes as they settle back and take in the Silence. The Silence of the Outback.

THE STATIONARY WIBBERLEYS OF TUMBY BAY

By Peter Morton

Introduction

I graduated in medicine in 1968 and did my intern year at Broken Hill. My wife and I were married that year and for ten years pursued our dreams of working in outback and rural Australia finally settling in Port Lincoln from 1979 until 2002. I then did various locums in many parts of rural Australia from 2003-2016 for about half the time.

Over the years in Port Lincoln I came to know or hear about doctors who were true stalwarts of their communities and professions. In no particular order Richard Jolly, Bryan Thompson, David Wibberley, Gerry Quigley, Dick Schoeman, Rufus McLeay, the redoubtable Ian Fletcher, Rob Oswald, Dennis Eaton and Graham Fleming come to mind, all men I have known. Others I have heard about include Murray Cotton from Streaky Bay and his successor Freddy Geisler.

I wrote an autobiography about my almost 50 years as a rural doctor but I did not come close to the stature and community involvement these doctors have achieved.

I have tried to distil the essence of a good country doctor that aspiring young doctors may emulate and who better to use as that model would be father and son doctors Brian and David Wibberley of Tumby Bay from 1920 -1999.

I entered medical school in 1961 and that year there was

a subject, Medicine and the Humanities, given by a tweedy, greying, gowned Oxford DON, Dr Harris for an hour a week. It was a potted history of mankind from the ancient Egyptians, the Fertile Crescent, the Renaissance, Harvey and circulation, the Hunter brothers and so on. I loved the course as I had read about many related subjects.

When pondering the weight of this task with 90 pages of Wibberley history in front of me I remembered that William Osler, 1849-1919, the doyen of his time, 'Father of Modern Medicine,' one of the four founders of John Hopkins Hospital and so on featured in this course for many cogent reasons. Osler stressed that doctors, whilst they must be scientists, should also be humanists, well read and involved in matters outside academia. As a bibliophile he recommended books aspiring doctors should read to achieve balance in their lives.

It struck me that the two Wibberleys and their wives were deeply rooted in their communities, cultured, caring and had a range of other interests just like Osler recommended. There is another side of this. Many people, including me, believe that longevity of doctors in rural practice is dependent or proportional to the amount of interests they have outside medicine or a special interest in an esoteric part and essentially the happiness and involvement of their spouse in their community.

BRIAN WILLIAM 'BILL' WIBBERLEY
MBBS, BSc, MC
Born: 1891
Died: 1973
Served in Tumby Bay 1920-1957

His father was Reverend Brian Wibberley from Derbyshire who, with his wife, settled in Brighton, Victoria in 1887 where their son was born in 1891 and daughter Annie in 1892. In 1897 they moved to the Wellington Square church, in North Adelaide. In 1912, when Brian Junior was 11, they moved to Moonta where he applied for a scholarship at Prince Alfred College in Adelaide. He had never studied maths but with coaching by his mother he not only gained the scholarship, but in his final year at school, now called matriculation, he topped the state in Maths.

His son David, when a scholar at the school 30-40 years later, noticed his name on the academic honour boards in the Old Assembly Hall many times and he also won prizes for gymnastics. He received another scholarship to study Medicine and the University of Adelaide and on the way earned a Bachelor of Science presented to him on the same day as his skilled and knowledgeable Reverend father, a musician and author, received a Bachelor of Music.

As was the life of the clergy Reverend Wibberley was moved to the General Methodist Mission in Perth but Brian stayed in Adelaide to finish his studies. In 1914 he was in final year when World War One started.

Brian's wife to be was Margery Rebecca Godlee born in 1895. She had a much tougher time in her life being one of eight to a widowed mother. She won a scholarship to the University of Adelaide and graduated with a BA degree and later was a teacher at Walford House.

Brian had been courting Margaret since she was 16 and announced their engagement as he and another House Officer were relieved from duties to enlist. They went to England in

May 1915 for training and in July they were in Europe with the Loyal North Lancashire Regiment. On the first of July 1916 the Battle of the Somme took place and Brian Wibberley was there.

The following is a direct quote from his son David, 'My father did not often speak of the war, but occasionally, if the mood took him he would launch forth with fascinating and horrific tales of the war. Stories of these frightful conditions they endured. Mud in the trenches, stories of bravery and comradeship and of the fatalistic attitude they developed to help overcome their natural fear of death. He wrote to his sister Mary of the battle of the Somme where he barely slept for three days and won a Military Cross that was presented to him by the King at Buckingham Palace.' There is no doubt he was lucky as was any one who survived those battles. He was with his batman going from A to B and came across a group of soldiers sleeping in a farm house. Tempting though it was they pushed on and yes, it was shelled and all killed.

A moment of reflexion. The battle of the Somme lasted from July 1916 to Nov 1916. The initial attack by General Haig's troops resulted in them suffering 60,000 casualties including 20,000 deaths. By the time the battle ended 600,000 British and 400,000 Germans had been injured or killed. The walls of trenches were riddled with bodies blasted to smithereens by artillery and never identified. That is horror on an unimaginable scale.

Another awful thing is that the soldiers had to carry 66 pounds or 30kg. These were small men by today's standards, maybe 5'5" or 165cm and weighed 10 stone or 140 pounds at the most, so 66 pounds of kit was perhaps half their body weight. One of the saddest things I have read about this war was that smaller soldiers with these loads often slipped from the duckboards and drowned in mud

At the end of the war he was asked to stay in Europe to help find Australians in German hospitals. He must have wanted desperately to go home but as he did speak German and French duty called so he helped tidy up and returned to Australia in 1919. When Dr Brian Wibberley returned home, his wife to be said 'Bill is ok he is his old self.' An extraordinary man by any measurement.

When re training at the RAH he ran smack into the Spanish Flu epidemic that killed William Osler, mentioned earlier, in London.

He and Margery were married and despite some to-ing and fro-ing he decided to settle at Tumby Bay in 1920. He played a huge role in starting and maintaining what became high quality and stable medical and hospital services more than 100 years later.

David wrote:

'The thirty-seven years my parents lived in Tumby Bay, was, in my opinion a time of uncompromising dedication of service, not just my father's medical role, but by two people to a community.

Brian and or Margery were members or founded the literacy society, the Dramatic club, the CWA, girl guides, the Red Cross, Gymnastic, life-saving and Mickey Mouse clubs. Brian was President of the school committee from 1922 to 1952 and a strong member of the Masonic Lodge and the church. Many pregnant girls appeared in Tumby Bay knowing that they would be treated with love and care. Then we come to hobbies such as gardening, history and photography and a string of weird wonderful and interesting motor cars each one with a story. His life was that of service and maybe noblesse oblige is fitting but as a Christian person he may have believed he had survived hell and was forever grateful.'

DAVID JOHN WIBBERLEY
MBBS, FRACGP, DORCOG, OAM
Born: Tumby Bay 1932
Died: Tumby Bay 2016
Served in Tumby Bay 1957-1999

David knew he would be a doctor as long as he could remember. 'Living with my father and seeing his conscientious and caring approach to human beings and the way he selflessly conducted his practice was the finest example that an aspiring medico could have.'

David found school easy but boring in Tumby Bay and received a rude shock when he went to PAC as a boarder in first year of high school aged 12. His mother helped him during school holidays so the stayed in the A form and went from being dreadfully homesick to greatly enjoying the life of a boarder when he left in 1949.

Already he was steeped in literature, rural pursuits, fishing, cricket and football and other Tumby Bay things like being part owner of a boat and was accepted by the University of Adelaide to study medicine in 1950. For the first four years he barely passed but had a lovely time boarding with his widower uncle at Millswood and thrashed the tennis court and billiard room.

Fate was catching up with young David though and he moved to live at the new Lincoln College as a resident for the last two years of his course, 1954-55. 1n 1956 He was a lowly RMO at the RAH but that did not matter in the eyes of a lovely theatre nurse Shirley. The next year David and Shirley decamped to the Adelaide Children's Hospital where lo and behold they were soon engaged and married that year 1957. Pictures of the couple taken at the time show a handsome man and beautiful woman whose good looks persisted well into their senior years.

David had planned to study paediatrics including the obligatory 'I have been to England' studying experience. But they didn't as David's father was not coping so David took over. It must have been like a leg spinner taking Shane Warne's place. David has often been asked whether it was a good thing or not to pick up that cricket ball but realistically he knew all about people and their backgrounds in Tumby Bay, a very tight community then and now. I can imagine a couple of old farmers with schooners in front of them at of one of the two pubs in Tumby Bay sucking on smokes when someone inferred David was not as good as his father. One of the men drew on his cigarette, exhaled and said, 'Aye, but he's one of us.' The other man swallowed his beer, picked up his hat, put it on and as he left he looked at the complainer and said, 'And don't you, ever, forget that.'

There was a huge crowd at David's funeral from different places and occupations. He was a loved and respected man. Dr Dennis Eaton spoke at the funeral and I quote in part, 'Dr David Wibberley practised in Tumby Bay from 1957 for eleven years on his own until helped for six years by Bob

Wadsworth and then Dennis Eaton from 1975 and Graham Fleming in 1979. Dennis still works at the practice but Graham left in 2019 to undertake what can only be termed errands of mercy, attending to medical matters at Kimba and elsewhere on Eyre Peninsula where there is now a paucity of General Practitioners. The clinic was well served by Judith Degener 2002 -2016, and Dr Hemmel, Dr George, Dr Xiang Lay, Dr Roeger and Dr Hamilton over the last 10 years.

I first met David in 1979 or soon after. He was a gentle, unhurried man who listened and a great leader, enormously respected. I sought his advice on occasions and he would always listen. I only ever saw him cross once and that was when I asked his nonagenarian fishing mate David Jones about some of their fishing spots. No more Mr nice guy.

Dennis and Graham are wonderful people and with David have three different personalities but the mixture worked. Tumby Bay must have one of the most successful rural practices in Australia. I can make no stronger comment than my wife and I regard Dennis/ Graham as our family doctor/s.

Shirley Wibberley is an extraordinary person and willingly gave permission for me to try this impossible task to adequately describe the amazing lives of the Wibberley two that should be the Wibberley four beyond a doubt.

David wrote, 'I must pay tribute to my wife Shirley who was a Tumby Bay Board Member from 1971 to 1986 and deputy chairman for many years, a delegate to the SA Hospital Association and the National body as well. She helped me in the practice for years and after our youngest child left home did a course in Social work.'

And of course Shirley was in many other groups and an

original member of Port Lincoln Chicken and Chablis Club as was David in the Beefsteak and Burgundy Club.

When David met Shirley in 1956 she had a 6-year-old child. I grew up in the 1950s and I know how hard that must have been but love found a way. David has described the financial chaos in his father's practice. Once a year after harvest his father would send out bills. His patients could come at any time, literally and there were poor, if any, medical records.

To retrace my steps. Shirley was a theatre sister. They live in a world of sterility, order, organisation and the capacity to respond to crises. Everything has a place and everybody knows their role. Accurate filing and records are absolutely essential. Shirley took on the job of sorting out the above deficiencies of the practice and set up appropriate systems and worked for and with David for many years.

After their third child had left home Shirley did a course in social work about the time I arrived at the Investigator Clinic in Port Lincoln in 1979. Shirley went from being a theatre nurse, practised in the scientific basis in health where, pun intended, everything is cut and dried, to social work with its social basis of health a much harder field in which to work because there are so many variables impinging on peoples' health and welfare and of course those people have become clients, no longer patients!

When I first came to Port Lincoln part of my work was to be involved with the Community Health Centre attached to the Investigator Clinic, a deliberate strategy of the Clinic and the SA Health Department. In my previous job as Director Medical Services at the Warrnambool Hospital I was responsible for allied Health Services so I was asked to do that at the Port Lincoln Community Health that was deliberately built next to and accessible from the Investigator Clinic. I had been to an excellent seminar in Adelaide about Strategic Planning, easily the most logical I had seen. It was about Goals, Strategies and Tactics—each being in different columns because they are different but invariably mixed up. Anyway, I thought this was great but none of the Health Centre people did. I recall Shirley, well dressed as always, give a theatrical loud sigh and pillow her head on her forearms resting on the table.

I don't remember much about the Health Centre because soon after that I became Director of Medical Services at the Port Lincoln Hospital for almost 20 years and had a lot to do with Shirley. She had identified a need in Port Lincoln /Tumby Bay and did something about it. Well, she is a nurse and they fix things!

I have mentioned my ideas that longevity in rural practice is often due to doctors who have an interest outside the standard patient doctor consultation. I have also mentioned the importance of a good relationship between a community and their doctors. The Tumby Bay Hospital board and doctors have a symbiotic relationship and as David has written,' The Board has never denied a reasonable request from the practice.' In the 1990s the Federal Government established Divisions of General Practice with several aims including building links between doctors and their communities and part of this was to fund projects outside the fee for service system. Graham was the second and long serving Chairman of the Eyre Peninsula Division of General Practice and I was the

GP Director.

Graham put together a project to investigate youth suicide in Tumby Bay but that did not happen without support from his practice and the Hospital Board. When medical students graduate they do so as Bachelors of Medicine and Bachelors of Surgery, the word 'Doctor' means ' teacher' and probably goes back to Hippocrates. Someone who does the required original research in Science is awarded a Doctorate of Philosophy or Ph.D. for example. As a Medical Graduate Graham was awarded a Doctorate in Medicine or M.D. so I suppose we should call him, Doctor, Doctor! As a matter of interest, the Division facilitated two other Doctorates to Medico David Mills and to teacher Peter Harvey who led the academic medical research for the Division. Richard Watts also achieved that distinction through other sources. There were about a dozen GPS in Tumby and Port Lincoln and four Doctorates is an extraordinary feat.

Last but certainly not least I quote the moving words from Dennis at David's funeral and reflect on the measure of the man and the stature he earned in his duty and devotion to the Tumby Bay community.

Dr David loved what was known as 'his hospital' for which he had worked so hard for so many years. It is fitting that in his declining months and weeks he was able to be cared for in the hospital he had called his own. In his final days he was in a room overlooking the sea he loved, with excellent care from staff and fellow doctors with whom he had worked so long. He went peacefully to sleep one night and did not wake up. That was his wish. Vale David, your legacy will live on in Tumby Bay.

THE AMAZING ROBERT BEDFORD FROM KYANCUTTA

By Peter Morton

In the memoirs of Dr David Wibberley of Tumby Bay he recounts various stories of his father's exploits, some hair raising. One of the most extraordinary involved a man who, like Dr Wibberly, became a legend in his own time.

That was Mr Robert Bedford who had come from England to Kyancutta in 1915 and amongst other things established an impressive museum, exchanging pieces of meteorites with other museums throughout the world. He also built a weather station. He had limited training as a doctor but set up a cottage hospital. David's father respected his skills and went out of his way to help him when necessary.

In 1926 a woman was taken gravely ill and he was asked, by telephone, to help. 'It was a very wet winter and the roads between Cummins and Yeelanna and to the north were impassable.' Bert Kschenka drove 175km to Kyancutta guided by fires lit by farmers alongside the road and they made it in one piece, though God knows how long it took.

Mrs Bedford was the sponge nurse and after several hours in an ether-soaked environment with a fire to keep the patient warm, the operation was successful. Decades later David discovered, in what was a dilapidated museum, a specimen jar of spirits with the ectopic pregnancy removed from that lady.

INTRODUCTION AKA BLIND FAITH

By Peter Kennedy

Looking back, it is unbelievable the situations my employer sent me into. I would like to say it was because I had shown great promise and maturity but I had worked for them barely 3 months and was a foreigner to boot. I suspect the reality was that they were in a situation where they only had me and they had to send someone, so they crossed their fingers, hoped for the best and put me on a plane. Blind faith played its part!

It was the very early 1990s and I was working for Marco Marine in Seattle, Washington. I had done a four-year apprenticeship as a hydraulic engineer at the shipyard in Port Lincoln, South Australia, my home town. After a couple of years at the local shipyard I found myself relocated to the USA, working for one of the world's largest tuna fishing equipment manufacturers. I had an office in the 'engineering building' and was one of two 'field service engineers' – despite not having an engineering degree.

Marco was a large outfit with offices in several countries around the Pacific but with the head office in Seattle. It was a union yard and had strict demarcation between zones where employees could or could not go, depending on which department they worked. Engineers, for example, were allowed in the assembly shop, but not on the waterfront.

Tradesmen were allowed on the waterfront and assembly shop, but not in the engineering building etc. I had the somewhat unique ability, as a 'field service engineer' to go wherever I needed to, so got to experience all the little worlds inside Marco.

I had been at Marco about three months and starting to feel my way around. Most people were getting used to me, to the point they understood 50% or better of what I was saying. Seems the Australian accent was quite popular at the time, but very few could interpret it fully. One of my bosses called me into his office and told me they were sending me to Samoa to overhaul a MARCO W1062 winch.

"OK," I said, "where is Samoa?" having absolutely no idea.

"Other side of Hawaii, you'll figure it out when you get there."

"OK, then what is a W1062?" having no knowledge of that either.

"You'll figure it out when you get there."

"How long will I be gone?"

"Come home when it's finished."

And with that, I was off. The first of many trips to unknown places to do unknown jobs.

It turned out that American Samoa is one of the most beautiful places on earth. A volcanic rock sticking out of the ocean in the middle of the South Pacific, 21 miles long and 3 miles wide, but spectacularly mountainous and covered in thick, green lush vegetation, surrounded by beautiful coral reefs and the bluest water. The people are some of the largest and strongest on the planet and welcoming and friendly. They have largely abandoned their head-hunting ways.

Working there however, brought its own set of challenges. It is HOT and STICKY with torrential rain. One spectacular day it rained 6 inches in 20 minutes, the blue water of the harbour turned brown with mud. There was all kinds of furniture and debris washed into the harbour along with a couple of dogs, who made it back to land ok.

I checked into the RAINMAKER hotel, that was something out of a movie. As everything does in the tropics, the hotel had that familiar smell of decaying wood throughout. Tall steep roofs made of woven grass over frames of bamboo with no ceilings. Walls of brown lava rock surrounded by neatly clipped grass covered in an abundance of green frogs. No air conditioning, but large and effective fans. All the staff, male and female, wore floral printed lava-lavas, which are basically skirts made by wrapping a sheet of cloth around the body and tying in a knot. Tropical flowers in the hair were mostly limited to the female staff.

Communication with the outside world was an unusual experience. This was in the times before cell phones and there were no public phones. Computers were reasonably common, but there were not yet laptops or internet. Fax machines were the latest in technology, but few people had them. And I needed to order parts – from overseas – and get them on a plane...

The communications building was a large white brick and typically government building in the village of Fagatogo. To make a phone call, you got in line to book a phone call, after taking the bus to Fagatogo of course. When your turn came, you gave the receptionist your name, the place and name of person you wanted to call, the phone number and how many minutes you wanted, then took a seat and waited... and waited. When your name was called, they would tell you which of the five booths to go into where there was a telephone, and when you picked up the receiver, the person you wanted to talk to was usually on the end of the line. It actually worked pretty well, but there was no such thing as making "a quick phone call".

So, in due course, parts arrived on the plane from Honolulu, were installed in the W1060 winch (which I was now becoming quite familiar with). It ran, and I was able to book a seat back to Seattle.

On the six-hour flight to Honolulu, I was feeling pleased and relieved that I had survived my first episode of working in the remote tropics. I started to think I had a bit of a handle on how things worked. Little did I know...

THE SOLOMONS

Time went by and several trips to Samoa later, I had again finished a job and was packing my bags for the flight home. A message was brought to my door to call the office urgently, BEFORE getting on the plane home. So, I called the office, only to be told that yes I would be getting on a plane, but not the one bringing me home. Instead, I would be getting on a plane back to Australia, where I would stay in Brisbane until I could catch a flight to Honiara in the Solomon Islands.

Details were a little thin, but I was to overnight in Honiara, then find my way down to the docks and find a ferry going to Tulagi, and get on it. Someone would meet me in Tulagi...
Things went fairly smoothly, considering, and in due course I did find the ferry going to Tulagi. It was an old ex-Japanese

ferro-cement pole boat and looked pretty dodgy.

The captain was pleased to see me and enthusiastically asked, "Hey, are you a marine engineer?"

"Er, well, no, sort of..."

"Great, you can be the engineer for this trip, our engineer didn't show up..."

One look in the engine room confirmed the worst and I spoke to the Captain again, "I can't be your engineer, I don't know this boat and I'm not qualified to take her out..."

"Don't worry," he replied, "Everything will be fine," and the ropes were thrown off and we were away before any more could be said.

It was about a two-hour ride across "Iron Bottom Sound" from Honiara to Tulagi, with all manner of people and livestock on the deck of this decaying, smoky old boat, but we arrived without fuss and there was in fact someone to meet me on the dock.

Tulagi was the scene of some fierce fighting during WW2 and there are remnants of this strewn about all over the place. Rusty landing craft and tanks littered the shoreline, piles of bullets and bombs had been heaped up in various spots about the place, guns small and large still pointed at the sky. "Iron Bottom Sound" had been named in honour of all the ships that had been sunk in a huge naval battle, and now lay resting on the ocean floor.

There was not much about, certainly nothing resembling a hotel, but down at the dock was a little purse seiner crewed entirely by Solomon Islanders and that's where we headed. Turns out this boat had been made in Australia and looked to have been a great boat in her day, but she had been worked hard and was in dire need of some TLC. I was told I would be staying in the Captain's room, and everything I needed – including meals – would be supplied on board.

So, I got to work. There was plenty to be done and most of the parts I needed were surprisingly on board already.

The galley came as a bit of a surprise. I'm sure it would have originally been built with a standard gas or electric cooker, but this was long gone and had been replaced with a large gas burner with what looked to be a cauldron hanging above it. Even though all the crew ate every meal from this cauldron, it was never emptied. The cook simply added vegetables, meat of unknown origin and cans of God knows what. It simmered away continuously. Whenever anyone was hungry, they simply ladled out how much they wanted of this brown soup/stew and the cook continued chopping and simmering.

I was a little concerned. I don't consider myself a fussy eater, but this lot was stretching my limits. Getting sick in the tropics, half a world from home, is a miserable experience. Then I remembered that, unusually, there was a chicken hutch up on the top deck with at least a dozen chickens in it. I checked it out and found a supply of beautiful fresh eggs. I asked the cook if he would fry these up for me, and he did so happily. So that was food sorted for this trip, fried eggs, three times a day for the time I was on that job.

The old ferry that had brought me to Tulagi chugged back and forth once a day, every day, except weekends. I had been working on the purse seiner all week, and when Friday rolled around there was still plenty to be done. The old ferry was due to leave on its last trip for the week back to Honiara,

Friday lunch time, and I was supposed to be on it, then wait in Honiara for my flight out on Monday. Given there was still a lot of work to be done, I asked whether there was a fast boat that could collect me Monday morning instead, allowing me to get a couple more days work done, but still making my flight home. This was arranged, and the old ferry wheezed its way out of the bay without me, heading back to Honiara.

I thought nothing more of it, and Monday morning, true to their word, a big fibreglass fast boat came to collect me.

"You're bloody lucky you wanted to come with me instead of the ferry," the skipper called out.

"Why's that?"

"Bloody thing didn't make it, she sank on her way back to Honiara."

Turns out it truly had sunk. Fortunately, all passengers were picked up by another boat – some of the livestock wasn't so lucky though.

I made it home fine.

THE PHILLIPINES

Still in the early 90s and the Marcos regime in the Philippines had ended some time ago, but things were still a bit "iffy" and security was taken very seriously.

My Boss was on a sales trip there and had found some customers that needed technical help, so he sent for me.

It was quite normal for a "winch package" to be put together in Seattle for a customer and a container load of components sent to whichever shipyard their boat was in. The yard would typically install the equipment to the best of their ability, then as they were getting close to finishing,

Marco would send me to the yard to do the finishing touches and commission the system. This was the case with my first job in Manila, and things went fairly normally at the start. We spent about a week finishing and testing the hydraulic system.

This was not a new boat, but an old one being refitted and as is quite normal on the scheduled "finishing date" many jobs were only half done and the rushing starts. A large party was booked on the finishing date to be held on board the boat.

The party started with a priest blessing the boat and then leading a procession of every person who had worked on it around every nook and cranny, stopping in every room for every member of the procession to throw salt over their shoulder – for good luck, or to protect from evil spirits – or both perhaps. Then the party lunch was under way with masses of rice, fried chicken and Coca Cola. Sea trials were also scheduled for that afternoon – after the party. So off we went, no preparation, no safety equipment, to make a sea trial.

The old boat made pretty good speed and after about 3.5 hours we had left Manila bay, passed Corregidor Island and were in water deep enough to shoot the net off. I had the chance to look around the boat and wasn't entirely pleased with the situation. Having left unprepared and in a hurry, we had no watertight doors leading out to the back deck, in fact there was still a big hole in the bulkhead where a generator had been installed. There was no drinking water – just some Coke left from the party, no food – just some chicken also from the party, there were no life jackets, no flares, no fire extinguishers and the radio did not work... and now we were out at sea...

Funnily enough though, the two sub machine guns in the wheelhouse looked to be in good working order. From memory one was a 9mm and the other a .223. Apparently pirates were a bit of an issue...

Anyhow, the trial went quite well, the hydraulics performed as they were supposed to and before long we had shot the net away, pursed it, hauled it back on board and turned for the run back to Manila... then the main engine stopped, and stayed stopped.

It was getting quite late at night now, the sun was long down, but the engineers could not get the engine to start again. There was the thought to call for a tug to pull us back to Manila and actually THIS was the point where we realised the radio didn't work. So, it was decided to drift for the night, everyone could get some rest and tackle the problem with fresh eyes in the morning. That tactic seemed to work, early next morning the engine fired right up and we were headed back to Manila, or so we thought.

We made good speed and everyone was happy to be headed back towards food and water, aches and pains from sleeping on the bare deck were soon forgotten, for about an hour...

The main engine played up again and overheated. It didn't stop this time, but could only manage an idle, any attempt to bring up the speed quickly resulted in overheating again. So, we idled all the way back to Manila, for about 14 hours.

We eventually arrived back in port, nerves a bit frayed, but all was good. I spent the next couple of weeks touring around the Philippines, visiting various fishing companies and shipyards, before I ended up back in Manila on my way home.

I had done several jobs for the owners of the boat that had broken down on trial and they seemed happy with what I had done for them. They invited me to a farewell dinner to celebrate and I keenly accepted. So, off we went to a local Filipino style restaurant and all sat around a large round table, when the menus came out – all in Tagalog. Back then I didn't understand any Tagalog, so I asked my hosts to order for me. They decided we would get several plates and all share.

Filipino food is most delicious, but to the untrained eye can be quite difficult to identify. I had sampled from all the plates and asked one by one what each plate was. All was going well, this plate was beef, that plate was chicken, another of pork, some goat etc. – then we came to the last plate. Of course I asked what it was, but this time I didn't get a straight answer, my hosts started looking at each other and seemed to be a bit uncomfortable about the question. Their English seemed to take a sudden turn for the worse, and as best as I could decipher, it was dog.....

So that completed the first of many trips to the beautiful Philippines. On to Guam...

GUAM

Marco had a branch office in Guam and with staff holidays etc., found themselves caught short for mechanical help, so I was sent there to relieve for a couple of weeks. The trip started in a quite straight forward way and was quite relaxing in fact, just working the standard 8-hour days with the weekend off!

Guam is another lush tropical island that saw a lot of fighting during WW2, and I spent a fabulous weekend scuba diving on sunken aircraft and shipwrecks.

Things started to turn during my second week there. There was report of a storm on its way. Storms are nothing unusual and the office had a set of wooden shutters which we put up to protect the windows from flying debris.

Around midday, the sky started to darken and the wind to blow, so we decided to head back to the house to sit this one out. I was staying with the Branch Manager on the third floor of a strongly built concrete apartment building, so felt quite secure there. Except that it kept getting darker and darker and the wind was getting stronger and stronger and the rain heavier and heavier.

Eventually the rain was driven horizontally and it was so dark it was impossible to see anything. The wind had gone from a howl to an endless scream – this was no ordinary storm. The changes in air pressure played havoc with one's ears and ceilings began to fall down. We sealed around the doors and window frames with duct tape in an attempt to keep the rain out, but eventually the rain was driven between the walls and window frames and we became quite flooded – on the third floor.

And just like that, it was over... In the space of five minutes we went from screaming wind, torrential rain in pitch darkness, to quiet and calm, the sun almost came out from the clouds. We went outside to survey the damage – and there was a lot! The poor sods on the ground floor had torrents of water flowing through their apartments, with both the front and back doors blown in, with all their worldly possessions being washed down the street. We scrambled down and sloshed about in the waist deep water collecting what we could and dragging items up to the second floor where they might be a bit more secure.

Then there was a slight puff of wind, only a puff, but everyone ran for cover, so I thought best do the same. Within another five minutes, the darkness had returned, along with the rain and the screaming wind – this time from the other direction.

We were ok on the third floor, the noise was incredible, water was flowing in around the window frames and the floor was flooded, but the water ran out again under the door and our beds were dry. There was no power, so no lights or a/c, but we had torches and food, so settled in for the evening and even got some sleep that night.

Everything was calm next morning. The rain and wind had stopped. People wandered about looking for their possessions and pets, but everyone was fairly calm. It was a scene of almost complete destruction. What had been lush tropical forest next door to us was now bare ground and twigs. Every leaf and every blade of grass had been swept away. Power poles and lines were down everywhere. Many poles had flying sheets of iron embedded in them. Away in the distance where several high-rise buildings were being constructed, the buildings were still there, but all the cranes had been blown away.

We wanted to get to the office to see how it had fared. Fortunately, our car wasn't one of the many that had been blown away. The dockside was a mess. Pleasure boats had been blown out of the water and lay strewn about on their sides, upside down or just smashed to pieces. A four-storey hotel had been blown off its foundation – it was still standing as though nothing was wrong, it was just in a different place to where it had been the previous day. What had been a full car park at the hotel was now a huge pile of twisted cars.

Seven tuna boats had been smashed against the dock until they broke up and sank, but the office itself – not a scratch.

We had a good-sized generator at the office so dragged it back to the apartment to keep the freezer and A/C going.

Funnily enough, many of the locals lived in wood and iron shanties, which of course simply disappeared during the storm, but within a day or so they were able to salvage plenty of wood and iron lying about to simply nail their houses back together.

So, the "storm" turned out to be not only a typhoon, but a "super" typhoon named OMAR, and the eye had gone directly over us. At the time nobody could say what the maximum wind speed was, as all the recording equipment had reportedly blown away. Many millions of dollars damage was done and it took years to clean up, but amazingly nobody died on Guam. And I made it home ok ☺.

A MISSED CHANCE

By Brian Mills

Editor: When I was gathering material for this book I bumped into Brian Mills, the retired Regional Manager of SA Water, in Port Lincoln where I had done some consulting work and we have common interests such as cricket, quiz nights and the English language particularly the written word.

At the time over a cup of coffee we discussed the current state of Australian cricket and drifted into the lives of some of the all-time greats of the game. I asked Brian if he had heard of a South Australian and test match cricketer from the early 1900s named Bill Whitty I had recently read about for the first time. To my surprise, Brian said that he had met Bill and after some discussion he agreed to write a story about him for this new book.

This is Brian's story about Bill Whitty. He has unearthed connections between Bill, English bowler Sidney Barnes who had a long career beginning in the 1890s and who is still widely regarded as the best bowler of all time and Victor Trumper who also played from the early 1900s, who some people say was a better batsman than Sir Donald Bradman.

It is difficult comparing sporting people from different eras and Brian does a wonderful job.

Dear Peter,

Bill Whitty, born in 1886, was a South Australian fast-medium left-hand bowler with an excellent test match record. Obviously comparing statistics from different eras is like the proverbial comparison between apples and oranges, but despite that, there are only nine regular bowlers in Australian test match history with a better bowling average than Bill's 21.12. Also, regardless of era differences, this was a better average than all of his contemporaries playing for Australia around that time.

Bill Whitty came from and played for New South Wales but was recruited to South Australia by Clem Hill who was the S.A. captain and also an Australian Test captain. Bill played for South Australia for the rest of his career and lived for much of his life in Tantanoola, a small township between Mount Gambier and Millicent in the south-east of South Australia.

The greatest bowler of all time has often been considered by many to be the Englishman Sydney Barnes. He opened the attack, bowling at medium pace to fast-medium. The latter-day cricketers I would class as being medium-pacers would be Steve Waugh and Shane Watson. The amazing thing is that Barnes could spin the ball at that pace and reputedly obtain swerve from spin as well as in the traditional manner when bowling fast-medium. The expression "hat trick" was born in this era; a hat was passed around the crowd to collect money for someone who had achieved three wickets with three consecutive balls.

In Don Bradman's 1950 book "Farewell to Cricket", he says that for him, the two greatest bowlers to that time were the New South Wales leg-spinner Bill O'Reilly, who of course had bowled to and for Bradman, and Sydney Barnes, because of all that he had heard of Barnes; he did not play against him! O'Reilly was quicker through the air than most spinners, but Barnes, when spinning the ball, would have been significantly quicker than O'Reilly.

Barnes' career spanned well over forty years and yet he played only 27 test matches. He played his first game in the English county competition for Warwickshire in 1894, aged 21. He retired from playing as a professional at the age of 67. Barnes chose to play in a minor league for the first part of his career, probably for financial reasons. However, his ability was so evident that he was selected to tour Australia in 1901, having played less than ten games for Warwickshire over those seven seasons. He was a difficult man to get along with and because of his clashes with authority, he chose to play many games for his home county Staffordshire which was not in the main county competition. Despite his interrupted test career, in only four of his 27 test matches he failed to take at least five wickets in an innings. His test match average is an astounding 16.43.

Jack Fingleton opened the batting for Australia, including with Australian captain Bill Woodfull in the infamous "bodyline" series of 1932/33 in Australia against the touring English team. Fingleton has the very respectable test batting average of 42.46 and was an excellent journalist. In his book "The Immortal Victor Trumper", who was an opening batsman for Australia from 1899 to 1912, he argues that Trumper was a better batsman than Bradman and what is more, was the greatest batsman who ever lived. That seems extremely odd when comparing test averages (albeit still like comparing apples and oranges) where Trumper's is 39.04 against Bradman's which is 99.94. No other batsman who has played at least 20 test match innings has an average greater than 65. It has been alleged that Fingleton didn't like Bradman much and if so, that would have been an incentive for him to push his case for Trumper.

Fingleton was no doubt influenced by Trumper's undisputed skill on wet wickets, with which he had to contend for his whole career. Bradman did not perform as well on a wet wicket, but wickets were able to be covered for the latter part of his career. A Trumper highlight was his second tour of England in 1902 when the summer was ridiculously wet and his tour aggregate of 2570 at an average of 48.49 (with eleven centuries) was not bettered until Bradman scored 2960 on his first tour of England in 1930. The Wisden Cricketer's Almanac (the "Bible of Cricket", which is published annually in England) stated that Trumper's batting on that tour stood alone in its brilliance. On the tour of England in 1921, Australian Charlie Macartney made 345 in four hours against Nottinghamshire. A newspaper report said that his batting was reminiscent of Trumper's. Macartney said that the comment "was absolute rot and as a batsman I wasn't fit to tie Vic's bootlaces."

Trumper's method seems to have been always to attack. English captain C.B. Fry said, with tongue in cheek, that Trumper "played a defensive stroke as a last resort." Barnes said that Trumper "always gave you a chance, almost daring you to get him out." Barnes also said that he "had more trouble with Trumper than any other batsman."

Australian captain Warwick Armstrong said "He could hit as quick as lightning all around the wicket. One could never place a man against him to stop his onslaught." Victorian captain Bill Woodfull made a similar comment to New South Wales captain Alan McGilvray about Bradman during a Sheffield Shield match in 1933: "Just how do you stop this man?"

Ex-commentator and author Johnny Moyse played against Vic in Sheffield Shield games and said, "I was amazed at his artistry. It made one wonder whether he was playing a game that he had made up for himself."

Renowned English journalist and author Neville Cardus wrote "He was a genius. He was master of all the strokes and he could use almost any one of them at his pleasure, no matter the manner of ball bowled at him".

Test match players Frank Iredale and Herbert Hordern were opposed in a Sydney grade match in which Trumper was batting with Iredale. After Trumper had played another spectacular shot off Hordern, Iredale complained to Horden "You never bowl that rubbish to me." Hordern replied "Frank, the ball that Victor belts for four is exactly the same one with which you can barely make contact."

Despite Trumper's reported inclination to attack the bowling, this doesn't imply that he lacked finesse. It is because of his perceived unmatched combination of grace, ease, style, power, quickness of foot, artistry, his wet wicket skills and inventiveness that Trumper was considered to be supreme. Some players and historians have classed him as the greatest batsman of all time but most of those attributes would also have been applicable to Bradman.

Considering the Englishman Jack Hobbs, who is routinely included in various "greatest team of all time" selections as one of the opening batsmen (including in Wisden's best team of all time), a comment from Australian ex-test captain Monty Noble is interesting. He said in 1936 (which is obviously after Bradman's record-breaking efforts on the 1930 tour of England) that Trumper was the greatest and he ranked Hobbs with Trumper. He based his opinion on Hobbs' record-breaking performances and the combination of Trumper's achievements (although statistically less impressive than Hobbs') and his classical, superlative batsmanship. However, referring purely to overall batting ability, he rated Trumper above Hobbs.

Around the Trumper era, many said that he could have made a lot more runs than he did, but he seemingly wasn't obsessed with scoring heavily and often appeared to be satisfied with a "small" century whereas by comparison, probably most and certainly Bradman were not.

Statistically, Trumper is the fastest-scoring regular Test cricket batsman with 40.1 runs per hour. Bradman is 5th with 37.6, Macartney 6th with 36.3 and Adam Gilchrist is 10th with 33.6. It is amazing that the fastest-scoring player was an opening batsman. That validates the preceding exalting comments from those who had seen Trumper bat, and also suggests that with less "attack" in his batting, he would have had a much better batting average.

When Jack Fingleton was writing his book about Victor Trumper, he wanted to speak to Bill Whitty. Bill was eight years younger than Trumper, but they were good mates and opposed each other in ten innings in NSW v SA Sheffield

Shield matches in 1910/11 and 1911/12. In those ten innings, Bill dismissed Vic seven times, Vic being not out on the other three occasions. Of those seven dismissals, Bill "clean bowled" Vic four times. He bowled Vic for a duck at Adelaide in 1911/12 with what he reckoned was as good a ball as he ever bowled. So with left-arm Bill bowling to right-handed Vic, the ball swung late to the off side and came back off the pitch to hit the stumps. To make an interesting "best ball" comparison, I refer to an Adelaide test match, in which a ball from the great English fast-medium right-arm bowler Alec Bedser dismissed Bradman for a duck. The ball was in line with the off stump, swung in late to pitch on the leg stump and then cut away to hit the off stump. Bradman said that that was the best ball to have ever taken his wicket. Considering these "best" two Whitty and Bedser deliveries, in the way that they deviated as well as the two bowlers' predisposition for left and right arm respectively, they are an exact mirror image of each other.

No Australian has dismissed Victor Trumper more times than Whitty. Sydney Barnes took his wicket 13 times, more than any other bowler. Whitty dismissed the great Jack Hobbs four times, and another legendary Englishman, all-rounder Wilfred Rhodes (who deserves to be named in a "best England team of all time") five times.

In the Sheffield Shield competition, Whitty dismissed test match batsmen Warwick Armstrong, the captain of the famous 1921 test team, ten times, Herbie Collins seven times, Alan Kippax and Vernon Ransford six times and Warren Bardsley four times. So Bill performed well against the very best.

In test and Sheffield Shield matches, 48% of his victims were "clean bowled" which is a very high proportion for that mode of dismissal. Some bowlers who are exceptionally fast will often "clean bowl" batsmen by beating them with sheer speed. However, Bill was of fast-medium pace and his comparatively high proportion of "clean bowled" dismissals indicates his great ability to make the ball swerve in the air and/or deviate after hitting the pitch. He was six feet tall and that undoubtedly helped. Whitty also toured New Zealand and played against them at home, and also played against South Africa in Australia.

When test cricket resumed after World War One, Bill was 34 and the first of the great Australian fast bowling pairs, Jack Gregory and Ted McDonald, had appeared on the scene and this saw the end of his test match career. Ray Lindwall/Keith Miller, Dennis Lillee/Jeff Thomson and Glenn McGrath/Jason Gillespie are considered to be the three greatest of the subsequent Australian fast bowling pairs. *The current group of Australian fast bowlers might have something to say about that! Ed.*

Bill Whitty last played at first class level in 1926 at the age of 39. The year before this, a South Australian team, containing some state players, visited Mount Gambier. Bill played for the locals and took 7/30.

I don't know if this was the first of the country cricket carnivals, but at such a carnival when Bill was 41, in a match against Port Lincoln, he took 8/22 and 8/14. In his last club game in Mount Gambier at the age of fifty, he took 6/27.

Bill Whitty is surely one of the best of the pace bowlers ever to represent Australia, considering at least his excellent test match average and his successes against the great Victor Trumper.

Peter, this has been the introduction. I now come to the highlight of this epistle. My wife Sue grew up at Tantanoola, also the home of the Whitty family. On a trip to see her parents in about 1970, it was arranged for me to visit Bill, who was then aged over eighty years and the only surviving member of the Australian cricket teams to tour England in 1909 and 1912. This was a rare and exceptional opportunity for me to meet an Australian test cricketer from that era.

I went to Bill's home and we had a great afternoon. He showed me all of his memorabilia, including a souvenired linen tablecloth autographed by all those seated at his dinner table during one of his tours of England. I can recall only one of those signatures, that of the legendary English cricketing colossus Dr. W.G. Grace, whose career spanned forty years from the 1860s. So, the beginning of W.G. Grace's career was over 150 years ago and when the young Bill Whitty was dining in the company of the great man, "W.G." was aged in his 60s.

I regret not taking even more advantage of my time with Bill. At the time, the only reference to Barnes that I had come across was Bradman's. I have since read more about Barnes in recently published books. Regardless, surely Bradman's opinion should have been enough for me to ask Bill if he had played against Barnes and if so, to ask him about Barnes' bowling as Barnes did dismiss Bill in a test match. There would have been very few people in Australia then with the interest and opportunity to ask this of the only Australian test cricketer still living who had faced Barnes. I missed that chance.

Something else I failed to ask Bill: A possible Trumper/Whitty contest had not occurred to me. First-hand comments from Bill about Vic's batting would have been unforgettable, and even more appreciated as I learned more about Vic (as I did about Sydney Barnes) in later years.

There is yet another regret. Regarding Jack Fingleton's book about Trumper, it is clear that Bill's experience in bowling to Trumper would have given Jack some wonderful material to include in his book. Fingleton had made a preliminary arrangement to journey to Tantanoola for this important conversation with Bill. However, in due course he received a letter from Mrs Whitty stating that due to a sudden decline in Bill's health, he unfortunately would not be able to assist Jack. Very shortly after this, Bill passed away. So that lost occasion really did matter a great deal, because Jack's book, good though it is, would have been made so much better by including Bill's input about so many aspects of Trumper's batting.

When I met with Bill, and Jack was probably planning to do so, Bill would surely have been the only cricketer in Australia still living who would have bowled to Trumper at first-class level.

So that covers the two intended visits to the Whitty home; mine, despite being a wonderful experience for me, occurred without full advantage being taken, and the other, by Jack Fingleton, sadly did not occur at all. Regardless of my failure to mention these absolute legends Barnes and Trumper to Bill, I am most grateful for my memorable and hugely enjoyable time spent with a pre-World War One test cricketer.

Bill died in 1974 at the age of 88.

Sydney Barnes died in 1967 aged 94.

Tragically, Victor Trumper died in 1915 aged 37.

Part VI

ADVENTURERS

THE LADY WHO LOVES A CHALLENGE!

By Sue Bishop

I was born in Adelaide on the 10th of November 1952, the eldest of Eleanor and Lyndon Trott's three children. My brother Timothy was born in 1954 and my sister Annabel came along in 1959. We had a happy, busy childhood, being involved in numerous extra-curricular activities and sports. I was a Brownie, Girl Guide and then a Ranger Guide; I did ballet and piano lessons, and I followed Tim in becoming a member of firstly Kensington and Norwood, and later Burnside swimming clubs, where I developed my life-long love of swimming. We trained hard, sometimes both before and after school, and competed in carnivals all over Adelaide. Tim and I also competed a couple of times in the 'Swim through Adelaide' in the now dirty, polluted River Torrens: we started by diving or jumping into the river from the Torrens Weir and swam to the Adelaide Uni footbridge – a distance of one mile and 200 yards or nearly 1.8 kilometres. I have to admit Tim achieved better results than I did – he was faster than I was but I always completed the event! Mum still reminds me what my coach at Kensington and Norwood said about me: "Put her in the River Murray at Renmark and she'll swim to Goolwa!"

Mum and Dad both loved the beach and swimming too, so we had a beach holiday every January – in the early years various houses were hired at Encounter Bay, and in later years at Aldinga Beach. In my teenage years I completed my Queen's Guide Award, and the Gold Duke of Edinburgh Award. The activities I enjoyed most of all during those times were camping and bushwalking, both of which I still love, although I prefer more upmarket accommodation than a tent on hard stony ground these days!

During my early childhood my best friend at the time and I would play with our dolls for hours on end, and of course we played schools! My choice of a career path was an easy one – I had always loved young children, so it was either Kindergarten teaching or Primary School teaching. I chose the latter, and never regretted my decision. During my time at Wattle Park Teachers' College I elected to do the Rural Head Teachers' Course, which provided extra activities to help prepare participants for the challenges of teaching in one-teacher schools. Our world view was broadened by visiting places such as the Youth Detention Centre at Magill, and sleeping rough (just in sleeping bags – no swags, in July!) while staying for a week on Anna Creek the world's biggest cattle station, which was a fabulous experience!

As soon as we had finished Teachers' College in 1972, four friends and I headed off on the overnight train to Melbourne, and from there to New Zealand, where we hired 50cc motor bikes and toured both the North and South Islands for about three weeks. This was certainly a challenge for us all - our 1st overseas flights, travelling without our parents and with communication limited to Airmail letters, being responsible for keeping our bikes in good running order and packing all our gear into small pannier bags. I remember when we were riding down Baldwin Street in Dunedin, which is officially the steepest street in the world, my bike overbalanced because I had too much luggage! Luckily, neither bike nor rider was damaged. I'm still not good at packing lightly when I go on holiday! A wonderful time was had by all: landing in a light plane on the Tasman glacier, which runs alongside Mt. Cook, was a particular highlight for me. We stayed in Youth Hostels, met some great people and shared lots of laughter. I seem to remember we were more interested in the opposite sex than in the beautiful scenery for which New Zealand is rightly renowned! Another vivid memory I have is of Christmas Day at the Youth Hostel at Te Anau: we were sharing a very different Christmas lunch to what we would have been enjoying at home when it started snowing, which turned a very ordinary meal into a very special one!

My first teaching appointment was to a one-teacher school at the tiny gypsum mining settlement at Stenhouse Bay, at the foot of Yorke Peninsula. When I was there, it was the smallest school in the whole state - the school had a grand total of seven pupils! After I had been there about three weeks the 'Sunday Mail' sent a journalist to write an article about the town and school. The entire school was able to be photographed on the swing-set, and I remember that my hair was nearly as long as the very short dress that I was wearing! It was hard not having anyone to confer with or to guide me, especially in my first year out of College but I muddled through the year and my students did make progress! On occasions, I used to bundle all of my seven pupils into my little Datsun 1200 and we'd venture into nearby Innes National Park looking for birds and their nests, native animal tracks, wildflowers etc. No-one worried about consent forms in those days! Sadly, my Dad died during that year, so I applied for a transfer to be closer to Adelaide and my Mum. My next appointment was to Delamere Rural School on the Fleurieu Peninsula, another one-teacher school but at this school I was in charge of 36 pupils from Reception to Year 7! It was very much a family affair, with the older pupils helping the younger ones. In the year that I was at Delamere, teachers' aides (now called SSOs or Student Support Officers) were introduced – I was allocated two hours a week! Although it was hard work – I also had to do all the administration and the cleaning - I had a wonderful year with those delightful farm kids and their very supportive parents.

I married Ian Bishop, my protective and loving husband of 46 years, at the end of my time at Delamere and taught at Heathfield Primary School until I went on maternity leave. We produced three wonderful, healthy and lively sons in the next 10 years, who have given us seven gorgeous grandchildren! When Ian's job in Adelaide became redundant we decided to buy the General Store and Post Office in the little farming district of Wharminda on Eyre Peninsula. This was indeed a challenge, as neither of us had had any experience at running our own business - our learning curve was steep! We also did a mail run three times a week; for two years we had the manual telephone exchange; Ian delivered bulk fuel to farms and managed the local silos and I did some relief teaching. One entire wall of our office was covered with licences – we needed a licence to sell bulk fuel, a licence to sell fuel from a bowser, a licence to sell cigarettes, a licence to sell milk etc etc! Every so often a Government Inspector would appear to check that our scales were accurate. I will never forget the first morning we were on our own in the shop. It was about 7:30am and Ian was outside pumping fuel into the truck to deliver to one of our customers and the phone was going berserk - the farmers used to make a lot of calls early in the morning before they went off for the day, as we were to learn. I stood at the back door, in my dressing gown, yelling at him to come and help me as I couldn't keep up with the calls and went into panic mode! We soon got the hang of it however, although it was not a part of the business which we particularly enjoyed: we much preferred to be serving our customers, who had to wait if the phone rang. The phone exchange was such a tie: for 14 hours a day, without a break, every local and trunk call had to be recorded, and when our customers were making a trunk call we had to interrupt them every three minutes to ask if they were extending the call! We had fun and games during thunderstorms - the little doors just kept dropping down, accompanied by the incessant, loud ringing of their bells – not conducive to sound sleep! On the other hand, it was a good feeling to be able to help out in an emergency situation. For all this we were paid the grand sum of $2.80 an hour, $1.40 each! After much hassling by Ian, Telecom as it was then known, brought forward their plans to switch the exchange to automatic, and we were very pleased to be without it! Mouse plagues were another part of country life which I definitely did not enjoy – I hate mice! One long weekend (we did not open the shop on Sundays or public holidays) early on in our time at Wharminda, Ian had taken the boys to Adelaide and I was left to run the shop and telephone exchange - during a mouse plague! I remember having to stand on the desk in the office to operate the telephone exchange as there were mice running everywhere! Ian kindly informed me on another occasion that mice had run over my pillow during the night – I'm glad he didn't wake me and tell me that! An amusing memory we have of our time at Wharminda – although it wasn't funny at the time - was a time when Ian had gone out to deliver fuel to one of the farmers and had taken two-year-old Lachlan with him for the ride. While he was pumping out the fuel, it started to rain, heavily; when Ian went to get back into the truck after he'd finished he discovered that Lachlan had locked all the doors of the truck, and it took some time for him to convince Lachlan to open them so he could get out of the rain! Chris and Matthew, our eldest two sons, very much enjoyed their time at Wharminda (Lachlan was too young to remember very much) - they loved having a swimming pool in the back yard, having chooks and collecting the eggs, and most of all having pets – dogs, kittens and even a tiny rabbit! They did very well at Wharminda Primary School where they received almost one-one tuition, especially when there were only six students at the school for a couple of years! All in all, however, despite the challenges and long hours, we enjoyed our time at Wharminda serving the local farming community and playing in the local sporting teams.

We sold the business after nine years and moved to Port Lincoln, where I was offered a full-time permanent teaching position. I loved my job and never considered changing careers: the sweet innocence of young children, their desire to learn and their rapid progress made my job very rewarding. I enjoyed researching and teaching new topics and am proud of my efforts to instil a life-long love of learning in my students by being a good role model. I worked alongside some wonderful teachers - we were a very cohesive and talented group - and also parents. After a few years I applied for, and won, a couple of short-term leadership positions, namely a Co-ordinator's position in Assessment and Reporting, and a Deputy Principal position. These were both challenging of course but I relished the opportunity to enhance my skills and try something different. As society changed, we seemed to have more and more complex students in our classes, the curriculum became fuller and fuller, and there were more and more administration and assessment tasks to be done with less and less time to do them in. Teaching was very different by the time I retired at the end of 2014 to what it had been like when I started my career in 1973, when we had a lot more time to teach and a lot more input into what we taught! Being presented with a *Rowan Ramsey MP School Community Award* for "dedicated service to the education and care of children at Kirton Point Primary School" was a real thrill for me and a nice way to finish my teaching career.

However, the next challenge was soon awaiting me. Within three months of retiring I had a cycling accident, resulting in a badly broken leg, collapsed kneecap and a broken collarbone! A few months later I received an email from Breast Cancer Network Australia with the subject line *Trek the Great Wall of China for BCNA!* It read "If you or someone you know is looking for a challenge, this could be just what you are after!" **China had never been on my bucket list, but trekking the Great Wall with a like-minded group** sounded like a fabulous idea – I love a challenge, I love walking, travel and history so it ticked all the boxes for me. It was to be even more of a challenge for me to be fit enough as I was barely back on my feet after my accident earlier that year. The trek was organised by a company called Inspired Adventures, which is an adventure fundraising agency which partners with Australian and international charities to organise challenging trekking and cycling adventures in Australia and around the world. I mulled over the idea of doing the trek for a few weeks and by the time I rang Inspired Adventures there was one place left - it was meant to be! I signed up for the trek, taking myself right out of my comfort zone - I didn't know anyone else who was doing the challenge; in fact I was the only participant from South Australia. Each participant had to raise a minimum of $4,000 as well as pay their own travel costs. I spent some sleepless nights thinking "What have I done? How am I going to raise that amount of money in a small regional city when there are so many other people all trying to raise money for worthy causes?" However, Inspired Adventures assured me that I wouldn't have any trouble raising the money because breast cancer is such a well-known cause and that proved to be the case as I easily exceeded the $4,000 target. Family members and a small committee of very supportive friends helped me, and we were overwhelmed by the generosity of people in Port Lincoln. Inspired Adventures also set up an online fundraising page for each of us. Fundraising was time-consuming and a lot of work but it was very rewarding and lots of fun and we all got so much more out of it than we put in.

The trip lived up to all my expectations – I loved trekking on the Great Wall, especially on the original, unrestored sections, even though it was hard, and SO steep. The steps were relentless. We had to watch where we were putting our feet all the time because the steps varied so much in height and width; in some places we had to walk sideways like crabs because they were so narrow; in other places the easiest way to come down was on our backsides because they were so steep! One day we had to climb 1400 steps just to reach the Wall! Some sections were literally like goat-tracks, with sheer drops on both sides and nothing to hang onto - there was no wall in those places! The enemy would have had a hard time scaling the mountainous terrain on horseback to reach the Wall in some places! In all we trekked about 35km over five days, the majority of which was steps! The views from the Wall in every direction were sensational. I was the oldest participant, but I had trained hard and am proud to say that I kept up with much younger participants. In all fairness though, most of the younger trekkers were still working and/or had young families so they didn't have as much time to train as I did. Beijing was noisy, bustling and chaotic but the elegant, colourful, ancient buildings were beautiful. Famous sites like the Forbidden City and Tiananmen Square were fascinating. China is certainly a country of contrasts - between ancient and modern, traditional and western ways. It was an honour and a privilege to have been able to undertake this challenge with such an inspirational, supportive and friendly group. We formed a very close bond as a group, having shared so much, and came away with 22 new friends.

My next adventure challenge came three years later, when I joined four other members of Dragons Abreast Port Lincoln (DAPL), including my sister, to tackle the Ord River dragon boat marathon. I had joined DAPL after I had recovered from my broken leg, and I absolutely love the paddling, and the camaraderie of the group. We joined forces with ten paddlers from Bunbury in Western Australia. The marathon entailed paddling down the mighty Ord River from Lake Argyle to the town of Kununurra, a distance of 55 kilometres, in one day! Our normal training paddles, once or twice a week see us paddling about 5 kilometres. The event was hosted by Kununurra Dragon Boat Club in conjunction with Dragons Abreast Australia.

There were 120 paddlers participating in the event, in 8 boats – each boat held 14 paddlers and a sweep, the person who steers the boat. Several boats had paddlers from all over Australia paddling together.

We had a very early start to our day – we were picked up from our accommodation at 4:45 am and transported by bus to Lake Argyle Resort, where we had breakfast and then we were taken to the starting point, just below the Argyle dam wall, for our 7:00 am start. There was great excitement as we drove over the dam wall and saw the starting point and all the boats lined up! The first section of the marathon saw us paddling 21 kilometres through the steep, spectacular gorge walls and three small sets of rapids, which was quite exhilarating and unlike anything we have paddled in here at Port Lincoln, before our first stop, for morning tea. After two and a half hours of paddling, we were very glad to get out of the boat and stretch our legs and move around! Our next paddle of about 11 kilometres seemed to go quite quickly – with magnificent scenery to look at, whistling kites soaring above us and the occasional freshwater crocodile sunning itself on the river bank, there was plenty to take our minds off the paddling! Throughout the paddle we regularly changed sides, and rested seat by seat for a few minutes – this gave us an opportunity to have a drink and take a few photos. After we had paddled for an hour or so after our second rest stop, a support boat pulled up alongside us, secured our boat to theirs and handed over our lunch to eat in the boat! We would have liked to get out of the boat and eat our lunch in the shade as this was the hottest part of the day, but we did have the luxury of being towed for a few minutes while we ate our lunch! Our final stop was about 10 kilometres from the finish. The last section was the hardest part of the paddle as we were tired, it was hot and there was absolutely no current to help us. There were several pleasure boats from Kununurra motoring along the river in this section as well, many creating a wake as they weren't going slowly and at one point we nearly capsized! We were counting off the kilometres one by one, and got a new lease of life when we turned off the Ord River with about 3 kilometres to go, into a channel connected to Lake Kununurra where we would finish our marathon. We were overjoyed to see the finish line. About 300 metres from the shore we waited for all the boats to arrive and paddled in as one in a show of unity and strength as the event was a challenge, not a race.

Celebratory drinks and a magnificent dinner awaited us as dusk fell and all paddlers reflected with pride and relief on what they had accomplished. The camaraderie amongst the paddlers was palpable. All our hard work and extra training had paid off and we had achieved our goal of completing the marathon. Although all five of us relished the opportunity to participate in such an awesome event, we all agreed that it is an event that we would take part in only once as it was such hard work!

Later that year I travelled to Europe on a long-awaited trip with my best friend. One component of our fabulous trip was a 98 kilometre walk over 7-days in the Cotswolds in South Western England, organised by a small company called *Foot Trails*. Its founders and consultants have lived in the area all their lives, and custom make independent (self-guided) walking trips which go 'off the beaten path' and to lesser-known places for people seeking an authentic and individual experience. After consulting us about our interests and the length of time we wanted to walk, they sent a proposed itinerary, which we altered slightly, and then organised accommodation and transport to and from our daily start/finish points. We were provided with maps and detailed trail notes for each day's walk. We started in the northern Cotswolds in a small town called Chipping Camden, over the course of the week passing through charming historic towns and villages such as Stow-on-the-Wold, Upper and Lower Slaughter and Tetbury before ending our walk in Bath. We stayed in historic country inns along the way which were full of atmosphere and served great food! We absolutely loved our walks through farms, on public walkways and narrow country lanes. The scenery was magnificent, with glorious autumn leaves and views over hills and valleys which took our breath away! On this trip it wasn't the actual walking which was challenging, except for a couple of very steep hills as we approached Bath, but muddy, slippery tracks and waterlogged paddocks! In the days before we started our walk it rained and rained and rained some more, which caused flooding in some areas. It took some organising to even get to our starting point as some trains had been cancelled because stations were flooded, and substitute buses had to do lengthy detours because many roads were impassable. Bledington, where we stayed for two nights, had been deluged with their annual rainfall in just three months, and the room we stayed in at the hotel had been flooded two days before we arrived and the guests had been evacuated in the middle of the night! Some of the tracks we had to walk on had turned to creeks, gates we were supposed to go through were underwater and we plodded through thick, squelchy mud, sometimes holding onto fences for dear life! Our challenge was to stay upright, which we managed, although we nearly lost our footing on a couple of occasions! In spite of the wet conditions, we thoroughly enjoyed the walk: it is a great way to see the countryside and become immersed in its history.

My next planned adventure challenge is to walk part of the Camino trail, the ancient pilgrim route, in Europe with my sister and another friend - if COVID-19 is controlled and we are ever able to travel overseas again! We plan to walk parts of the trail in Switzerland, France and Spain, including crossing the Pyrenees on foot. This will be a challenge for us all as we plan to sleep in albergues (similar to Youth Hostels) and carry our luggage on our backpacks - well some of the time anyway - so I'm going to have to learn to take a lot less gear! The walking will be much harder than it was in the Cotswolds, with many more hills and mountains to negotiate.

Meanwhile I plan to keep on enjoying life and making the most of every day and every opportunity! Port Lincoln with its laidback lifestyle is a wonderful place to live - we are blessed with beautiful beaches and bush nearby, and plenty of open spaces and fresh air. I am fortunate that most of my immediate family, four of my seven grandchildren and my closest friends live here, and that I am able to participate in activities which I love, including dragon-boating, golf and singing. I feel sure more challenges will present themselves, and there are still plenty of places in Australia and overseas on my bucket list to visit if I have the opportunity!

SLING YOUR HOOK – HOME IS THE SAILOR

By Capt. Rob Cobban

Where to start? Born Aberdeen, early education in Portsmouth UK, mid 1950s embarked *SS Otranto* with brother Gerry and three other lads bound for a migrant children's training farm in Australia and arrived at Dhurringile (near Tatura, Victoria) to complete a rudimentary education at Shepparton Technical School.

Dhurringile was something of a salutary introduction to the realities of life facing youngsters in a church run 'home'.

Apart from fending off the unwanted attention of some male staff members there were many kindnesses shown by locals far and wide who would take many of us into their homes for school holidays etc. Life was far from being miserable if perhaps not exactly ideal.

There was a 'home' pipe band comprising two outside 'Scots' mature age tutors with the appropriate experience on pipes and drums, with the boys then making up the bulk of the band. It was seen as an ideal way of getting outings around the state including competitions in Melbourne and Daylesford. We travelled long distances in a Ford Thames truck with a canvas cover. The seats were hard planks and the wind was cold on the evening returns. Still with a few singsongs and the resilience of youth it fell under the heading of fun.

My education terminated at the Intermediate level and I moved onto a series of jobs including, joinery assistant, apprentice printer, farm hand, timber milling and bulldozer operator, tool setter, spare parts binner.

From an early age in Portsmouth I had developed an interest in the Royal Navy so I took the nine-year introduction offer to join the Royal Australian Navy as a recruit seaman. Following basic training and additional gunnery training I attained the dizzy heights of ordinary seaman/gunner.

Navy life was a great experience, a continuous round of joining and leaving ships, mastering the art of hammock entry and exit within a ship that moved the moment one cheek was lowered. I acquired staunch shipmates who would rotate through my nine and half years of service. Most of my sea-time was spent in the far east which included the hostilities of Borneo/Malaysia and Vietnam. The lot of a service person is when not actively refining talent for fighting the ship we trained to do so. One such training event was a gunnery target for other ships. The 'firing ship' would acquire the target ship by radar computers of the day and then calculate the range, bearing and future position of the target. Ideally before guns were layed onto the target a calculated 'throw off' would be applied and a salvo would be fired. This fall of shot would usually a safe measurable distance clear of the target. On this particular occasion the target was straddled, a rapid radio message to firing ship to " cease firing " was met with the reply " the next salvo is in the air " - fortunately the second salvo landed where it was supposed to but there were a few tense seconds on our bridge. The shells being used were six-inch practice rounds, with no explosive but still dangerous.

Sadly, I lost my only brother, Gerry, to the *Melbourne/Voyager* accident in 1964. Another accident but tragic for four score men and their families.

At one point during my navy service at sea, we had a Royal Navy exchange gunnery officer who related a story (probably apocryphal) about Prince Albert (later King George VI) when a midshipman under training. He had a speech difficulty and was aboard a cruiser with a flight deck carrying out parade training of a squad of marines marching resolutely toward the edge of the flight deck. With the dedicated marchers getting ever closer to the edge, the gunnery instructor training them said "For god's sake man say something even if it is goodbye!" Some years ago I saw the movie " The Kings Speech ', this related the prince's speech therapy before he replaced his brother, who was abdicating as King and Emperor of the British Empire and Commonwealth.

Navy shore time was mainly promotion training and then a period instructing new entry recruits during 1964/65 then back to sea for 1966 and 1967 training in waters around Borneo and Malaysia.. Then followed a year shore based in Darwin before more promotion training in 68 and back to sea as a Petty (as in small!) Officer, more south-east Asia service and occasionally off Vietnam. This was followed by a period of instructing at Gunnery School at the shore depot HMAS Cerberus at Westernport in Victoria. My instruction role was mainly gunnery subjects to male sailors, but someone applied questionable trust and had me instructing 'lady' sailors.

As a reward for putting up with parade ground duties and the added hardship of instructing female sailors I was given the role of small arms instructor at the rifle range. A great final six months in the RAN ! When not instructing we were intensely involved with volley ball matches, eating very well at this semi-remote area and I improved my 9mm pistol and F1 sub machine gun skills by shooting rabbits in the surrounding sand hills.

Following my naval service of nine and a half years I secured a job as seaman and diver with the Commonwealth Lighthouse Service. This was supplying and servicing both manned and unmanned light houses as well as navaids. I was onboard the Victorian based vessel. A smart little one of three ships, of around two thousand tons called *MV Cape Pillar*, handily equipped with crane, cargo hold, work-boats and up to two Light Amphibious Resupply Ships or LARCs.

It was an interesting six months onboard ranging as far west as Rowley Shoals (Imperious Reef) off the North west coast of WA where we sunk footings and erected the first section of a 30 plus metre light house, to help iron ore ships Port Hedland bound from Japan. During this period I decided to study for a Second Mates Foreign-Going Certificate of Competency. This I kicked off with Radar Observer's Certificate, Life Saving and Boat operators, First Aid Certificate etc. As the qualification was a merchant one my military sea time was only counted in part. I was lucky enough to secure a berth as a Navigating Cadet with the then Australian National Line in order to acquire the remaining six months cross-over sea time before becoming eligible to sit for examination. I successfully completed my 2nd Mates in early 1972 and then did the rounds of shipping company offices in Melbourne. When I approached the Blue Star and Port Line office (UK company) I was told " we will give you a berth but it will be a month or two ". They rang me the next afternoon asking me to join a ship in northern Tasmania the next day.

Spent a busy 24 hours packing uniforms, selling my car before flying to Launceston to join *SS Tasmania Star* then loading apples. Ship was a 5 refer cargo holds and two general holds built around 1950 of about 12,000 tons – my first vessel as a brand-new Third Mate. Never mind I knew enough about the merchant navy to be dangerous! We loaded in Beauty Point before completing our apple loading in Hobart - week of parties with a bevy of girls for dancing the nights away. Sailed from Hobart bound Cape Town, south of 40-degree weather bad for a week, I kept the 12 to 4 watch, afternoon and night. First night out I was wrestling with 'obsmeteo weather reports' in the chart room, vessel rolling heavily when a beanie clad head appeared around the chartroom to the bridge doorway requesting a coffee, I initially took this to be a crewman but closer inspection revealed an attractive lady passenger. Night watches became a treat and I thought this civilian navy is way more appealing for bridge watchkeeping than the RAN.

The voyage was via Capetown and thence to Hamburg where we part discharged our cargo of apples before making for Cardiff, Wales where I signed off and left the 'Blue Star Line'. I journeyed by train to Colchester, Essex (north of London) and visited my mother after a parting of 18 plus years, a warm reunion which went well, I stayed for five weeks or so and then re-joined BS Line via a ship completing cargo in Ghent, Belgium. The next few months saw me in South American ports including, Rio, Santo (Sao Paulo),

Montevideo, Buenos Aries etc. some memorable trips on these freezer cargo ships with up to 12 passengers.

One notable Captain was a chap named Ian Smith, who had served during WW2 and was master of a ship discharging via barges at Port of London. He had a confrontation with a barge skipper. It was the practice to close all overboard discharge valves, particularly toilets. This was to be done ahead of cargo barges laying alongside the ship. The report I received was via the Purser who was in the Captain's office when an irate barge operator stormed into the Captain's office clutching an ominously brown stained piece of 4 x 4 paper, this he slapped down on the Captain's smart polished desk replete with a pristine blotting pad. The cockney barge skipper said "erre, ooo owns this then! This just came down on my barge, oowu ohns this then?" The captain lifted an immaculate ruler and pushed the offending stained paper off the immaculate blotting pad.

The Captain stated " I really do not know who owns it but, if no one claims it by end of the day, it is yours!

Loading a whisky cargo in Glasgow was something of trial. Instructed by the Chief Mate to supervise within the hold, the finishing off of loading pallets of Scotch I was treated to the gangers (wharfies) broaching the cargo and drinking the scotch. They were initially oblivious to my presence but then told me to FO before I got hurt. Towards the latter part of the shift the wharfies were unable to climb the hold ladders to come up on deck, this was the last day for our loading and no Scotch was being loaded for a few days so they were topping up. They were lifted out in a cargo net ! When I later related my experience to the Chief Officer he replied " Never go down the hold on the last day when loading whisky. Argentina, Montevideo and Brazil were all interesting places, Brazil was always a tad risky to go ashore by yourself but Argentina was generally ok. A return trip to Europe which included ports in France and Germany before heading for a dry docking in Newcastle, worked by the ship for a few weeks before a months plus leave in Aberdeen, Colchester and Portsmouth. A call from manning Blue Star Line in London saw me and a few others flying out via London to LA then overnighting in San Francisco before a flight north to Eureka, joining the MV Timaru Star.

I Remember the Chief Mate telling me to get some sleep as I would be supervising Mate on deck that night loading bulk paper for NZ, it was snowing. From there we headed up to Vancouver, weather bleak till we reached Juan De Fuca Strait. Vancouver was working cargo but still enough time to join some old shipmates on an Australian vessel in port, we spent an afternoon skiing on Grouse Mountain. Next few months saw calls at six NZ ports, Fiji and New Caledonia, Honolulu, LA/San Pedro, San Francisco, Portland, Oregon, Tacoma (Washington State), thence down to San Francisco before final port was calling back at Los Angeles returning to NZ to do another round trip.

In all I spent nine months on this vessel, a good crew of West Indians out of Barbados made for at times, some interesting moments, their main interest was playing wharf cricket and chasing girls. At the end of my time onboard this ship I had accumulated enough sea time to present myself for First Mate (FG) studies back in Australia. I opted for the Sydney Techs nautical and aviation section at which to study for the department of transport examinations. Following on a successful examination and a two-hour oral exam and six months down the track I returned to sea initially with Associated Steamships before returning to Aust National Line fold. Serving on a variety of ship types including, container ships, bulk carriers, tankers, RoRo (roll on/off), trading mainly around Australia but also to my old area of South Pacific and west coast north America and Canada. By this time I was sailing as second mate and secured enough sea-time to make a tilt at studies for Master Mariner (FG/class I).

This time I opted for studies at Warsash Nautical College in Hampshire, this being part of Southampton University in the UK. Allowing for interludes in Greece and trips to Germany as well as trips around the UK, it took some sixteen months of sporadic effort to get it done. Having friends in London and a fast car weekends in London ran into 3/4 day breaks. This I did knowing full well that even the smart guys were not only attending the lectures but studying well into the night. Finally with the likely prospect of a return to Australia empty handed, I applied my modest academic abilities and crash studied night and day for some months to get the job done. Was lucky enough to satisfy the UK Department of Trade I was competent to hold a Master Mariner Foreign Going Certificate of Competency. Thereafter followed a few days of sleep catchup and a drink or two at the "Old Ship" pub at Bursledon. Packing up was mainly textbooks and car tools. Curiously at the time initially I felt immense relief followed by an anti-climactic feeling of returning to 'real' life with the prospect of going back to seafaring.

Fare wells in the UK were made in late April 1979. The 911 car delivered to a freight company to travel by ship to Sydney and I caught a flight home to Australia. I was happy to return and my employers who had been paying me six months at two thirds salary plus some four months leave, were keen for me to return to the company ranks. This was to a previous ship running to west coast states and Canada, still as second mate and I could not have been more pleased. Still, one quick round trip of six weeks saw me sent on leave ahead of being elevated to Chief Mate on a coastal RoRo vessel, short distances between Port Kembla, Westernport (near Melbourne) and Adelaide and much less 'appealing ' than the USA coast.

A six-week swing saw me take some leave ahead joining a ship loading grain in Adelaide for discharge in Nakhodka (near Vladivostok). This was in 1980 just ahead of the Moscow Olympics. Nakhodka was a somewhat sombre place at this time although the girls were friendly. Geographically it is close to Japan and a tri weekly ferry ran to Yokohama. Nakhodka had a rail head to connect with Siberia. I had some local shore leave and was walking into the city by traversing the rail yards, as I was approaching the relatively small railway station I encountered some civilians milling around.

As I approached this group of people, apparently just off the overnight ferry from Yokohama they went quiet and parted as I (a lone perhaps sinister figure), neared them. They were all still quiet, I studied them as there was something vaguely familiar about them, I realised they were dressed in typical Australian style, jeans, RM moleskins etc. When in their midst I said "G'day how are you going!" Great rejoicing by people who had been away from Australia for about three days but delighted to see a face from Australia. Australia actually had an embargo on trade with Russia at that time, we even snubbed the Olympics - something to do with the Russians being in Afghanistan. The Aussie tour group were also surprised that I was on an Australian ship in the port. I guess they had a story of a lone Aussie sailor in Russia, to relate later as I do about them. It was fun to see their faces.

We spent a month alongside in Russia. We were allowed day shore leave, but had young guards checking us off and then back on the ship. Shore leave was over at midnight. Plenty of night clubs selling 'rocket fuel' being passed off as cocktails. Still the crew had fun even with 'Cinderella leave'.

We sailed in June and traversed Japanese waters Indonesian waters and home to Australia to sign off in Newcastle. Home to Sydney for me for, a few weeks leave snow skiing etc before my next ship. This next ship was running between north Tasmania, Melbourne, Geelong, Point Henry, Sydney, Brisbane, Townsville, Darwin, Groote Eylandt. As coastal runs go this was great, as the Mate it was about as good as it gets. The officers onboard, had got together over time and built a 'Bronzewing' catamaran, with both cargo and stores cranes we were able to store and launch this for leisure moments. I do not think there would be much of such moments in present times. It was a tad unique even then.

Whilst in Darwin in 1981, I learned that a local company had a new small ship entering Darwin, Borneo, Timor, Malaysia and Singapore trade and were looking for a Captain with a Class ! Masters Certificate. I made the approach and secured the role and then had two plus years in command of a very varied trade of livestock, general, drilling gear, containers, and manganese. As an early farm boy and worker, I managed the transition to cattle carrying ok but confess NT cattle and buffalo could and did 'fizz' up a little more than southern cattle.

The operation of this Darwin based company was transporting up to 840 head of cattle and/or buffalo taking a route up through the Indonesian and western Philippines Archipelagos. The welfare/condition of the cattle was paramount, so the route taken was to the Master's discretion regards weather and avoiding pirate active areas. Had a really good group of officers with a generally content crew. Ship was purpose built to allow for cargo loading from the beach, the vessel was only 80 x 16 metres with a draft of 4.5 metres total crew was 11 plus a stockman. Steady work at times but interesting ports. During this time I was living in Neutral Bay, Sydney and would commute for a nine-to-eleven-week swing, this equated to two northern trips.

At the end of almost two years I got word that the then Marine & Harbours SA were looking for a harbourmaster/marine pilot in Port Lincoln. I had visited Lincoln on two ships over the years so found the job prospect appealing. Made an application, did a preliminary interview when off Borneo by HF radio, a final interview was organised when my ship returned to Darwin about May 1983. I packed up my kit and flew down to SA for two nights, secured the job and flew back to Sydney to organise an uplift to Port Lincoln. On arrival Lincoln the incumbent Pilot escorted me through four in pilotages and three outs. It was a little stressful to return to manoeuvring ships of 180 to 225 metres LOA (length overall) and usually one tug to assist. Use to think I wonder what the Captain of the ship would think of my most recent background driving an 80-metre ship. When I was at sea I had a few experiences when my embarked pilot would abdicate his role because I questioned approach speeds or voiced another concern, somewhat alarming the first time.

For the most part piloting in Port Lincoln was straight forward but could be character forming when the ships were large and/or empty with a strong wind. My first 25 years were with only one tug assisting. Tug skippers were highly competent and worked industriously to keep their pilot out of bother.

We pilots were also required to work other ports when free in our base ports, I also held licences for Proper Bay, Whyalla and Thevenard which I thought kept me gainfully employed but some other colleagues maintained and worked regularly in five plus ports.

Over the thirty years I worked in various ports as a marine pilot, there were several events that kept my ego in check.

Port Lincoln was extremely problematic for one's ego. This was a result of the berthing basin amphitheatre like setting, virtually half the town have a ringside seat to not only one's great feats of pilot brilliance but also ones less streamlined manoeuvres i.e. stuff-ups.

A large number of pilots have sailed as Captains and we know how Captains sometimes will have great trepidation, when handing over the control of their ship to this unknown interloper, even when he is kitted up to look like a pilot. Ship Captains in recent times, are encouraged with their bridge team members to challenge their pilot over genuine safety concerns which they have with the ship's intended track and progress. Given the vagaries of wind and tide it is not always easy or advisable to make a very slow approach to the berth, that being said the extremely nervous Captain can be a distraction to one's concentration.

Occasionally, when fielding yet another query about approach speed and knowing one cannot safely proceed any slower, I have given out the following, " Captain I always know when I am approaching too fast, the men on the wharf will run away ". Best said with a smile if not sure about the Masters knowledge and appreciation of Australian humour.

As pilots, most of us will know that our next incident may occur on our next 'job'. The reasons for incidents are many and many may be beyond our certain control, but we are being paid for both the good and bad days and one can take action to effectively minimise accident damage.

In 2010, I had covered a colleagues night work load in Thevenard so he was able to attend a family event in Port Lincoln. Having worked during the night I could not safely continue the almost four-hour return drive in time to meet an early afternoon pilot commitment in Lincoln. The other pilot was assigned the ship *MV Grand Rodosi*. Long story shortened, the engine failed to run astern and continued to run ahead. Lincoln's smartest and most expensive fishing vessel saved the wharf and grain conveyor from certain crippling damage but was sunk in that process. As I drove into Port Lincoln I was asked by phone to escort police on board the *Grand Rodosi* in order to conduct breath analysis. All clear from effects of alcohol or drugs.

A few days later I was piloting an Australian tanker into the port, the Captain, who I knew from previous visits asked what happened. I said it was not me, he said "we know that" I gave the outline of events and at the end added there were two golden factors on the day, he asked what they were, I replied "nobody was hurt or worse, and I was the not the effin pilot" (language detuned).

Many ships later I hung up my VHF radio and flotation safety jacket for a return to warmer parts in July 2013.

Chiang Mai was the city of choice with yearly returns for an Australian summer - pre Covid 19.

Part VII

TRAVEL

LEAVING ENGLAND

By Lisa Morton

As I grew into my teenage years, I had a feeling I would move overseas. Our family, mum, dad, sister and I nearly moved to Canada when I was 11 years old as my Grandparents lived there at the time. The emigration applications were filled out, but my mum had second thoughts and didn't want to leave her family in England. Eventually my Grandparents from Canada moved to England. Maybe that's why the idea of moving overseas wasn't that scary to me. I liked adventure and change and for some reason I just could not see myself settling down in England.

I did a lot of travelling in my 20s. I visited New Zealand and Australia and worked on an amazing children's Summer Camp for five summers in America. I was back and forth flying, travelling, working and having a great time but feeling unsettled. In 2004 I met Tim, an Australian who was working at the Summer Camp and had a great feeling about us being together. Tim travelled to England after Camp and we stayed in touch, but he eventually went back home to Australia.

We missed each other quite a bit as we had become good friends. I asked him, "Why don't I come to Australia?" If I remember correctly Tim was concerned that I was making such a big move. I wasn't scared at all, I was ready for an adventure and if it didn't work, I had plan B which was to go to New Zealand and stay with my sister as she was studying in Dunedin on the South Island at the time so I had an exciting back up plan.

I packed my back pack with a few essentials and importantly, a photo album of my family, pets and my gorgeous English country. My parents had bought an old 4 room house in Great Totham, Essex, England and my dad built an extension and renovated the lot. Mum helped where she could and worked hard in what became a beautiful garden. My family and I actually lived in a caravan in the back garden for 2 years and it was the best experience for us growing up. My sister and I have many fun memories of that time especially with all our pets.

September 5th 2005 I arrived in Adelaide and was met by Tim and a big bunch of red roses. We had a great time settling in together at Glenelg a famous beach in Adelaide. Tim showed me around and I met all his friends and heard all the stories that went with them. I had been to Australia before with a few of my friends in 2001/02 we lived and worked in Sydney for a few months, travelled to Melbourne, to Adelaide, across the Nullarbor to Perth up the West Coast to Exmouth then on to Cairns and down the East Coast, that was a great experience. I had spent so much time in America and being around the American wildlife and cities that I absolutely loved America and was quite disappointed by the Australian wildlife and the outback, I didn't really like it I am ashamed to admit but that's just because it was so different. I love it now and certainly appreciate all of Australia for what it is and never get bored seeing a kangaroo in the wild.

After a few months in Glenelg Tim decided he wanted to

move back to Port Lincoln and take me 'home' to where he grew up after we had done a few trips to see friends in regional South Australia as Tim just wanted me to experience the small community feel. We rented a friend's house in Port Lincoln for a while and 'oh I mustn't forget to mention Tim's beautiful black Labrador 'Barney.' He was two years old when I first met him and we become the best of friends instantly, probably because I wasn't working so we spent a lot of time together going on walks.

Port Lincoln was gorgeous, such a beautiful isolated spot. And that's exactly how I felt, isolated, alone and foreign... Everyone was into sport, watching sport, playing sport and talking about sport. I am an outdoors kinda girl and enjoy being active, but sport, nope not really interested, so weekends were hard for me at the start and after sport, you drank. I liked a drink or too and dancing yes but every weekend the same thing. It was hard to get used to. All the locals were very nice but they just didn't really understand me. 'G'day' was 'Hello' and for me 'Alright' is 'Hello' but every time I said 'Alright' to someone they just looked at me with a very strange looking face and with no reply. Sometimes I would get an answer like 'yes I am feeling fine' thinking that I was asking them if they were feeling ok!

Another memory that sticks in my mind from those early Port Lincoln days were 'sausages and champagne', all it seemed we did was eat sausages, drink champagne and watch sport. I felt extremely out of place and missed my family and England very much. I called home a lot and spoke to my mum and dad and about the differences between the countryside in England and regional Australia, it is so different and I wasn't quite sure if I could ever get used to it. Eventually I started working and made some friends of my own. Two of my new girl friends were from overseas. One from England the other Canada We knew exactly how each other felt and understood all our similar feelings of being outsiders. It was comforting to know I was not alone in this beautiful but isolated town. *In social surveys done in PL isolation is high on likes AND dislikes! Ed.*

A few years passed and Tim got the adventure bug again and decided it was time we moved on. We didn't go far, to Whyalla, 3 hours up the road! Now if you said that to someone from England they would think that that 3 hours up the road isn't far, that's like a trip on the M25 sitting in traffic going on a yearly holiday I was finding out that 3-hour drive covers somewhere around 300 km. We travel a long distance in Australia and it's no big deal, I kinda liked that. We had a great few years in Whyalla and again it was isolated, dry, red and dusty and so different from England but I was starting to enjoy the life that country South Australia had to offer. Slower pace and outdoors all the time because the weather was so good. Not many rainy or cloudy days, whereas in England there were not many sunny days! Oh and we did have our first baby, Laila, at Whyalla.

We soon decided to go on more adventures so we moved to Nhulunbuy, an Aluminium mining town in the Northern Territory. I thought South Australia was different but wow the NT, especially Arnhem Land, was a whole lot different again. Luckily, I had been to Australia before and had an understanding of how vast it was and how the states were completely different to each other. The, climate, the scenery, the landscape, the fauna and flora. And even community lifestyles are different in each state. When I remembered that Australia was the same size as the USA, except Alaska, it made a lot more sense.

Tim and I loved it and hated it, you needed permits to live Nhulunbuy, a permit to drink alcohol, just one shop for food and if the barge didn't arrive that week that meant neither did the food. It was hard and at times depressing, oh and no epidural at the local hospital to help with Harry's birth!!! It was as remote as you could get, only one vet in town and if she went on holiday then no care for your pets. The upside to this strange simple way of living was the most spectacular scenery, nature, no crowds and the aboriginal history was amazing. Living in Nhulunbuy made you appreciate what Australia is all about, you felt honoured, privileged even to be allowed to step onto Arnhem Land and be a part of the community. Even though we couldn't wait to leave when it was time to go, we would go back there in a heartbeat, that place just gets stuck under your skin and our sweet dog Barney is buried there.

We then moved to the cowboy country of Chinchilla in outback Queensland. Horses and rodeos everywhere but we didn't find our elusive dream so we moved on to Shepparton in Victoria. 'Shep", is dry in summer but cold, lush and green in winter. The beautiful mountains of Australia's Great Dividing Range are nearby and the Goulburn River runs through the town. Compared to the other places we have been there are many small towns and other attractions nearby to explore.

One day we would like to move back to South Australia

where it all began for us. It will be great for our children to show them the lifestyle Tim had growing up and we know that they will love it.

Australia is a multi-cultural country and I love that about Australia but I still love it when I hear an English accent, whether it's on the street or on TV, I love watching English shows on TV, it just warms my heart a little hearing a familiar accent and reminds me of where I grew up. I still call England home even though I am an Australian Citizen and probably have seen a lot more of Australia than many Australians. I have loved moving around and exploring new towns and the surroundings, it's amazing how many locals don't travel much even around their own town where they grew up. I have met many new friends who live in an area and yet I have seen more of the area than they ever have. To me that's strange.

It has always been lonely living in these small towns with the locals who have their families around them to go to for dinner, to have as babysitters and to spend time with at weekends. I get sad when people complain about their family members when they live so close and mine don't, these people don't know how lucky they really are. As much as family can be a pain sometimes, family is everything to me. My parents and my sister and her family live in New Zealand which isn't too far for a visit, better than having to fly to England, I haven't been back to England since I left. I miss my childhood friends; I miss where I grew up. It's hard to explain but it's almost like a double life, I had one life in England and now I have this life in Australia, I feel like two different people, I don't like to think of it too much as it does make me feel sad.

One day we would like to take our children to England and show them where I went to school, where I lived, see my Aunties and Uncles and Cousins. Sadly, I don't have any grandparents left now both my Nans have passed away since I left England. Thank goodness for Technology, it has made moving overseas that little much easier by being able to send photos, emails and even do video calls. My memory is slowly fading of England maybe that just comes with age!

Leaving England was easy, settling into Australia was hard and took time. I feel lucky to have been able to travel and move around Australia, I have learnt so much about Australia and its people. I love everything about Australia's natural beauty and its wildlife. I have lived in Australia for 16 years now and where ever we have lived locals have always said to me 'when you reach 20 years you are a local' I guess I'm getting close.

A MOTOR HOME ADVENTURE

By Chris & Ann Watts

We have both been school teachers all our working lives. In October 1984 on our first long service leave we made our first family trip to the east from our home in Western Australia. We sent the car to Adelaide on a truck. Chris and the two older children (11 and 8) took an overnight bus from Perth to Adelaide while Ann flew to Adelaide with the 3-year-old. We bought a caravan in Adelaide and holidayed in South Eastern Australia until Christmas. Chris particularly enjoyed the trans-Australia drive. Ann not so much, to say the least.

In 2003 we moved to Deniliquin in NSW and worked there for three years and in 2007 to our current home on the Bellarine Peninsula near Geelong. Since then Chris has had a variety of jobs and we have made many trips to Perth to see friends and relatives. It is no secret that Ann prefers flying to driving.

Since retiring from full time work in 2007 we have had several overseas and Australian holidays and enjoyed the flights necessary to fit cruising schedules and other destinations overseas. However long-haul travel in economy, crowds and the waiting at airports have definitely taken the lustre from air travel and the reality of Covid 19 diminishes the appeal of cruising.

But all is not lost. We have found another way to enjoy travel.

In mid-2019 Chris was itching to drive across the country and being the organiser that he is arranged a deal with *Imoova* rental vehicles to drive a Britz motor home from Adelaide across the Nullarbor and relocate it in Perth. Ann relented with this compromise and actually looked forward to the new experience as one of her friends was a great fan of these vehicles. The deal was very cheap – about $5.00 a day and six days were allowed to complete the transfer. The *Imoova* was an almost new 6 berth Mercedes diesel and we were to leave Adelaide on a given Saturday and deliver it to their depot in Perth the following Thursday.

We left home two days before the pick-up in Adelaide. Our eldest daughter, domiciled in Melbourne with her partner and their three little boys, was completing genealogy studies through a Tasmanian University and suggested that we explore some of the family history on our trip. We had planned to stop at Casterton, the home of the Kelpie sheep dog, in Western Victoria where there was a family connection at the nearby towns of Digby and Merino. Ann's grandmother, Annie Haworth, was born on New Year's Day 1868 in Digby. The family later moved to Merino in 1876 where Annie's father took up the licence for the Digby Hotel. We detoured through these cute little towns and saw the Digby Hotel but no evidence of the family history.

One of the delights of travelling is to find accommodation gems that pop up out of nowhere. We left Casterton Thursday afternoon and made our way via the Coorong and Wellington ferry to Milang on the shores of Lake Alexandrina in South Australia where we had pre-booked accommodation in what was a 1960s-style motel. We parked by the office to be joined by the man who had been cutting long grass, but now diverted to be the Motel Receptionist. Prior to departure we had negotiated a reasonable rate but the motel would only accept cash and there was no change available. The room rate was negotiated downwards to the paper money we had without resorting to coins. Despite this bizarre start, the room was very comfortable with an enormous bed and a huge television set and after our big day we slept well. An in-room continental breakfast was included and was better than many buffet breakfasts at up-market hotels. The trip was shaping up well.

Early Friday morning we purchased some morning tea at a nice bakery in Milang for Ann's 91-year-old brother who lives at Aberfoyle Park in the Adelaide Hills. The one-hour journey through Strathalbyn and Kangarilla was very pretty along a winding and hilly road. We did wonder how a motorhome would handle this as we did have some similar hills to face as we approached Perth through the Avon Valley. We spent the morning with Ann's brother then accompanied him to a nearby nursing home to visit his wife who had dementia. It was a short visit but we planned to see them on the way home. Later that afternoon we made our way to a motel near the Adelaide airport and the Britz Campervan depot in readiness for our Saturday morning departure in the motor home.

With supermarket supplies in hand, we made our way on Saturday to Britz for our instructions on how to pilot this, new to us, vehicle. The training session took about 20 minutes and was mainly concerned with the gas appliances, the cassette for the toilet, delivering the vehicle full with diesel and awareness of the 'Number to call if you get into trouble.' The important mechanical issues like changing wheels and normal daily vehicle safety checks were overlooked! With motor home loaded and car parked at the Adelaide airport we were on our way on the new freeway. The vehicle was very easy to drive and after a couple of hours Ann had a drive and enjoyed the experience as the road was reasonably quiet, the weather good and the after a while it seemed the motor home was as driveable as a big car. It was clear we would be at Kimba, half way between Sydney and Perth, our preferred destination for the evening, well before dark. Britz rules stipulated no driving at night on country roads and speed not to exceed 100kmh. As we approached Port Augusta, it was clear we would need to refuel. Chris had a preference for a servo other than the first one we came to. We also needed to make sure the servo had toilets. Aware of these requirements, Ann kept driving and refused to detour to the opposite side of the road to go to a servo – she just kept going! Ann surrendered the driver's seat about 100km west of Port Augusta and Chris became alarmed at the low fuel gauge. As the gauge got lower and lower, Chris was contemplating, the 'Run out of fuel' story we would have to tell Britz. Would we have mobile service? Would the RAA be available? Surely Kimba has diesel! Should we turn back to Port Augusta? At least we had food, water and accommodation! The atmosphere was rather silent as the gauge moved to empty. Mercifully though, we made it to Kimba where they did have diesel and we resolved to ensure the vehicle was at least half full at all times.

The journey across the Nullarbor proceeded smoothly and

we were soon calm and relaxed. Planning for breaks improved. We stopped and prepared our drinks and snack before opening the doors to welcome the flies and insects. A bonus of this strategy was to observe the birdlife, undaunted by our trespass, displayed magnificent colours as we enjoyed our break. One bird in particular was tiny, much smaller than a budgerigar or canary, with bright yellow plumage, digesting the produce of a bright green tree near our vehicle. The Nullarbor scenery is captivating with the elevated position and big windows enhancing our view of the vastness of the desert, the starkness of the isolation and the magnificence of the Great Australian Bight from the strategically located vantage points. The views of and from the coasts are breathtaking and it is a pity that our opportunities to stop were limited by the inflexibility of our timetable. The random wildlife presenting during this trip was limited to birdlife whereas on previous trips we had seen many kangaroos and once thirteen Wedge Tailed Eagles attacking one carcass, and enormous flocks of budgerigars. The obligatory fuel stops gave us an opportunity for casual interaction with fellow travellers and those motivated to spend their lives serving the travelling public while domiciled in some of the most remote settlements in the world.

The well-known milestones along the Nullarbor prompt reflection on the vastness of the land. Perhaps the most poignant are the aircraft landing strips painted on the road at key intervals. The lines prompt questions. Do aircraft other than those of the Royal Flying Doctor Service ever use this landing and take-off facility? How is the road cleared of other vehicles to facilitate landing and take-off? Is it possible for police to attend to supervise aircraft movements? The road features a stretch of 145.6 km without a bend between Caiguna and Balladonia. It was nice to chat and we played some games such as, what happened to people forced to abandon wrecked vehicles and caravans along the way? These questions pervade the minds of travellers as they observe the landscape. For some it is interesting, for others, monotonous and some scary. As you arrive at your overnight destination though, excitement mounts. News and TV to update football results as radio, mobile phones and TV have yielded to CDs and compromise the tranquillity of the quality time with one's partner of 51 years. Eucla was the most interesting stop as Ann's grandfather in his career as a postmaster had been stationed there. Is it in WA or SA?

The Border Village is in SA so as you proceed west, your first port of call is the quarantine station checking for pests, weeds and diseases. The WA Department of Agriculture requires travellers to surrender fruit and vegetables. All vehicles are checked by officers in a friendly yet authoritative manner. It takes a little longer when you aren't all that familiar with your vehicle!

After the Border Village we made good time and by about 4:00pm we were about 10km short of Norseman and a decision had to be made as to whether we should press on to Kalgoorlie. The decision was made for us by the sun in our eyes as we were heading west and three rather large kangaroos jumped across the road– the first live 'roos we had seen on this trip. We slowed down and resolved that Norseman would be a prudent place to spend Monday night.

With an early departure from Norseman we remembered

the genealogy assignment about Anne Haworth our daughter had given us. By 1891 Anne, having commenced her teaching career in Digby, had moved to Mildura where she remained until moving to Broome, WA in 1900. After landing in Broome, Anne married Fred Tuckett who was post master at La Grange Bay where we taught in 1970. Fred Tuckett went on to an appointment at Kanowna, near Kalgoorlie, before a posting to Halls Creek in 1911.

It was at Halls Creek in 1917, where he became famous for his part in promoting Rev John Flynn's establishment of what became the Royal Flying Doctor Service. James Darcy, a stockman, suffered injuries to his urinary tract in a mustering accident and Fred Tuckett received instructions transmitted by Morse code from Dr John (Joe) Holland in Perth, to "Operate or he dies" and that is what Fred did and Darcy survived. After Fred's operation with primitive instruments and anaesthesia, (likely a bottle of rum) Darcy showed signs of recovery but Dr Holland was worried about deeper injuries than Fred could reach let alone deal with and journeyed from Perth to Halls Creek. It took 3 weeks. A voyage to Derby and then by a Model-T Ford across rough tracks to Halls Creek. Darcy died from malaria the day before Dr Holland arrived – that must have devastated Dr Holland. One of many times that an operation was successful but the patient died. This was just one of the stories that inspired Rev John Flynn in his work with The Australian Inland Mission and RFDS. *see footnote p 219*

Reverting to our genealogy assignment. We discovered the Eastern Goldfields Historical Society in Kalgoorlie. They were extremely helpful and directed us to some publications and relevant sections of the abandoned Kanowna town-site and cemetery that we investigated but we were unable to help our daughter other than a few photos and a person at the Historical Society who established direct contact with her; a more reliable and effective form of communication than Mum and Dad.

Kalgoorlie is one of our most fondly remembered teaching appointments. Chris was appointed there in 1978 and found it to be a most welcoming community. The husband of one of his teaching colleagues went on to become a member of state parliament, a government minister and more recently the Mayor of Kalgoorlie-Boulder. I asked at the Historical Society if by any chance they knew him and indeed, one of the volunteers worked at the Council offices and gave us his personal mobile number. We visited his wife that afternoon and the following morning we had breakfast with him and his wife as they launched his successful program for re-election to the position of mayor. While at breakfast he suggested we should wander down to the ABC office in Hannan St where the ABC presenter, Ivo, recorded an interview with us for his segment *Songtales*. Chris was asked about his memories and recalled an interview he had recorded for Four Corners in 1979 in Perth about the achievements of a delightful indigenous student who, despite losing the lower part of all limbs had meticulous handwriting, with a hand fashioned into a claw and represented the school in netball. The song Chris chose was Keith Michell's *Captain Beaky*, popular in 1978, especially with children. Ann talked about her sporting achievements, especially in tennis and teaching young indigenous adults. Her song was a Cilla Black selection, *Step*

Inside Love.

But we had to go and made our way along the Great Eastern Highway to Northam where we arrived just before sunset. In planning our last day, we had to ensure we arrived at the Britz depot between 2:00pm and 3:00pm so we were able to visit Toodyay, a marvellous town in the Avon Valley where we spent two years of our teaching careers in 1989-90. At the time, Toodyay was a thriving town. During the year there were a number of community events that attracted people from Perth and even interstate. These included mid-week horse race meetings, the Avon Descent and the Toodyay Folk Festival. The school had grown remarkably after its reclassification and the community spirit seemed to be much as it was 30 years before. Some people even remembered us and that was nice. As well as meeting the new school Principal, we were re-acquainted with two of the staff who were there in 1990 and another former staff member at the tourist bureau.

The motor home handled the hilly terrain with aplomb, no concerns at all.

With an extra 2500km on the speedo we arrived at the Britz depot on time, the vehicle intact and with a resolve that we do more travelling in such a vehicle whether it be the Nullarbor or other likely places. After a week in Perth with family and friends we flew to Adelaide, retrieved our car, visited Ann's brother again before an uneventful drive home with an overnight stay in Keith.

What fun! Bugger cruising and bugger aeroplanes. Bite the bullet and hit the road in a Motorhome—way to go!

Footnote

It is November 18, 2020. Last night I watched 'Outback Ringers', a series about catching wild bulls in the Northern Territory on the ABC. This must be one of the most dangerous jobs on earth as demonstrated by the casual comment, 'We all get horned'. Handling cattle of any sort probably kills more people than any other rural industry but this is frightening to watch. One of the ringers was horned in the penis, clearly not funny but only centimetres away from getting permanently damaged sexually or killed. He was looked after at the camp for 2-3 days keeping the wound clean and eventually was seen by a doctor, at Borroloola perhaps, who said it was healing well and to come back if he had problems. How long after the injury he was filmed I don't know but he certainly was sprightly and said his girlfriend reckoned 'It worked ok so that is all that matters.' He had other scars from horning that again were near misses. So, it still happens in the bush. Ed.

A NAURUAN FUNERAL

By The Silver Fox (aka Aileen Pluker)

Through European contact almost all of Nauruan culture has been destroyed or debased. The final ritual, however – that of death and burial – has retained significant aspects of former times. Though covered with a veneer of Westernisation and Christianity, enough of the original practice has remained to be recognisable.

Death is an ever-present visitor among the people of Nauru. Western lifestyle diseases such as diabetes, heart, liver, and kidney failure, coupled with an alarming number of traffic fatalities for such a small island with only one circular road, touch every family.

I have attended several funeral masses but, until recently, the people were only names. Last week, however, I was personally involved with the death and burial of a colleague and friend, Gabby Garabwin.

Gabby was afflicted with a number of medical problems caused by over-eating, excessive drinking, and lack of exercise, like so many in Nauru. When I first met him Gabby was already in a wheelchair, having had one leg amputated. During the time I knew him he had several visits to hospital where progressively three toes and finally his remaining foot were removed.

This year it was evident that Gabby's time with us was

limited. Still, he remained cheerful and gratefully accepted any invitation to do a days' relief teaching when he was able.

On the night of his death I went to visit him in hospital. His entire family, sister and brothers, nieces and nephews, and a number of the third generation were there, sitting in groups around the bedside or taking a break outside. They softly sang hymns and favourite songs in Nauman and English, prayed, and talked among themselves about his life and the times they had had together.

There was no thought of excluding the younger children. They moved in and out between the ward and the veranda, a little more subdued than usual but showing a lively interest in everything that was going on. Family members took turns to provide food for everyone. It was eaten in shifts so that there would always be a number with Gabby even though, by this stage, he was barely conscious and was relying on mechanical devices to keep his bodily functions going. Nurses and doctors would monitor his condition from time to time, but otherwise did not intrude.

Eventually, about 10.30, Gabby's life came to an end.

A collective sigh went out from those in the room while those outside were quickly called in to say their goodbyes. Nauruans are not demonstrative people, so there were none of the obvious signs and sounds of grieving, but luminous brown eyes became liquid with unshed tears. Some spilt over and ran unchecked down bronze cheeks.

Because of the heat, and because there were no distant relatives to wait for, he was buried next day. Two hours before the funeral the staff at Kayser went to Gabby's house, where his body had been laid out for viewing. It had been lovingly prepared by female family members and lay in a simple wooden coffin made that day at the Nauru Phosphate workshop.

Before we went we had been provided with small rosaries, holy pictures and medals to place in the coffin as a farewell gift to our friend. There were many other gifts both religious and worldly in the coffin, for there had been many visitors before us. After praying and saying our farewells we went outside and partook of refreshments.

The funeral mass was conducted in the Urebo Church according to the Catholic rite and was identical to one at home. Afterwards the coffin was loaded onto the back of a utility to be taken to the cemetery. In former times the body would have been wrapped in a mat and carried to the site by nephews, but now it is sufficient that they carry the body from the church and drive the utility. The grave, which had been dug by male family members, had been Gabby's mother's grave, and there was evidence of her remains still visible.

After the short grave side service we returned to his house, where female family members had prepared enormous quantities of pork, beef, fish, and rice. There were a number of soft drinks there, but nothing alcoholic. Later in the evening male family and friends would go to another family home and there spend the evening in reminiscing over glasses of a more potent brew.

On the third day after Gabby's death we were invited, along with relatives and friends, to yet another meal. This was to be Gabby's final send-off. Everyone had stories to tell of strange happenings: machines that suddenly stopped and then started again, a tree with furiously waving branches while all around was still, dogs that stood suddenly with raised ears as if listening to an unseen sound, and coconuts and breadfruit that fell beside where people sat. There was no sense of apprehension or fear, just an acknowledgement of Gabby's presence among us.

At the end of the meal there was a gift-giving, Gabby's final farewell to his friends. The gifts in the coffin had been collected and were now presented to us as mementos. When my name was called I was amazed to be presented with a lovely silver watch.

To say I was overcome would be an understatement. I realised the honour that had been given me. Everyone smiled, happy that Gabby had been given a gift suitable to be presented to one in my position. An old family friend who also happens to be a minister in the government was also there, and we were referred to by our official titles all night, because our presence would add to Gabby's prestige.

I was impressed with the comforting acceptance of death among: these people. There was a wonderful sense of community and an acknowledgement of death as part of the pattern of life. Perhaps in our society we have so sanitised death, and hidden it behind so many euphemisms, that we lack the ability to accept what, after all, is just another step towards eternity.

LOCATING THE CENTRE OF MAINLAND AUSTRALIA

By Neville Gregory, Terry Hill, Rod McLeod, Ron Potter

Introduction

I was friendly with Peter Malycha at Medical School and through him his Loxton friend David Simpson and their friends at Wentworth, the late Rod McLeod from Kelso and Terry Hill from the adjoining Netherby Station on the banks of the Darling River. On New Year's Day 1966 at Netherby was the only time, in very good company I might add, I managed to drink a carton of beer in a day.

I have kept in touch with those guys over the years hence this story. I have not met Ron Potter, owner of A and G Engineers in Griffith and Neville Gregory a jewellery in Gladstone Queensland. Rod and Terry became very successful in the wine industry since 1969 and built Buronga Hill Winery with partners in 1984. Terry now owns a private Hospital in Mildura.

They have a catalogue of interesting adventures on most if not all continents including Antarctica between them this is but one.

AUGUST 2000

From Australia's National Mapping Agency we were given six locations:-

1) **Central Mount Stuart** – nominated by Sturt as the centre in November 1845, but not reached until 22nd April 1860 when John McDouall Stuart planted the British Flag there.

   "Sunday, 22 April 1860, Small Gum Creek, under Mount Stuart, Centre of Australia - today I find from my observations of the sun, 111° 00' 30", that I am now camped in the centre of Australia. I have marked a tree and planted the British flag there."

   Mount Stuart is approximately 210km north of Alice Springs and just a few km west of the Stuart Highway.
   The precise point of Stuart's flag planting is, of course, very uncertain. We selected a peak, complete with a national survey benchmark, to which our GPS gave the co-ordinates:

   South 21 – 59 – 00
   East 133 – 27 – 00

2) **Centre of Gravity.** More than 50,000 digitised points representing the coastline of mainland Australia were assigned a unit weight. The moments were calculated assuming equal units of latitude and longitude, the latter varying with the cosine of latitude. The result of this calculation gave the centre as:

   South 23 – 7 – 00
   East 132 – 8 – 00

   Located about 15km north of Derwent Homestead, which

is about 190km WNW of Alice Springs and 25km east of Papunya. This location was pegged by The Jones family in 1992.

Our Garmin 12 GPS co-ordinates matched the co-ordinates given and marked by Jones in 1992.

3) **Furthest Point from the Sea**

A series of concentric circles drawn on transparent material were moved over the top of 1:5-million scale map of Australia until one circle was found to touch the coast at three points. The centre of the circle was then marked and the co-ordinates scaled from the map. This method resulted in a good agreement with the centre of gravity method.

We located and marked this point some 10km north of the Centre of Gravity Point, still on Derwent Station.

A peg and plate was placed on the fence-line 26 metres west of the actual point.

To our knowledge we were the first to visit, and certainly to mark, this point.

South 23 – 2 – 00
East 132 – 10 – 00

Note: Cecil Madigan – first to cross the Simpson Desert in 1939 – calculated the Centre of Gravity Point to be in this general vicinity.

4) **Median Point**

The Median Point was calculated as the mid-point between the extremes of latitude and longitude of the continent, giving the following co-ordinates:

South 24 – 15 – 00
East 133 – 25 – 00

This point was located and marked, by two "Garmin 12" GPS instruments, some 70km south-south west of Alice Springs and 4km west of the Stuart Highway.

Hitherto, this point has been of a theoretical nature only and has not been physically identified. The route to it is over rough, rocky and difficult country.

5) **Lambert Gravitational Centre**

In 1988 the Royal Geographical Society of Australasia determined, as a Bicentennial project, the geographical centre of Australia. A monument was erected to mark the location and named in honour of Bruce Lambert, a former director of AISLIG, for his achievements in the national survey, levelling and mapping of the continent. Similar to the centre of gravity method, the location was calculated from 24,500 points at the high-water mark of Australia's coastline. The computed result was:

South 25 – 36 – 36.4
East 134 – 21 – 17.3

The monument is located in sandhill and mulga-scrub country about 17km north of the Kulgera-to-Finke Road, 25km west of Finke.

Both our Garmin 12 GPS readings at the monument were:

South 25 – 36 – 522
East 134 – 21 – 710

This gave the true location of the point as 950 metres west on a bearing of 282. The position was located and pegged.

6) **Australian Geodetic Datum – AGD**

The Australian Geodetic Datum was proclaimed in the Australian Commonwealth Gazette of 6 October 1966. This proclamation included the parameters of the local ellipsoid known as the Australian National Spheroid (ANS), which defines the adopted size and shape of the earth, and the position of the origin point – Johnston Geodetic Station.

This trigonometric survey cairn, situated about one kilometre north of Mount Cavenagh Homestead, was built by officers of the Division of National Mapping in December 1965 and is the central reference point for all Australian surveys. It was named after Fredrick Marshall Johnston, former Commonwealth Surveyor General and first Director of National Mapping.

South 25 – 56 – 54.551
East 133 – 12 – 30.077

Our Garmin 12 readings at the cairn, which is located on a singular, bare, and most imposing rock, were both:

South 25 – 56 – 819
East 133 – 12 – 576

The actual point, which was located and pegged, is therefore, we assume, 680 metres to the north-west on a bearing of 313. The Johnson cairn is near Mount Cavenagh Station, 20km south of Kulgera on the Stuart Highway.

7) The National Centre for Social Applications of GIS in

Adelaide also provided the co-ordinates for what they calculate to be the Geographic Centre of Australia:
South 24 – 53 – 443
East 133 – 23 – 06
Located on Indracowra Station, this point is on plain country, almost midway between the Stuart Highway and the Central Australian Railway line, about 160km south of Alice Springs.

The position was for the first time located by Garmin 12 GPS and pegged.

The discrepancies between our GPS readings and those of the various professional bodies is interesting. A possible cause for this, we feel, is the Datum employed. Our GPS was initialised to Datum WGS 84. In the case of Johnson and possibly Lambert, the cairn may have been placed in the most convenient and prominent position and referenced to the actual point.

Variations were:
Centre of Gravity – Nil
Lambert – 950 metres on bearing 282
Johnson – 680 metres on bearing 313

It must be stressed that our group is without any training, or experience, in survey work.

Ed. As this wonderful work may have actually be done last century and only reported this century I checked with Rod Smith who graduated with Geology/Physics majors in Science.

He compliments these adventurers but is unsure whether they have actually achieved their aim in the true sense. He mentions that there has been no mention or consideration of the Central Australian tectonic plate on which Australia sits or the Geological/paleontological centre of Australia. I passed this message to Terry yesterday (Mar 18 2021). His reply was, 'Ask him where those bloody things are and we will go and measure the bastards.'

ADULTING IS HARD

By Mary Gudzenovs

I left Australia for England, aged 24, in the early autumn of 1994 having never travelled alone before. It was exciting but beyond terrifying for a quiet, small town girl.

The solo journey was a culmination of a series of life changing events and in a way a final test of how well I could cope with being alone and in charge of my own destiny.

Ten years earlier my father, Len, had died suddenly of a massive coronary in the Port Lincoln Hospital. Although sudden and devastating at the time I concluded later that this was the better way to go with no hanging around waiting and being in pain. It was awful. His death was only ten days after the birth of his first grandchild, and twelve days before the wedding of his oldest son. The impact on our family was enormous.

After that, it was me, Mum and Grandma. My siblings, all at least ten years older than me, had left home and were getting on with their own lives. At 15 I knew I had to step up and help out as far as I was able.

A couple of years later I bailed out of Year 12 after only a few weeks and drifted into looking for work, which was almost impossible to find. A night job at the local market video store put a few dollars in my pocket and gave me a sense of being an adult.

The best thing to happen during this time was that I enrolled in a Creative Writing course at TAFE. Out of that course grew Eyre Writers Inc, which has been a large part of my life for the last 33 years. I have served as President, Secretary, Treasurer, Competition Secretary and deputy to all those positions multiple times. I have formed long-term and close friendships among its members.

When I finally moved out of home into my own space when I was 21 a friend and I decided it was time to go back to school and complete Year 12. It should have been an easy year, with sharper concentration thanks to my own decision to be there, but it turned out to be anything but settled.

In the new year of 1992 my mum, Joyce, had fallen backwards while trimming a tree at home and hurt her back. Her health went downhill from there and ultimately to a diagnosis of terminal renal cancer during the first school holidays and her death and funeral in the second school holidays. I passed, just, but really didn't consider it a priority at that point.

I inherited the growing care of my grandmother, Minnie, who was almost 60 years older than me. In some ways we got along great, but in other ways our tastes and interests were poles apart. I had lost my mother and my grandma had lost her only child. We just had to get on with it.

When the dust had settled I received a share of my mother's estate and after investing for a short time I decided I should do something definite with some of the money instead of frittering it away on life's necessary expenses.

I can still remember the look on my brother's face when I announced that my passport had been ordered and it was on its way. 'You're really going?' he asked.

Yes, I really was going.

I researched and planned, booked flights and bought train and heritage passes. My best friend was following me over later with plans to stay on a two-year working visa. She had been living with me in the meantime, so I had a built-in dog-sitter for my Dobermann x Kelpie, Dee Dee. Grandma was to fill in for the last few weeks – she adored all her four-legged grandchildren.

After thirteen hours of turbulence between Singapore and London, finally, I landed at Heathrow Airport at six in the morning and disembarked into a five-degree dismal day.

I had booked a Walkabout airport collection and London City Tour for my first day. It was a relief to see my name on a cardboard sign and know that I didn't have to find my own way into the city. He was late, but at least he was there.

The hotel I had booked for the night looked fine in the pictures but they failed to mention that the nice neat building on the corner was connected by narrow, lumpy corridors to the decrepit building alongside. And of course, my room was on the decrepit side. There were wires hanging out of the walls where there should have been lights and the heating wasn't great, but the bed was ok, the TV worked and the shower was hot.

The Walkabout tour of London was only a couple of hours but it took in the iconic places and my first view of Tower Bridge is a memory that will stay with me forever. The chatter of the group suddenly ceased and we all gazed in amazement at the construction we had seen so many times on TV screens and in tourism brochures. We really were in London, England.

When we returned to the depot my bubble of happiness was promptly popped. The 'helpful' lady at the counter proceeded to tell me that I should be booking a tour because it was much better, and safer, than trying to find my own way. I wandered up the hill toward my crappy hotel room with a huge knot in my gut. I was an untold number of miles from home, knowing no one and with only one night's accommodation booked. I was crazy. I had to be to put myself in this situation.

But half way up the hill I stopped, took a deep breath and got angry with the woman at the Tour Company. This was my holiday. I had planned it to happen the way I wanted it and I wasn't going to let a woman who didn't know me at all scupper my plans. I found a café, bought myself dinner, went back to my room and poured through the Let's Go Britain and Europe book my friend had given me just before I'd boarded the plane. Right after dinner I called and booked a bed in a dorm in a Bed and Breakfast Hostel. I slept because I was tired. My first day on the other side of the world had been one of emotional turmoil.

I had five weeks to fill before my friend joined me in Manchester. After a couple of days in London I discovered that the English couldn't tell the difference between Australian, New Zealand and South African accents. And that I evidently looked lost and out of my depth because a few fatherly figures in the tourism industry had been generous and attentive. I didn't find London a comfortable place so from there I headed for Deal on the south coast and then on to Dover.

My next adulting challenge happened while travelling

between Dover and Salisbury when I had to change trains at short notice. The station staff were amused by my admission that I had stupidly left my train passes on my seat in the train I had left. I spent an anxious half hour waiting on the platform. There was no way I could afford to stay in England if I didn't have those passes. I was on a severely limited budget of 40 pounds a day to pay for food, accommodation and souvenirs. It would not stretch to transport as well. I put off planning changes to my travel timeline in hope I wouldn't have to.

I was lucky. The very nice station master told me the conductor had found my passes only a few minutes before school children would have boarded. Had he not, those passes would have disappeared and I would have been headed home much sooner than anticipated. The passes were put on the first train coming back my way and after a short wait I was back on track, if not on schedule.

I learned to keep my passes in my body belt with my passport and travellers' cheques. I was also learning that most people are kind and helpful. That didn't mean I was incautious. I still made sure I was at my accommodation by dark and didn't stray into places that were obviously dubious. But it did mean that I was more comfortable talking to strangers, knowing that I could trust my instincts, and had many fascinating conversations, and experienced wonderful diversions, as a result.

I worked my way across to Land's End in Cornwall and up to Edinburgh where I felt so at home that I returned only a few weeks later. While having an extended four day stay at Milton, (just up the road from Drumnadrochit – where a large green 'Nessy' sits on the roadside enticing drivers to turn off to explore to shores of Loch Ness) I was treated to a canine visit. I spent a happy half hour sitting on the kitchen floor with two golden retrievers, getting my doggy fix while missing my Dee, reminding me yet again, that on the whole, people are kind and just want to make you happy.

During that stay I also managed to unintentionally treat my Grandma to a Mother's Day phone call (the date is different in England and I had totally forgotten). And that reminded me that keeping in touch with family at home was important too. I posted half a dozen postcards from the Drum post office.

I spent my 25th birthday on the Isle of Skye, a wild, beautiful place, full of history and from there I headed back down to Manchester to meet up with my best friend. We spent three weeks doing stuff I wouldn't have done on my own – rode roller-coasters at Alton Towers, spent an evening in a pub in Wales with pen pals, climbed castle towers on foot-worn stairs... and I encouraged her to talk to strangers, ask for directions and enjoy the strangeness of it all.

I arrived home after eight and a half weeks with a greater sense of who I was, what I was capable of, and with a sense of optimism for my future. It turned out I would need that optimism to see me through the trials of life since then. And I will forever be glad that I gathered the courage to travel to England on my own, worked through the issues that I faced, and arrived home safe and sound. If I could do that, I could do anything.

Life goes on, and although I still remind myself that I can do anything, as I get older it doesn't get any less scary.

Adulting is hard.

Part VIII

PHILOSOPHY

MUSINGS ON THE YEAR 2020

By Dr Stephen Ballard

For several months, we have been hearing and reading a lot more than usual about "Rights".

One can generate an entertaining debate about whether these very Human constructs really exist. Let us, for this blurb, assume that they do exist. The usual corollary to this assumption is that a Right also carries a notion of responsibility.

Legal codices in several jurisdictions bang on about "Inalienable Rights". These do not seem to put any onus of responsibility on the part of the recipient of the Right. (I suppose that is one aspect of "inalienable")

Great examples of the confusion in the matter of Rights exist in Australia. Many presume that we have a Right to free speech, and that the Media have a Right to publish what they like. Australia's legal system accords us no such rights.

In fact, as is repeatedly held by the courts, even Truth does not automatically confer a "Right" for any person, or publisher, to say what they like.

More recently, in some ways due to these misunderstandings, large, wealthy media and social media platforms try to wriggle out of their responsibilities, by saying they are not publishers of what may be truth, or not; or vilifying, or not; or just plain rubbish…. That they are merely conduits, for the misguided to spread their questionable messages.

We need only to examine the bizarre processes involving Israel Folau's, and Rebel Wilson's legal actions and counter claims.

A good number of clear thinkers would have thought that the end results were difficult to comprehend whether they were pro or con the individuals.

Some would think that we might have some Right not to be assaulted daily with reports on these two's assertions, and the results.

Another area of contention revolves around the Rights of Aboriginal peoples, especially Land Rights. South Australia has long recognised the Rights of Aboriginal people to camp, live and hunt on their traditional lands. However, despite the hopeful good stuff that came out of "Mabo", and the Native Title act, we find that they have no say over whether nuclear materials repositories can be placed on their Traditional Lands.

This is little different from the long-held ability of Mining prospectors and Mining Companies to enter any property they think has something they want (i.e. make money from). They may have to offer a compensation, or pay Royalties, but that is a separate matter. In Law the Miners have all the "Rights".

In 2020 the various confusions over Rights have come to the fore around the World.

At this point, I should state clearly that I do not hold to the Gaia Hypothesis of James Lovelock.... that our Geo-biosphere is in some metaphysical way a single organism.

As though "Nature" was in some way striking back at the

evil Humans, who seemed to be intent on the destruction of the Biosphere, Humans are now grappling, rather haphazardly, with the so-called SARS COV2 Pandemic.

I can state categorically that this illness is not associated with driving Toyota Coronas, nor drinking a Mexican Beer with the same name.

Until 2002, there seemed to be about a dozen Coronavirids which afflicted Humans, generally causing a common cold. SARS took hold that year, but it seemed to be rapidly controlled so all relaxed, until the closely related MERS popped up in 2013. Doom and gloom again, but no pandemic. The Coronavirids are widespread in the animal world, producing a variety of illnesses, and have a propensity to mutate, as RNA viruses are inherently unstable. Most mutations are not viable. I suspect that there have been many other coronavirus species affecting Humans, over however long we might postulate that Humans have been in existence. Let us just use the last 100,000 years... from the time of the early modern Humans.

For almost all that time, Humans have lived in small family groups, or tribes, widely separated, and only occasionally meeting. Even a very nasty virus, crossing from a local prey... like a bat, or marmot, or civet, pangolin, or whatever, would rapidly affect a small group, with a definable mortality, but, because of the de-facto quarantining effect of the small isolated groups, the virus would die out, at least amongst those humans.

If viruses were capable of thought, and volition, they would regard killing off all their hosts as a poor survival strategy. Since about 10,000 years ago, humans in several regions started to cultivate certain plants, and animals, thence to develop villages, and within 9,000 years very large cities. It is thought that Early Imperial Rome housed as many as one million people. In the last 190 years, we have seen progressively fast mechanised transport, and vast conurbations, from which large numbers of humans can travel half-way round the planet in a day, carrying what they like, or do not know about.

If virus were sentient, they would say "Yippee"

Yearly, the Popular Media advise us of Killer 'Flu coming. A *very different* RNA virus, but it has at least some preventative immunisation available.... granted its being blessed with the capacities of genetic drift and shift.

Perhaps I should be allowed a minor deviation about "vaccinations". This has become, now, a semantically awkward word, as its original meaning was specific to the use of Cowpox virus, "Vaccinia" (... from the Latin "vacca", the cow), to prevent Smallpox (Variola) by Edward Jenner. Primary School stuff. Remember the old immunisation booklets many of us had, as migrants, or travellers. For the pedants.... those even worse than this writer... *bos, bovis*, is the Ox... a male cow, if one likes. Hence Bovine.

All the rest of the popularly called "vaccinations" are *active*, (or occasionally *passive*) "immunisations". In truth, even the use of immunisation is troubling, but at least it is general in concept. For completeness, as I know some of the readers will wonder, there are, now, *passive immunisation* strategies for the use of pooled convalescent antibodies in the treatment of severe SARS COV2 illness.

The above may seem to some to have been a

schizophreniform *flight of ideas*, but to continue the metaphor, there is a method to my madness.

I have a recollection that it was in late October of 2019, when reports dribbled out of the Peoples' Republic of China (PRC), regarding a SARS-like illness, and that the whistle-blower was an ophthalmologist. Initially, he was chatted by the Police for perhaps being subversive. Later, he succumbed to the disease. Near the end of 2019, the PRC came clean (ish), and we then had a few months of dithering by the WHO, and governments world-wide, before March, when New Zealand and Australia a little afterward, took what was then considered to be rather draconian actions. They closed their international borders. I was convalescing from a serious illness through February and March, so had a lot of time to watch the events and mull over them. No bastard 'phoned me for my views. I had plenty of time then.

I had then a view (like Python's Ron Obvious), that although the closing of international borders was good idea, it seemed rather late This was compounded by what we now know to have been difficult-to- explain lapses in quarantine processes in NSW and, later, Victoria.

I will get to the Rights issue... just wait... like Mel Gibson, in "Braveheart".

I still maintained contact with colleagues, who, being clinicians (doctors and nurses), were going to be front-line fodder, maybe. Victoria later showed how that can go badly wrong, though other countries had very different health-care worker SARS COV2 infection rates.

Bring on the Slogans, someone thought. And behold; we had "protect the vulnerable", "save lives", "prevent the spread".

These were notionally to support a platform of the oddest planks indeed.

At the outset, if a vulnerable group is identifiable, it should be far simpler to segregate them, and, we must accept, their carers. We have great evidence of what happens when we do otherwise. Worthy of consideration is that about 70,000 persons have contracted the disease since SARS COV2 reached our shores, and at the time of writing, about 500 have succumbed to it. That last group is strikingly over-represented by Aged Care Home (RACF) residents.

"To save lives", is illogical in and of itself, and is a notion worthy of a long debate. The idea has been partly applied to such things as tobacco smoking, alcohol misuse, and driving motor vehicles, with some success. So that what is really intended, in the nominated at-risk group, is postponing death in some way. Averages can be misleading, but in Australia, the average age at death from SARS COV2, is about 80 years.

If a child is dragged from a pool, pulseless and not breathing, subsequently resuscitated, and is sitting up to breakfast the next day, we would grant *that* as a life saved.

In our genes, we are programmed to live for a limited time, so the real impetus should be in prolonging wellness, rather than longevity. Indeed, the Hippocratic Oath says we should not *strive officiously* to prolong life, but to provide succour and comfort.

It seems to this writer that to arbitrarily cause one-two million workers to lose their jobs, and tens of thousands of businesses to cease activity, many not likely to resume, in order to "save" a much smaller group from illness or death (notionally prematurely) gives a very strong message that a large, mostly young group, which represents a future of some kind, is much less important than another, smaller, older group, who could have been isolated in other ways. The last two months in Victoria should make many ponder the effectiveness of the economic shut-down. I believe that, as a result of the delayed international border closures, and faced with at least a perceived risk of rapid penetration of the virus into the general community, an element of panic supervened. Philosophically, hedonism won out over utilitarianism.

It is often said that the Public Health Departments, and particularly their Heads, brought about the widespread business closures and restrictions. That is only partly true, as they do not ordinarily have such powers. However, the Emergency Management provisions allow the State to cede certain powers to the Public Health Authorities and do grant quite extraordinary powers. These will vary in extent and effect between jurisdictions.

Public Health Practitioners as servants of the State, can only advise Government on the Community Health aspects of any perceived threat. They are generally not trained in, nor required to consider the economic consequences of strategies they might suggest. I like the use of the "health prism" metaphor, in that the afferent light beam is the threat, and the efferent rainbow either its various effects, or actions needed to be taken. The economy is one of those.

Like it or lump it, the Government is responsible for its decisions.

As alluded to early in this monolog, the idea of quarantine has been with human societies for hundreds of years, often with little idea of how a disease was transmitted.

So, we now wade into the murk of "Rights".

Most "Rights" are an expression of the Golden Rule.

When did Humans start to outwardly express, and codify Rights? The earliest such codices arose in Sumeria, engraved on Hammurabi's stele or column. And some ancient Egyptian codices rather later. Thence to the Judeo-Christian, tradition over several hundred years culminating in the interpretations and teachings of Jesus, called the Christ. The Qur'an is more to do with obeisance to God, though does demand a lot of responsibilities to be met, which, when looking at how we deal with others can be taken as part of a codex of Rights.

Magna Carta was written into Law in 1215. Interestingly, there were several copies, and they are not identical. The effect was to take away the supreme powers of the King, and allow the nobles more autonomy, and more control over wealth, as well as placing a right to trial by jury of one's peers, if one was a noble. The peasantry and slaves were not included in any meaningful way.

The American Declaration of Liberty, and later Its Constitution laid down many Rights in Law, though they had a long way to go, and still do... at least in a practical sense.

I remember LBJ signing a Bill of Civil Rights.

Australia still has no Bill of Rights.

Enough History for now,

Is there a Right for any group within a Community to be especially protected from something which in fact threatens all members of the Community? In some ways, we do accept such an idea. For example; the act of driving a motor vehicle whilst under the influence of a drug or alcohol is strongly proscribed throughout the world, and if caught, the offender is liable to severe censure, even imprisonment, as the offences, as defined, are regarded as threats to the larger community.

To drive a motor vehicle, licensed or not, is considered by many to be a Right. That many are oblivious to the notions of consequence, or responsibility is portrayed weekly on Television.

We accept a right, within our community, for persons to consume alcohol, even to excess, but their responsibility is to not place others at risk. It is an aspect of the Golden Rule.

We are now aware that a small proportion of young SARS COV2 sufferers have died, at least one being a toddler. Further there is evidence of long-term post inflammatory consequences in some. SARS COV2 is far from unique amongst viruses in these associations.

Although the numbers are presented daily as though sports scores, the greater proportion of mortality in Australia has remained amongst those of advanced age, or those with multiple co-morbidities. These remain the usual suspects. Symptomatic heart disease, chronic lung or airway disease, diabetes mellitus, obesity, cigarette smoking, and immune suppression. These were true before the multiple outbreaks of SARS COV2 in Victorian Aged Care Facilities.

The rare deaths in those much younger suggest they were special in some other way.

Therefore, given much of the above, our Governments were placed in no-win positions.

Presented with a substantial perceived, and later actual

threat, the Government belatedly closed international borders. Aircraft are useless on the ground, and the already struggling Virgin Australia became non-viable. QANTAS, a rare investment class airline came to struggle.

Balancing a nominal Right for people to return to their homes against the Public Health imperative of stopping disease transmission (the Rights of the many to be protected) became an impossible task. This is an antithesis of what the Government did in causing the unemployment of 1-2 million workers. Clobber the many to protect the few. Essentially, our collective Governments' actions were the economic/regulatory analog of the way the body's immune system responds in those persons with severe response to SARS COV2.

We should understand that SARS COV2 is merely one agent that may provoke such a response in some of us. It just happens to be a very infectious one. An uncommon effect, but with a large pool of potential sufferers

In recognition of the plights of so many of our population, the Governments have needed to attempt to mitigate the social and economic effects of the regulatory changes.

It may surprise some readers that the Health and Welfare of Communities depends little upon Doctors. Many will have heard or read of the Social Determinants of Health.

These are chiefly, shelter, good tucker, safe water, Education and Employment.

Public Health Doctors are involved in population health; other clinicians work chiefly with individuals.

Back to the business closures. I believe it needs recognition that many of the businesses directly affected were providing non-essential services. That is to say; things we like a lot, but if being honest, we should allow that they are not essential. Coffee shops, Gymnasiums, Pubs, "Pokie" places, racecourses. Humans have long recognized that certain diseases spread less rapidly when a form of "social distancing" is practiced, so that, given millennia of normative Human behaviour, such actions made some sense, even though they run counter to the general gregariousness of Humans. However, the underlying premises remained false.

The virus is not as special as many believe. Saving the "lives" of a few at the expense of the welfare of many is a dubious aim, where we do not apply that ideology elsewhere with

rigor. Truth be known, Humans are much more likely to sacrifice a few to benefit a majority. That is what we do at war!

"Stopping the spread!" I always had a picture in my head of a tub of butter, or jar of Lemon Curd, in a circle, with a diagonal stroke through it. Jokes aside, next to the international border closures, this was an idea that quickly gained traction, had a logical basis, and by itself is not especially disruptive.

The problem with the Trident of isolation, quarantine and social distancing, is that we are trying to make humans into a different kind of animal. We have great variability in our capacity to adapt to change, and most would prefer to avoid change altogether.

Then we have the mask problem. The evidence remains conflicted, and depends very much on what the proponent, or opponent is talking about.

As an aside, can someone please tell me why, in South Australia, the authorities insist on calling filtration/barrier masks "respirators". They are not and cannot be respirators.

A good number of my doctor and nursing colleagues have been puzzled by notices and practice directions stating that in certain conditions, the use of specified *respirators* is mandated.

Meaning masks. Not ventilating machines. Not organisms which consume oxygen to burn carbohydrate.

Which brings us to the rather ugly interaction, screened round the country, between a woman and Police, over her not wearing a mask in public. She had tried to enter a Bunnings store. The store staff denied her entry, as she was not wearing a mask. Within a private property, the store staff had every "right" to deny her entry, without a reason being given. Her contention was that she had a Right to not wear a mask. She deliberately baited the police officers, who did not rise to her challenges. She should have been arrested for "fail to cease loiter", then sent home with a stern letter to her Mum.

She threatened to sue the Police officers, individually, for $60,000 each. She used an expression which included the word "kidnapping". This would have been a deprivation of liberty... a criminal offense, and the charge would be brought by the State. The woman later threw in the 1948 Declaration of Human rights, and other irrelevancies.

Should masks become mandatory? The evidence does not help the general public walking in a park or on the beach. There are however a good number of specific potentially high-risk activities where masks should be useful.

Let us think on "testing". Australians love medical tests.

We have high testing rates for SARS COV2. The standard is the test for viral RNA... its nucleic acid. Polymerase Chain Reaction, PCR. High sensitivity, in the symptomatic subject, but unreliable in the asymptomatic. High specificity when detected.

There are blood antibody tests, which only tell if the person has had the disease AT SOME TIME.... If IgM type antibody, in the last 3 months or so.

Should widespread testing be mandatory? There was a legal challenge against mandatory testing, some weeks ago in Victoria. I think the challenge would succeed, as taking a swab is a Medical intervention, and must have a valid consent. It seems, from my reading of the Emergency Health Management docs, that it likely cannot over-ride the requirement for valid consent. The ability of a Chief Public Health officer to mandate testing will likely be challenged.

It is difficult enough for Police to obtain Blood for alcohol testing from a person refusing the test.

I think it is a silly question, as Australians love medical tests.

Moving on.

Does the State have any "Right" to close borders? Are there rights allowing free movement across borders in all circumstances? No each-way bet.

In our cooperative Federal system, and under Emergency Management stipulations, the States can close borders, and no amount of bleating will change that. After that, it is a matter of degree and time. Are there special rights to freely cross borders? Of course not.

The effect of Federation on Borders was chiefly to abolish

customs and duties which then had to be paid on passing from one colony to another. It is noteworthy that WA was the last Colony to agree to enter the Federation.

Lines on a map, rather arbitrarily drawn up long ago. Borders change. Who knows which bank of the Murray is the border between Victoria and NSW? And that little blip at the NSW/Vic/SA border. Who ordered that?

And now we have a former Federal Senator, and nominally very wealthy bloke, trying to sue WA for a very large sum of money, seemingly on the basis that he and his companies are being deprived of a right to freely enter WA (to make a lot of money).

There are two unrelated actions he is taking, so the stories have become conflated.

This chap, who bragged on National television during an election campaign about his highly questionable activities as a youth. Way past the statute of limitations.

The man who, it is reported widely, ran a nickel refining business down to fund an election campaign, killed the business off, and whose workers are reportedly yet to be paid their entitlements, as there is no money left. The rights of the many, trampled by the supposed rights of the one? It only proves that Humans with resources have more "rights" than those who do not.

Sounds Orwellian. The inexhaustible capacity of the Bourgeoisie to protect itself against the needs of the Proletariat.

Did we ever hear who set fire to the dinosaur at his Sunshine Coast golf course?

Continuing with the border closures. For SA, WA, NT, and

Tasmania, is a relatively simple matter, one would have thought. Not many robust ways in or out, and Tasmania has a moat.

However, we are seeing a slow breakdown in Cooperative Federalism, in that some State premiers are demanding that borders be opened, but on purely economic grounds.

The NSW Premier was most shrill, then had to go quiet when the Victorian problems became severe. I note that she is now becoming more unhappy about Qld. Slow learner.

I would be regarded as an "at risk" person. I am fortunate in being able, after an unrelated illness, to return to work, as a clinician. Some would say that I have some right to be protected from SARS COV2. Dunno.

I feel a greater responsibility to serve the community, accepting that the whole of life carries substantial, but variable, and sometimes modifiable risks. Like being born, taking a first breath, driving a car in public, eating out.

Does any special group have a Right to be protected from a threat, over the needs of the majority? Doubtful. Some may bring up child protection. Protecting children does not involve impinging upon the valid needs of a community, and, in fact, supports its future.

Child protection has thrown up some bizarre legislation, where many of us are presumed guilty, and are required to undergo criminal checks, to be employed. So much for the Right to presumed innocence. We do have an increasing problem with respect to the presumption of guilt, in Australia.

Do we have special rights to cross borders at a whim? Of course not, this is arrant hedonism.

We do not have rights to enter any property without

permission, and crossing borders requires a permission, explicit or implied, in a similar way. The State is the Guardian of the Crown Land.

We cannot enter the APY Lands, without invitation, or a permit. There was, early in SARS COV2 story, a bizarre twist. Nganampa Health, based in Alice Springs, is a Government funded service, charged with the Health care of the APY Lands residents. Its Medical Director was based in Sydney, early this year, when a decision was made to transport the frail and chronically ill (which would be a majority within that community) from the APY Lands, to Adelaide, to protect them from SARS COV2. Clearer thinkers suggested, correctly in my view, that, although these people are chronically ill, arbitrary transport to a major city would have placed them at higher risk of SARS COV2 infection. In any event, the frail chronically ill elderly residing on the APY Lands, would prefer to remain on and die on country. Their chief hazard would be the free movement of some of their youth between Adelaide, the lands, and Alice Springs

We cannot enter the military reserves at Cultana, Woomera, or Yeppoon Peninsula.

It is concerning that there have been good number of "Compassionate Permissions" for individuals to cross borders, which again says to me that individual wants may take precedence over the perceived needs of the many. Hedonism again.

The rising tide of complaints, on chiefly economic bases, about business restrictions and border closures is placing undue pressure on Governments.

The earlier failure to act on borders resulted in the hard

attack on small business.

To now reverse those decisions prematurely would suggest to us that all those lost jobs and businesses really do not matter. The other downside for Government to consider is the much smaller workforce left to support, through taxation, the sudden increase in unemployed numbers.

Seen logically from the Health standpoint, having made the earlier questionable decisions, it would be reckless to jeopardize or sabotage the apparent low levels of endemicity of the virus in most of the country, by relaxing movement restrictions yet a noisy minority is demanding just that.

There is much being said about the Rights of people who live close to the borders to cross unhindered to work, plough fields, visit relatives, go shopping, seek medical care. There are no such rights or if there are the responsibilities must be substantial in this context.

The issue has been dealt with poorly, and inconsistent decisions made, and unmade or subject to un-heralded *volte face*. BUT, if we accept that borders can in some way be rubbery, just how rubbery can they be. For example, along the Dukes-Western Highways.... Kaniva, Nhill, Dimboola, Horsham, Ararat?

Coming the other way, Keith or Bordertown. And all those towns in NSW and Victoria within 40Km of the Murray. *Reductio ad absurdam.*

It has been frequently stated that the aims of the whole shebang are to have a low level endemicity of the SARS COV2; so that the inevitable infections can be dealt with without affecting the rest of the Health "system"; to allow us to stockpile adequate quantities of PPE; and to allow development of an active immunization and thence to its deployment. This last usually takes 3-5 years, for a successful agent.

Although there are about 34 candidate immunizations in the pipeline, and about 6 of these in phase 3 efficacy trials, we are still many months from the time of effective active immunization to be deployed. An unfortunate aspect of the need for time to demonstrate safety and efficacy, is the repeated statement from the boffins that although they can demonstrate antibody responses, they cannot yet demonstrate viricide. Or disease prevention. To keep saying this, for SARS COV2 specifically, tells the "Anti-vaxxers" what they have always wanted us to believe.... that immunisations do not work or are unsafe. Great.

Should immunisation be mandatory? The PM got himself into hot water when said he hoped they would be.

Of course not. Medical intervention requires valid consent. End of story.

But Refusers must accept that if *they have the right* to refuse, the Community has a similar Right to shower upon them whatever lawful unpleasantness it can. Like not allowing their children into kindergarten or childcare.

At this juncture, we could be forgiven in believing that perhaps the Governments have been making it up as they went along. As the rolling disaster is novel, there were few clear principles to promulgate. All of them relate to making Humans do what they do poorly. Keep away from each other, until our materials and biotechnologies offer novel long lasting solutions.

Unfortunately, there is an important minority who believe

that they have Rights to do what they like. So, through carefully studied indifference, or ignorance, they do exactly what they have always done, and sabotage the small gains made by the rest of the Community. It is suggested often that, although Humans might attribute the species' success to their thumbs, or language development, our chief advantage is our evolving a complex capacity to cooperate with our fellows, across many axes. We do have a good number who are not capable of this cooperative bent, to our greater challenge when under threat.

Some point to the inconsistencies in preventing free border crossings, but allowing re-entry of Australian Citizens, or Students from overseas. Yet, they are not remotely the same. The return of Citizens, or students is intended to be tightly controlled, whereas the other would be a free-for-all.

For some of us, even in March, the seeming arbitrary nature of the business lock-down gave us cause to wonder at the long-term social consequences of such a process. We therefore come back to the Social Determinants of Health.

In my early list were Employment and Education.

I have two daughters with University degrees. One, nominally an environmental scientist, runs a bakery-coffee shop. The other is an entertainer, who also teaches singing and voice. She is good at this, but Skype and Zoom, in her world, are challenging platforms for teaching, yet needed to be used during the prolonged school closures.

No live performing for 6 months. For many, the loss of employment carries not only the financial penalty, but also takes away part of who they are. Loss of confidence, pride, and self-worth. If they are employees, the Government supports help the financial side, but do not address the self-worth component if they are freelance, or not employed.

The widespread school closures, and the move to online teaching for university students has seen different challenges. For some, the isolation was seeming ho-hum, but for others, gravely challenging. I have two sons studying at tertiary level; one in engineering, the other mathematics and physics. For them, the logistics were relatively simple to resolve. But for others in performance, small group tutorial-based courses, or hands-on practical trades, their tasks have been made difficult.

We are hearing frequent anecdotes about mental health problems amongst students and the recently unemployed. A nursing colleague posited that the loss work and income contributed to the suicides of three young people she knew. One "Summer-swallow", aside, the association with a virus associated economic slow-down is seductive.

Economists, Sociologists, and Mental Health practitioners will be telling us a lot more over the next 3 years.

Misguided notions on Rights, the inconsistent application of restrictions which many believe run roughshod over individual Rights, and the minority who believe that the rules, however reasonable, only apply to people other than themselves, will together give cause to ideas that perhaps the whole process will prove futile.

The 3-6 months of restrictions touted from on high, at the outset, were always extraordinarily optimistic, and betrayed a serious lack of the simplest arithmetic capability, and ignorance of the way the biological world works.

Think 3-5 years.

We had two warnings, in 2002 and 2013. Then, there were surprising reprieves.

In 2020 the closely related SARS COV2 virus did not cause 1-2 million new unemployed to appear, nor close thousands of businesses, nor cause alcohol abuse, domestic violence, suicides, or shortened AFL and NRL seasons.

Humans brought these things about. On our behalf, well-meaning, in in the hope of protecting a defined few, and a much smaller less well-definable group.

I might be one of them. I am not sure that I will be comfortable in being an individual beneficiary of the challenges presented to our young new unemployed, or students, excepting that I am able to continue to work in the "Health" environment.

At the time of writing, SARS COV2 had directly affected 24,400, and killed 472 persons in Australia. Out of 23 million, and 799 thousand world-wide.

The social damages resulting from the Human responses will take years to determine.

That's all folks.

A WINDOW INTO THE CABRA SISTERS' DOMINICAN STORY

By Sister Angela Moloney OP

On the fifth December 1868, after a challenging journey of three months at sea, seven young Dominican Sisters arrived in the young colony of South Australia. Mother Teresa Moore was their Prioress. By the following February they had advertised and opened a Secondary school, with an amazing curriculum and philosophy of education for teenaged girls and a Primary school for younger children at St. Mary's, Franklin Street, Adelaide. This was a missionary endeavour that could have failed in the harsh conditions of a strange country where new predominantly British colonists were establishing a society. Like colonists in other parts of Australia they denied the Indigenous peoples their birthrights, despite the Letters Patent signed in 1836 by King William 4th, recommending that the new free settlers would respect the rights of the Indigenous Peoples as they created their new "Provence"[1]. Further, in this young colony a Catholic Diocese was dealing with its own growing pains, in a culture and climate strange to them.

Sadly, after becoming seriously ill, Teresa Moore, the "wise and loved leader" died on 14th February 1873. Life for the Community became extremely complex and difficult and the Sisters in Ireland wondered if this mission should be ended. One Sister had returned to the community in Cabra, Dublin and another Sister departed from the community. It is not known if she stayed in the colony or returned to Ireland. After seeking advice, the Dominican Leaders in Ireland decided to send two of their best Sisters, Catherine Kavanagh and Columba Boylan to help build and restore confidence in the struggling Community in Adelaide. Gradually young Australian women sought to join the Sisters, who so ably had educated them.

Twenty years later the Community under the leadership of Columba Boylan, had purchased land "in the country", now known as Cumberland Park! There they built a boarding school and a day school for girls. Down the decades young Dominican Sisters continued to come from Cabra, Dublin, to support the community. After some time young Irish and English women came across the seas to join the Dominican Sisters in their ministry of education and their Dominican way of religious life. Indeed, this practice continued until the 1950s. Both, St. Mary's College, Franklin St. Adelaide and Cabra Dominican College, Cumberland Park, continue to thrive in the twenty-first century as respected centres of education. St. Mary's, a College for girls caters for Pre-school to Year 12; Cabra is now a Co-education College from Year 7 to 12.

I was among the young women who came from Ireland in the early 1950s. We studied for our year 12 Certificate and then trained as Teachers with great Dominican educators, Therese Sweeney and Mary Vianney Horgan. They both loved the adventure of educating young people. They skilfully developed their students' sense of wonder, curiosity and imagination, while drawing out their innate creative gifts within a holistic curriculum. So we were fortunate to be inspired by these great practitioners who embodied the Dominican ethos. They certainly created in me a desire to educate the whole person, body and spirit, mind and emotions. In these years we not only met their students while doing practice teaching but some of these students chose to join our Dominican community after they had completed Secondary education. Down the decades our Sisters founded and taught in over twelve Parish Primary Schools in the suburbs and in country areas. During these years some of our Sisters conducted Summer Schools in country areas for Catholic children; others taught children with disabilities and others worked with adults with hearing disability.

And now, returning to the 1950s, when I, and the young women who came from Ireland with me, were participating in our Teacher Training. The, the Sullivan girls, Susan, Leonore and Jacqueline were attending Cabra College. Susan, was one of the students taught by Sisters Therese and Vianney. I want to name Susan because she too was greatly inspired, by these gifted educators. She later, with some of her friends, joined our Dominican community. Susan taught in our Primary Schools and at St. Mary's College, Franklin St and later, for many years Susan chaired the Board of St Mary's College.

Throughout 1987 our whole community chose to engage in serious study. We had decided to invite Christian Feminist facilitators to help explore from a Christian feminist perspective many aspects of the Catholic Church's traditions. We examined our own ministries as Dominican women. We critiqued received theologies and interpretations of Scripture. We saw more clearly that the patriarchal structures of society and church shape how we view reality and how we live in this world. We recognised that since Plato and Aristotle, reality in western cultures is hierarchical, divided into two layers, one superior and the other inferior. In this pervading view, man was, for example, perceived as closer to divinity and woman to the nature world. Consequently, man was thought to be superior. We grew in our awareness of the many injustices that result from this worldview in our lives and in all people's lives. Injustices that lessen the quality of life for women and men, for our fragile planet home and indeed for our understanding the Divine Energy in all of creation.

We unanimously resolved as a community at our 1987 Chapter[2] to be aware of this injustice whether in the classroom, or other areas of our diverse ministries and lives. We also resolved to create, if possible, a corporate expression of our chosen vision. To our amazement and delight and after much hard work, within four years we made this dream a reality. *Sophia*,[3] our Ecumenical Feminist Spirituality Place/Space was realised as a beautiful building adjacent to the Dominican Peace Garden. Now we needed to bring *Sophia* to life, to begin to embody our vision. For sixteen years, Susan Sullivan OP Co-ordinated with great dedication the organic growth of this new and timely ministry. Margaret Cain and I collaborated with Susan learning how to work together without hierarchy. We sought to embrace a holistic view of planet earth, the 'only home,'[4] of all who inhabit this fragile planet and the sacred spiritual/ divine energy that permeates all of the amazing cosmos. We knew that we were exploring new terrain, exploring a more holistic vision of our totally interdependent planet home. We welcomed to *Sophia* all who shared our vision and as *Sophia* grew and continues to flourish many skilled women gave and continue to voluntary give of their rich talents.

In 2021 *Sophia* will celebrate her thirtieth Birthday. The *Sophia* community is preparing to publish a community history of this wonderful venture that has touched their lives in so many significant ways. The *Sophia* space affords opportunity for women to 'hear each other into speech.'[5] Here each woman can find her voice because she is heard in confidence. In this space women grow themselves and strive to grow a better, more just and compassionate world around them. I am happy to say that a number of pro-feminist men happily partake in the life of *Sophia*. They too, yearn for a more holistic world where every person is treated with human dignity and the amazing, but fragile interdependence of life on this 'Blue Marble Planet'[5] is honoured by all.

1. *Coming to Terms, Aboriginal Title in South Australia.* p. viii
2. *A Chapter is an important community Meeting which takes place every four years. At this meeting we consider our lives together and make important for the future. Such decisions carry significant importance in the Laws of the Church.*
3. *We chose the name Sophia for our new ministry because Sophia is an ancient female symbol for God, both in the Jewish tradition and in the Christian tradition.*
4. *I am quoting the wonderful, David Attenborough, when I call planet earth 'our only' home.*
5. *Most of us have seen that wonderful photo of earth taken by one of the early Astronauts.*

Leonore's sister, Susan, sadly passed away too soon but her efforts and leadership have been recognised by the new library at St Mary's College, Adelaide being named in her memory.

Part XI

COURAGE

NOT THE GOOD TOWELS

By Sarah Holden

It was the dead of night; she woke feeling a familiar pain....no it couldn't be...it was too early. She tried to go back to sleep, but there was the pain again. She tried again to sleep hoping it was just a stomach ache, but the pains continued. She knew that feeling – she was in labour – 10 weeks too soon!

She frantically woke her husband.

He calmly called the hospital, and the nurse asked questions and then directed them to come in straight away. The contractions kept going and there was less and less time in between. The nurse realised what was happening and suggested they call an ambulance.

He called the ambulance: she could hear him talking and laughing – he laughed when he was nervous. The person on the other end was telling him that the baby could arrive any minute and to make her comfortable and to get lots of towels on the bed. All she could think was "not the good towels".

One ambulance arrived, but they had to wait for a second ambulance with more specialised officers. Why was this taking so long? She was praying the contractions would stop.

Finally, she was assisted down the stairs (in a very skimpy nightie) and settled in the ambulance. The pains were becoming more and more frequent and intense – she wanted the labour to stop – the baby wasn't ready! She could hear the ambos talking... 'We need to get to the hospital; this baby can't be born in the back of this ambulance'.

They asked her – 'Do you need to push?

'No' she said – which was a lie. She just wanted to make this stop. They arrived at the hospital and she was wheeled into a lift.

She was barely aware of her surroundings but knew her husband was right next to her. He joked again... 'Honey, I think I can see your first grey hair'.

She didn't react but was laughing on the inside. There was deathly silence as the medical staff glared at him... they didn't see the funny side.

She was taken to the delivery room and the staff tried to comfort and settle her. Within minutes she said 'I need to push'.

This seemed to catch them off guard. They called the doctor... he appeared like a shadow, delivered the baby and then disappeared.

It was a boy.

He was just 1.9kg and 45cm long... She held him for a minute. He had a little wool beanie on and his eyes looked like two dark holes not ready for the outside world.

They had to rush him into the humidicrib to assist his breathing and keep him warm. Her husband went with the baby. They needed to stabilise him on a different floor.

She just lay there in shock, listening to the nurses chatting away and cleaning up the room. They asked her who was her usual doctor and when she told them they proceeded to chat about how good looking he was in the old days.... She couldn't believe what she was hearing... She had just given birth to a premature baby and they were gossiping...

She had to ask for a drink and something to eat... Couldn't they see she was in shock? They also suggested she could go home within four hours if she was feeling ok... She was in no state to make any decisions.

Her husband finally came back and she broke down in tears – what a shock it was. The baby couldn't stay at this hospital – he was too premature and they had to find a bed for him in another hospital. That hospital, on the other side of the city, finally confirmed they had a bed for her and the baby. The baby was transported in an ambulance and she and her husband made the long journey to be with the baby.

The baby was settled in the Neonatal Intensive Care Unit. He was stabilised in a humidicrib with CPAP to assist with his breathing – his tiny lungs were not developed properly – this happens at 34 weeks.

She was resting in another room and was woken throughout the night to express breast milk. The next time she was woken was by the medical staff who informed her that there had been a complication with the baby's breathing. He had suffered a pneumothorax... part of his tiny lungs had collapsed... this was to happen three more times during his stay in the Neonatal Intensive Care Unit (NICU). This meant there were all sorts of treatments to save his life. The first being put on life support so a machine was breathing for him. There were so many tubes put in his chest (the scars still with him to this day), medications and blood transfusions.

Probably the worst day of her and her husband's life was when the baby had a brain bleed and the doctors couldn't report the severity of it for a few days but warned it may affect the movement in his legs. As a mother she was distraught – the baby should still be safely inside her. Finally, the results came in and the doctors announced that he was fine – they were so relieved.

The day she left the hospital to go home without her baby was another tough day... she hated the fact that she couldn't take her baby home, but knew the doctors and nurses would look after him. And so began many weeks of hospital visits, expressing milk and sitting by the baby's side and then back home to care for their other son – express milk – sleep – express milk.... You get the picture.

First cuddles didn't happen until he was off the ventilator and was about two weeks old. It was an exciting, but also an anxious, moment as he was so tiny. Once he was could breathe on his own he thrived. Although he was still being feed via a tube, his lungs were getting stronger and he was able to grow and put on weight.

Once he was over two kilos and was no longer tube fed, he could go home. This took six more weeks, so she and her husband and family continued the hospital visits and support. There were many milestones that took place at the hospital, like first bath, Easter and Mother's Day. As the weeks passed she found comfort in the fact that he was getting stronger and would be home soon.

After a few bumps in the road he was finally allowed home. Time to be with his family.

He is now 9 years old and strong and healthy – something that she could not have imagined on the morning he was born.

Dedicated to:

Our son Luca

Our best friends, the Menzs – who looked after our older son Max on that fateful morning, brought our car and a care package to us on the way to have their own baby! (Aleksis Jane just scraped in at 11.45pm on the very same day)

Luca's grandparents who had been visiting just before this and turned the car around and drove over 1000kms to be there for us and help care for Max for several weeks.

And all our friends and family members who helped throughout this stressful time of our lives.

The amazing medical staff at the Mercy Hospital who saved Luca's live and looked after him for so many weeks.

THE METTLE OF THE MAN

By Graham Fleming

Ed: I wrote about the amazing story of the Tumby Bay doctors particularly the two Wibberleys, Dennis Eaton and Graham Fleming who collectively served Tumby Bay for 186 years for heaven's sake. In writing that I remembered attending to Graham and his family after he hit some horses. I double checked this with Graham and he wrote the reply below. I decided to include this with his permission as there is a lesson here about country driving and the abilities of Georg Kiroff, the late Ian Fletcher and Anne Williams, and Graham has mentioned this but also that the Rural Medical services have deteriorated rather than improved. I have not worked in Port Lincoln for 20 years so cannot comment further but I knew and worked with George and Ian. There were world class surgeons. I remember George once joking that Ian should be on medication he had so much energy and he didn't know how he managed his workload. More pertinent was George's comments to me at Ian's funeral. He said, 'I have climbed the academic ladder being very good at thoracic surgery but Ian didn't want academic honours he just wanted to be a country general surgeon and he bloody well was the best.'

Graham has been very honest about his fears and the unpleasant experience he had and it was the measure of the man that he battled through this severe injury to work for another 30 years, an amazing effort.

At the time he was injured I was the Acting Medical Superintendent of the Alice Springs Base Hospital for six weeks so a lot of it was news to me as well as the readers of this story. I have always admired Graham as a person and a doctor and this letter only increases my respect. I wish him well.

Good morning Peter

I have had a number of serious car accidents but only two on the West Coast.

The first you are referring to when you looked after my family and myself was around 1979-80 and I was driving a blue 1977 SAAB back from Lincoln on a dark night. Our two girls were strapped in the back and my wife was holding a baby in the front of the car, before baskets were mandatory. I was driving at the speed limit when just before the Louth Bay turn off I saw a picket fence across the road and braked hard. It turned out the picket fence was the legs of a mob of horses. I estimate I hit them at 70-80km/hr.

The first horse I hit took out my headlights, crushed the bonnet in, smashed the windscreen and Gladys and child were smattered with glass. The horse then went over the roof and caved the roof in. The other horses kicked every side panel on both sides of the car so only the tail gate was undamaged. The dent in the bonnet cracked the distributor cap so the car was not driveable, but all doors opened and closed as if nothing was wrong. The car was written off but I had a call from the buyer who asked how the damage was done and were the seats belts worn as they would need to be replaced. The net result of the dreadful affray and carnage was out of the dozen or so horses one was dead and two were put down. It may not be surprising to note I went out and bought another new SAAB.

However, the worst accident was in June 1990. I had driven my 60 series Land Cruiser to the airport to drop someone off to catch a plane. On driving home I rolled the car immediately north of the White River bridge. The cause of the crash is unknown for certain but eighteen months later when I dropped something on the floor and could not reach it and released my seat belt to retrieve the object I found myself on the wrong side of the road. I recovered that time without incident but taught me a valuable lesson. On the 1990 occasion I believe I went off the road where there was a downward camber and as I pulled the car back onto the road it rolled. That I suspect explained the events that followed.

A car behind noticed I had moved across to the wrong side of the road and inexplicably rolled. I was seen to fly out of the car like Super Grover the Muppet and the car rolled several times. I was conscious at the time by reports. The Tumby Bay Ambulance was summoned because, 'The doctor's car had rolled and he is in need of assistance'.

Ross Hibble, the Tumby Bay chemist heard this on the CB radio and immediately rang Dennis Eaton, my colleague, who hot-footed it to the accident site. The ambulance was about to load me and take me to Tumby Bay but Dennis reversed that decision and sent them direct to Port Lincoln Hospital. He rang Ian Fletcher, who was about to leave the hospital to go to Ceduna for consulting and operating. He stayed behind, as did George Kiroff, who was also a resident surgeon who had moved there from the liver transplant unit in France.

No CT in those days. Body X rays showed I had broken my big toe and L scapula. All seemed well apart from the fact I was badly concussed and kept complaining of R shoulder pain and terrible abdominal pain. Ian put a needle in my abdomen and got a spray of blood. I was put to sleep by Dr Ann Williams an excellent GP anaesthetist while the two surgeons hunted around for four hours to find the cause of the bleeding.

An 11cm split in my liver was one cause but there was marked retroperitoneal bleeding and they could not find the source. However, the bleeding appeared to diminish and my blood pressure was creeping back especially after 4 units of blood which brought my haemoglobin up to a tidy 10.

To sum up: comprehensive soft tissue damage, two broken bones, a ruptured liver, bilateral haemothorax (although small enough to not require a drain) and a closed head injury which knocked out my balance if my eyes were closed.

I endured a week of Morphine IV in the Port Lincoln Hospital before being transfer to Tumby Bay. In Port Lincoln I had learnt urinary catheters are made of barbed wire and it is impossible to swallow a Ryle's tube and it is operator driven.

The second most humiliating event was when the nurse came to take me to shower me. To be washed by a nurse – how embarrassing. I can recall it quite vividly but by the time she got me on the wheelchair to the shower I was so exhausted I didn't care what she did as long as it was quickly because I wanted to be back in bed.

A week in Tumby saw some recovery and a mild pulmonary embolus and then I was chuffed to Adelaide when well enough to travel, to be seen by neurologists, neurosurgeons and ENT surgeons, and have complete CTs.

The radiologist remarked, 'Why did they dare open you up in Port Lincoln without doing a CT scan first?' The answer seemed obvious to me. In Adelaide they would have been CT-ing a cadaver.

It took nine months to get back to work mainly because I had damaged my semicircular canals bilaterally. It took eighteen months for that to recover but the further recovery caused me more problems. When listening to a heart I generally close my eyes to concentrate and most of the time I stayed upright but others I managed to fall on the patient's chest... most embarrassing.

The most humiliating consequence occurred about eighteen months later when I noted a yellow bag parked alongside my wardrobe out of sight. I opened it to find all the clothes I wore on the day I had been cut free – even my socks and jocks. Is there no privacy these days, I asked Dennis and the assembled nursing staff in the Tumby Bay Hospital on the morning ward round and hand over?

I explained how cavalier the Port Lincoln Nursing staff were to cut my jocks and socks off. Dennis explained that that didn't happen in the hospital but at the road side.

Now, I know there was a large gathering of people watching the ordeal from the road side, enough to sell tickets. Many said to me later I looked pretty crook at the time and wondered whether I would pull through. They also told me I was talking but not making a lot of sense. (How would they know that from normal I wondered?)

For a week I grieved and moaned with the thought of

everyone seeing me in my birthday suit. Dennis got sick of the moaning and groaning and said, 'You were in the ambulance at the time'.

It is a story of how, in rural hospitals with well-trained GPs and surgeons, many lives have been saved. Unfortunately, there are no Ian Fletchers anymore, the hospitals are being degraded, understaffed and clinically limited. I had a note from the Whyalla surgeons that they no longer do carpal tunnel release and the patients need to be sent to a hand surgeon. I could do the operation myself.

Life has its tricks and turns but I regret very little and have had an amazing run and I remain in good spirits and look forward to living at a more sensible pace.

Kind Regards

Graham Fleming

A TALE OF TWO MATES – HOW ADVERSITY BROUGHT TWO FAMILIES TOGETHER

By Peter Hawke

Richard (Dick) Churchill

Dudley (Hawky, Freddy) Hawke

Richard Churchill (my uncle)

INTRODUCTION
"On the 2nd April 1911 The Advertiser reported that the previous day a new born baby boy had been found alive in Churchill Street, Adelaide, shortly after 6 am. He was wrapped in two old blankets, a cotton sheet and a towel. Having been informed, the metropolitan police placed the infant under the care of the State Children's Department."

One can only imagine the sad and desperate condition of the mother to resort to abandoning her newborn babe. This tiny baby was a foundling and as such was treated by law the same as a vagrant and judged as a second-class citizen. He was taken to the Industrial School Orphanage, Edwardstown and given the name Richard Churchill after the street where he was found. There was no opportunity for him to be adopted as adoption wasn't introduced into South Australia until 1925.

Fortunately for Richard however he was fostered by a Mrs Rohlbush when he was just 8 days old. This was a mixed blessing. While Mrs Rohlbush treated him reasonably well during his childhood Mr Rohlbush took delight in giving young Richard a regular thrashing, for no particular wrong doing, to teach him respect and discipline.

Bath time was once a week, with Mr and Mrs Rohlbush taking turns, followed by their other 3 children then Richard last with the water by then cold and brown. Because he was a ward of the state he was required to go to church on Sundays. The Rohlbushs, however, were atheists and apparently found it a source of humour to give Richard laxatives on Saturday night so that in the morning the frequent call of nature would disturb the tranquillity of his church attendance.

When he reached the age of 14 the foster care money was stopped and as was the practice at the time for foundlings, he was indentured out to perform labouring type work. There was no expectation on the part of the employer to teach him a particular trade, as would be the case for an apprentice. Part of his wage was held in trust by the Department for Children's

Services until he was 21 to ensure he behaved. If the employer reported that he was lazy or his behaviour had cost him money, he could claim an appropriate amount back as compensation. It appears he had at least three different jobs over the next seven years. One of those was with a blacksmith, another brutal man who treated him badly and often beat him. Richard told the story of one occasion when things were so bad that he crept up behind the blacksmith working at the forge and pushed him forward so his hands landed in the coals. Richard was learning to stand up for himself and no longer meekly accept his lot.

Despite a cruel start in life Uncle Richard was strong and resourceful. He was happy-go-lucky, the life of a party and at the same time was a sensitive and caring young man.

Richard's Early Adult Life

A Department of Child Services record shows that when he turned 21 he was able to claim eight pounds eleven shillings from that department for wages held back in trust and he used this to equip himself for gold prospecting with some friends in the Adelaide hills at Cudlee Creek. At weekends .someone would stay to watch the claim while the others went to Adelaide. It was dangerous at times as Richard found once when he was on watch and had to climb a tree to avoid a flash flood. He was there for several hours before his friends returned to rescue him.

He always said *'I found enough gold to keep m'self in tea and baccy for my pipe.'* Whether that was a rueful or a happy comment no one knows but I like to think it was the latter.

One Saturday he went to a dance at the local hall and saw

the pretty Ruth Millington across the room. He asked her for a dance and she accepted his offer. They shared every other dance that night. The next week he sold a small parcel of gold to buy tickets and took Ruth to the pictures. On the way he gave her a bunch of Boronia that she greatly appreciated and the romance blossomed. The Millingtons were not particularly impressed with Richard as he had no social standing, a poor education and no particular future prospects but he was successful in impressing Ruth and she happily agreed to his marriage proposal. When they were married in 1937 Richard's friends provided the flowers which naturally included Boronia. On every wedding anniversary until his last days Richard gave Ruth a bunch of Boronia as a memento of their wedding day, the best day of his life. He was very much a romantic and even overseas during the war he would write to Marion, his sister-in-law, asking her to get Ruth some Boronia for that particular anniversary.

Richard had a motor bike and sidecar they used for their honeymoon in Victoria. The trip home took them south from Geelong to the Great Ocean Road. As they travelled that winding, windy narrow road with steep cliffs only a few feet from the edge of the road and the seas below the bike and sidecar started vibrating excessively. They stopped at the next town and discovered that the bolts holding the bike to the sidecar were loose and had all but come apart and thrown Ruth and sidecar into the sea. I can only imagine the thoughts that would have flashed through Richard's mind as he recognised the danger that had just been averted. *"What would I have said to the Millingtons?"*

There is a report in the March 23rd 1938 *Advertiser* of

Richard Churchill being taken to the Port Adelaide Casualty Hospital suffering from shock and head injuries. He told the police that, *"About 6.30 am I was riding my motorcycle and sidecar along Junction Road, Rosewater, when the front wheel of the machine struck a depression in the road surface. The outfit swerved across the road, jumped across the footpath and struck a galvanised fence and I was thrown off".*

When Richard told the story to his children years later it had taken a more dramatic image with the outfit tearing through the galvanised iron fence leaving a cut out the shape of a motorcycle, sidecar and rider. He was a bit of a larrikin who never let the truth spoil a good story.

Dudley Hawke (my father)

In December 1914, Amelia and Walter Hawke welcomed their third child Dudley to their happy family on their farm near Millicent in South Australia. Dudley was followed by Wally in 1916 and life looked rosy for this young tribe. Walter was a devoted husband and father. He was also well known in the district as a crack shot, having won many trophies for his marksmanship.

In 1918 Amelia was pregnant with their fifth child when Walter fell ill with the Spanish flu and was hospitalised. Although extremely sick he was concerned for his wife about to give birth and caring for four children on her own. Against hospital staff advice he discharged himself and walked the five miles home in the rain. His condition worsened so he was again hospitalised, but died from the influenza and pneumonia on that same day November 8th. Baby Reginald was born seven days later to a widow with five children under eight years of age.

Income from the farm was meagre and life extremely difficult for the next four years. As soon as the children were of age they would walk the five miles across paddocks to and from school. Edward O'Malley then entered the scene. He was a tall and charming newcomer who, unbeknown to the locals, had a police record for illegal gambling and embezzlement. He wooed Amelia and married her in 1922 and eventually sold all of her possessions, including the farm, to pay for his drinking and gambling.

Ted was born to the couple in 1924 and with things getting a bit "hot" in Millicent for Edward he packed up the family that same year and moved them to live in the Adelaide Hills. They were almost destitute at this stage and Dudley remembers sleeping on straw in the shed. The family were so hungry that at times they had to eat grass to survive. Somehow they managed to find accommodation in Norwood and in June 1926 Mary was born, but died seven days later.

When drunk, Edward was often violent and abusive to the children and Amelia. There were family stories of him dragging Amelia around the house by the hair. When Basil, the oldest son, was 15 he came home from work one day and found O'Malley beating Amelia and threw him out of the house. Police records show he was arrested several times after that episode for unpaid fines and begging in the street. Eventually a warrant was issued for his arrest in 1932 for unlawfully leaving his wife without adequate means of support. It appears O'Malley assumed an alias or worse and disappeared. No record can be found of him from that time.

Despite the chaos at home Dudley managed to complete year seven top of the class. He had just turned 13 and should have continued his schooling for at least another year but he needed to work in order to help support the family and frequently had to hide from the truant officer. The first job for this 13-year-old was as a strapper looking after the race horses at Victoria Park Racecourse. In the late 1920s he would collect horses that came into Adelaide by train and walk them through a tunnel (originally constructed for a train service in the 1850s) that ran under King William Street and came out just before Frome Road. He would then lead them across North Terrace and the East Park lands to the Victoria Park Racecourse. The handling of thoroughbreds gave him an interest in horse racing that continued throughout his life.

Throughout the Depression Basil, Dudley and Wally supplemented their meagre incomes with the sale of meat and skins from rabbits they shot in the Adelaide Hills. In the early 1930s Dudley began working for a fruiterer who would buy fruit and vegetables at the Central Market very early in the morning and hawk them around from door to door from a horse and dray. After a few years Dudley bought the business and ran it until he enlisted in the army in 1941. In the 1930s Basil somehow saved enough money to buy the family home in Norwood.

Clearly the resilience, responsibility and work ethic shown by these young men is a testimony to the love they had for their mother and the values she instilled in them in the face of the many challenges and hardships. Dudley, like Richard, had seen and experienced brutality, privation and injustice in his childhood but, despite, or perhaps because of this, he was a sensitive man who hated violence. His childhood and his experiences during the war left him deeply affected and so much so that he struggled to discipline us children. That was left to our mother.

World War 2 Enlistment line up 18th December 1941

At Keswick Barracks two strangers waiting in line next to each other started chatting and found that they had much in common. Both loved a good joke and a bit of chiacking, although Dick, as Richard was now known, was a little more outgoing than Hawky (Dudley). The friendship they struck up was such that Dick invited Hawky to his home for a meal and to meet his wife Ruth and baby Richard (Rickie). Marion, Ruth's younger sister, happened to be there after babysitting Rickie while Ruth plied her craft as a hairdresser.

Hawky took more than a passing interest in the vivacious and fun-loving Marion and by the time the men reported for duty two days later, Hawky and Marion had agreed to correspond and see how their friendship might progress during these worrying times.

Basic training was at Woodside in the Adelaide Hills followed by infantry training in the Barossa Valley. The site with its many wineries nearby tempted these two lads who were keen to develop their expertise, skill and resourcefulness in covert operations. One night they went AWOL and returned with a cache of wine for their fellow troops. Their mates reassured them that any senior officer discovering the venture would have applauded their efforts.

On 26th August 1942 they were sent to the Middle East on the troopship *Rajula* to join the 2/48th Battalion that had been fighting some of the bloodiest battles of the war at Tobruk and El Alamein. The ship was filthy and conditions on board poor so shore leave in Colombo, Ceylon, as Sri Lanka was then called, was most welcome. The two young men had seen nothing like this amazing place and bought a whole bunch of bananas, their favourite fruit, for a fraction of the price at home. Hawky threw the bananas over his shoulder and headed back to the ship. Fascinated by the sights, sounds and smells of the city the two were oblivious of the little urchins sneaking up behind them with their pen knives and cutting bananas off the bunch. The story goes that by the time they realised what was happening they had only one shrivelled banana left on the stalk. This was likely another of their stories that stretches the truth just a little short of breaking!

They disembarked at Deir El Adhaba in Palestine on the 8th October 1942 and were attached to the 26 Australian Infantry Training Battalion for desert warfare training before joining the 2/48th Battalion who were involved in the second desperate battle for El Alamein. On the 7th November the German and Italian forces were defeated and in full retreat. The 2/48th later moved on to Gaza in Palestine awaiting further orders. Having missed most of the fighting in that theatre of war Dudley's and Richard's section returned to Australia in February 1943 for jungle training in preparation to engage a new enemy, the Japanese, in New Guinea and elsewhere so close to Australia.

Dudley was Hawky to his army mates, but for some reason "Freddy" to his new girlfriend Marion. When they returned to Australia they were granted leave that gave Dick much needed time with his beloved wife and son, Rickie.

Freddy, now back in the family home in Norwood would cycle to visit Marion at her home in Prospect as often as he could. Freddy had to pump up the bike tyres much to the amusement of a pet sulphur crested cockatoo named Argus. The bird had the run of the yard and stood close by mimicking the hiss-hiss sound of the air as it entered the tyre. He also made a bobbing movement in time with Freddy's pumping action. Having completed the job Freddy went back inside to clean up only to find when he returned the back tyre was flat again. A little frustrated he proceeded to remove the tube and inspected it for a puncture. Finding none he reassembled the tyre and tube and pumped it up again with Argus adding the action and his version of the hiss sound. On returning from washing up a second time he found the tyre was once again flat. After pumping the tyre up again Freddy went back inside and looked out the window to observe any nefarious activity that might provide the answer to this conundrum. Sure enough, as soon as he was inside Argus hopped over to the bike and with his beak, deftly pushed down on the valve expelling the air from the tyre. He obviously enjoyed mimicking the pumping so much he wanted the game to continue. It was one-sided entertainment with Freddy losing valuable courting time. On his now frantic ride to Prospect, he rehearsed an apology to Marion. Smugly he parked his bicycle and then thought, *"My goodness she will think I am mad, a liar and stupid to think such a ridiculous excuse was acceptable."* He never did remember what he said but it must have been accepted.

After leave the 2/48 Battalion reassembled near

Townsville in Queensland to undergo jungle training. Dick and Hawky were in different platoons. Dick was in the rifles and Hawky machine gunners, but they got together whenever they could. Hawky was good with maths and gained proficiency as a "G3 Range taker" for a machine gunner who he had to tell the distance to a target and load and feed the belt of rounds. The big drawback for Hawky was that they were known as "mug gunners" as, in combat, they often had to go in advance of the platoon to soften up the enemy in preparation for an attack.

Their next posting was New Guinea where they would need to make river crossings and landing assaults from the sea and it might be handy to be able to swim. Hawky had never learned to swim and this was considered by his mates to be dangerous. Dick, being a considerate mate and always ready to assist in providing good training, took Hawky out to the end of the jetty in Townsville, tied a rope around his waist and with the help of others threw him into the sea. Whilst he never mastered a good Australian crawl stroke, the keen novice did manage to learn how to gasp for air each time he bobbed up to the surface and eventually, to everyone's credit, a useful form of dog paddle.

New Guinea

Dick had always wanted to be a journalist and kept a diary on tissue paper and recorded this period of the war. It was kept in a cigarette tin and discovered some years after his death by his daughter, Mary. When typed, the diary was a 300 page, almost day by day journal of events only interrupted by the days of heaviest fighting. Some understanding of what they experienced during this time can be drawn from a few brief excerpts from his diary.

They landed at Milne Bay on the 6th August 1943 for a month of further training including amphibious landings, shooting and grenade practice. After one the grenade practice sessions Dick writes.

"Terry and Tren are in the tent when I get back. My grenade looks very greasy so instead of going through the safety precautions, I took the pin out. As the spring clicked both Terry and Tren stood rooted to the spot and I was dumb founded myself as I looked at the grenade in a dazed sort of way. I said calmly looking at it in my hand, "I wonder if it is primed?" it broke the tension for they both made for their end of the tent in a terrible hurry. I threw it at the doorway of the tent but it struck the upright and Terry and bounced back. The four seconds were up before I threw it. It wasn't primed so we still live. I will make sure next time though that I unscrew the plug and see whether the grenade is primed with the detonator".

On the 4th September the 2/48th participated in the division's amphibious landing at Red Beach north-west of Lae and fought in the battles around Lae, Finschhafen, and Sattelberg. They initially thought they were facing 3000 Japanese, but records later showed there were 5000 enemy in this area. The fighting was intense particularly the taking of Sattelberg on a high ridge. Neither man wrote or later talked about this period except for an entry in Dick's diary where his rifle unit were coming up to support the machine gunners who had been on the front line in the taking of Sattelberg. It's a poignant example of how dangerous the battle had been and how close my father had been to losing his life.

"Graves (Australian), must be well over a dozen along the road and six here side by side. Gee! We are going close. Here we are now and we have to dump our gear alongside of the road. **"Hawky? You dirty looking so and so." "I know Dick, but I haven't been able to have a wash for ten days. I haven't even had time to wash my knees."**

"Our Machine Gunners were lucky. They had just been relieved by those of the 32nd when Tojo got on to the nests with his guns and blew four gun-posts to smithereens."

Within a few days of this Dick put in for a transfer to Hawky's machine gun unit which was approved and the two went through the rest of that campaign together.

In December an anxious and very excited Dick received news that his daughter Mary had been born. He couldn't help himself shouting the news to the rest of the platoon. However, as Christmas approached, missing his family, he became rather pensive and wrote in his diary, *"The others yarned but I will sit on the side of the hill next to my doover and I think about my daughter. There were some red tracers flying around way out to sea. Hawky has come and sat down beside me and is doing some heavy thinking too."*

"New Year's Eve I thought a lot of Ruth and Rickie and thought of Rickie on his knees saying "Gentle Jesus meek and mild."

Both men spent several stints in field hospitals with malaria, dengue fever and other tropical diseases that took a huge toll on them physically and was compounded by the mental trauma of the conflict. Dick was especially affected. By the time he returned to Australia in February 1944 this 6-

foot-tall man weighed only 6 stone and was lighter than a jockey. He was admitted to Daws Road Military Hospital in Adelaide for three months rehabilitation before being discharged from the army on medical grounds.

Hawky, my father, went on to see service in Tarakan (Borneo) where the Japanese put up fierce resistance with mines, booby traps and suicide raids to halt the Australian advance. Two months before the Japanese surrendered in August 1945 Dad's offsider and closest mate Ray who had been with him from the earliest days was killed. They were taking shelter in a foxhole when Ray, who had acute hearing, said he heard a whistle and stood up. It was a mortar bomb which landed close enough to kill him. The others were shell shocked, but survived the blast, at least physically.

Following the Japanese surrender Dad was transferred to the 2/3 Pioneer Battalion staying on in Borneo to perform garrison duties and to bring in Japanese soldiers who were unaware the war had ended. This action was quite dangerous and required patrols to take Japanese prisoners with them to try and convince their comrades to lay down their arms. He was finally discharged in April 1946 an emotionally broken man. The tragedy of losing a close mate, the other horrors of war, along with the lasting effects of malaria had a profound effect on my father to be. Some eight months later he married his sweetheart Marion and the following year I was born.

Much more could be said about the circumstances that cemented a lifelong friendship between my dad and my uncle Dick whose lives fortuitously intersected that day in the enlistment line up. From early childhood my cousins, sisters and I learnt a lot from these two men who were to us caring, fun loving heroes. From my uncle Dick, it was his never say die attitude and determination. For example, he handmade thousands of bricks and with limited assistance built his own home while employed full time as a trolley bus driver. From my father one of the lessons was resourcefulness. He was a determined do-it-yourself person. He made toys for us kids, grew most of our vegetables and spent months mixing concrete in a hand cranked concrete mixer, then laying the concrete paths and driveway in our new home, occasionally assisted by his own child labour.

Both men managed to hide from their children the sadness and horrors of their childhood and war time experiences. They chose to live in the present and focus on the opportunities presented as did thousands of others from that era. Despite past challenges and the occasional failure they were successful in the most important parts of life. They both cherished their wives, raised children who were well provided for and knew the love and joy in two happy, healthy families.

Having shared stories with cousins and siblings, researched old newspaper articles, war archives and medical records and my uncle's war time diary, these men who were once childhood heroes now stand even taller.

Editor's note: During the course of World War 2, 2,838 men served with the 2/48th Battalion, 343 were killed in action or died on active service, 675 were wounded and 20 captured.

According to the Australian War Memorial the 2/48th Battalion was "Australia's highest decorated unit of the Second World War".

Part X

OLDEN DAYS

PORT HEDLAND – 50 YEARS AGO.

By Peter Morton and Ian Phippard

I asked Ian Phippard to write some stories about Port Hedland where we met in 1970. It made me think about Leonore's and my experience there so I thought I would join Ian and see what happens when we put our stories together.

In June 1969 Leonore I were married in Adelaide in the middle of my intern year at Broken Hill, after which I was appointed as a District Medical Officer in Broome for six months and then transferred to Port Hedland in September 1970.

We soon made friends with Ian and Lyn Phippard. Lyn was a nurse and my first memory of her was her calling me about a patient who had been playing with her boyfriend and a potato or perhaps vice versa and said potato had become stuck in her vagina. Lyn in her soft and gentle voice, asked, 'Would you like me to remove it?' 'Yes thank you,' was my reply.

Then I met Ian with severe tonsillitis and I sent him to have an injection of penicillin. Unfortunately, he happened to line up with people having shots for venereal disease given by one of Lyn's colleagues and got a right bollocking from her for getting that awful disease. It was sorted out in due course. How could we not become friends with those introductions and we still are 51 years later.

In the mid-1960s vast iron deposits were found in the Pilbara. The Chief Geologist for Kaiser Steel reported, 'There is enough iron ore to last the free world 20,000 years, it is like trying to measure the air.'

Soon there were frenetic activities in the Pilbara, as the wartime ban on exporting iron ore by the Commonwealth and Western Australian Governments, had been lifted. That activity has slowed but not stopped ever since. Ports were enlarged e.g. Port Hedland, or built e.g. Dampier and towns were built at mine sites, Mount Newman and Tom Price or nearby like Karratha in 1968. Knitting all this together was a rail network of many hundreds of kilometres of railways.

Port Hedland was one of, *The Ports of Sunset,* a book written by Ernestine Hill in the 1930s that I have read, a most evocative book and indeed I have been to most of them and lived in two as mentioned.

It was named after Peter Hedland the first European to sail there in 1857and used by the pearling industry after1888, and later was an outlet for the Pilbara tin and gold fields being connected by rail 1912-51. During WW2 it handled tin, tantalite, columbite and manganese from the Pilbara.

I am trying to recapture what Port Hedland was like in 1970-72 when we were there. It was big, noisy and dusty, with huge cranes, gantries, loaders, massive heaps of iron ore and salt with a channel between the Goldsworthy ship loader on Finucane Island and the Mount Newman/BHP one on the mainland and trains coming and going to and from the port. There were was about 30 million tons a year of iron ore exported in my time. The town was filthy dirty and dusty. One of the town leaders ,Angas Richardson, was the Shire

President, owned a car yard and the local butcher shop and famous for telling an ABC journalist, 'I'll worry about the dust when it blocks up my cash registers.' South Hedland was barely under way. Lang Hancock, who started all this when he found iron ore in the Hammersley Ranges some years before, was said to be paid $10 per rail truck of iron ore. There were five trains of 150 trucks a day so he may have earned $50,000 a week and that was 50 years ago

The wages and costs were high. As an intern in Broken Hill I was paid $5000 a year compared to Adelaide Hospital's $3000. That was it. No overtime or special rates. In Port Hedland $7000 a year with accommodation and a car. We paid $20 a week rent and about once a month received a cheque for $50 for non-existent travelling expenses from the WA Health Dept. I just realised that worked out at a dollar a day rent. Apparently the Australia Tax office was not pleased with almost free accommodation that was initially planned and the good old WA mob sorted it.

I met a chap who had worked at the Brighton Cement Works near my family home in Adelaide. He was shift boss/foreman or similar and was paid $3000 pa. In Hedland for similar work it was $10,000, plus accommodation plus transport to work. For people, self- employed or working for organisations not so generous, a caravan in the park was $50 a week. Cabbages and cauliflowers were more than a dollar.

Like many other companies Bell Brothers a transport, construction and mining company invested heavily in this boom particularly in Port Hedland. Once they had an order in place for the next 80 MACK or Kenworth trucks to come into Australia. Other than Scammell trucks operated by DFD

Rhodes they were the only trucks capable of handling the Pilbara terrain.

Ian told me one day that he had started with Bell Brothers in Perth at their head office in1964. In 1967 he was sent to Port Hedland as Transport Supervisor and promoted to Transport Manager for the Port Hedland Area 1968 under Depot Manager Harry Brenton.

One day I looked out the window of my office towards our workshops about 30-40 metres away and Harry Brenton was walking towards me and came into my office and sat down and started talking some work matter. Harry then jumped up and pointed at a welder walking towards the toilets 50-60m away.

His name was Miladand, for the story, from one of the Slavic countries as were most of our welders. Harry blew a fuse. 'He is a bloody malingerer. He must go to the camp toilets five or six times a day, come with me Ian. I am going to sort this bastard out.'

With that he stormed out of the office with me in tow and confronts Miladand who was 5'10" and 16 stone (178cm and 102 kg) and two axe handles across the shoulders, in the middle of the yard. 'Where do you think you are you going Miladand?'

With a look at Harry that could kill Miladand, in broken English, answered, 'Mr Harry I am going for a sheet.' I took a step backwards because I thought there would be blood on the ground and I did not want it to be mine.

Well Harry really goes to town now. With steam coming out of his ears he yells, 'Miladand you have more shits a day than the rest of the workshop put together. If you want a shit that badly, you shit right here, right now and Harry pointed to the ground. For 20 seconds there was a dead silence and I feared for the worst but there was no violence. Miladand turned around and stormed back to the workshop and there after only had one sheet a day. But he did square up. He was looking for Harry one day and couldn't find him so had a swing at me but I was too quick for him and I only copped a glancing blow on my shoulder.

The work was a huge challenge and I was pleased to be made the Depot Manager in 1970, the youngest in Bell's operation at 26.'

I was busy at work, we had great fun fishing and partying with the Phippards and other friends from the hospital and patients we met socially.

Our first child, Kirstin, was born in December 1971 and still considers herself a Sandgroper. I did a fair amount of flying in RFDS planes, some emergencies but almost all to Mount Goldsworthy doing clinics and was there when she was born. I had a can of Courage Beer on the way home to celebrate and learnt not to open a can while airborne in an unpressurised aircraft. I proudly announced her birth to the civil aviation world on our plane's radio with the call sign Foxtrot Delta Juliet or FDR

We had been in Port Hedland over a year and it was obvious that the town and port was expanding. I drove from home to work and vice versa along the Esplanade and there were always ships at anchorage on the horizon. As medical officers we had an interest in the ships because most of them had to be boarded by a doctor to check the crew for smallpox. We looked at their bare forearms where smallpox starts and examined vaccination cards. So we knew the size of the crews and if interested the tonnage of the ships.

I learnt to estimate the size of the ships and they were 30—50,000 tons with a crew of 20 or more in the first year I was there. And then there were one or two more much bigger ships and the first 100,000 tonner was welcomed with its crew of 12-15. Very soon that was the general size with an occasional bigger ship again. The biggest was *Fukakawa Maru* from Japan of that could hold 160,000 tons the biggest ever to that point and I did the quarantine check. It was 900 feet long and I walked across the engine. The 6-8 cylinders were well over a metre wide and probably the same distance apart, as I remember. I checked the 2021 size of vessels to use Port Hedland and it is up to 286,000 tons. It was a long time before 200,000 tonners came into frequent use after the 160,000 tonner I mentioned and maybe not until this century. It certainly was nothing like the progression during the two years that I witnessed.

It was brash, noisy, rough and tough. Men and money attract camp followers and there are consequences. We dealt with much alcohol abuse and venereal disease. I do not remember other drugs being a problem. Many times I saw big drunk blokes, with related injuries and often angry but I never felt in danger and countless times saw these guys do what the nurse told them to do such as 'Sit down and be quiet.' Ambulance patients were admitted directly to a treatment room but all other patients were assessed over a simple counter. This was the same set up in Port Lincoln, where I have lived and worked since 1979. By 1990 the Emergency Department was secured with gratings and locked doors. A consequence of drug fuelled behaviour. I know of an example in a Victorian Hospital where I worked in 2015 of a small young woman around 55kg who went berserk with 'Ice' and it took three police officers and three ambulance officers, all or most were male, to control her.

Back to simpler times in Port Hedland. There were many drunk and injured patients and they were managed accordingly. There were also chronic, end stage boozers, who we admitted, to get them off the grog and treat the inevitable DTs. I remember one dear old bloke who was a 'frequent flyer' in what was a demountable building about a metre off the ground where we admitted people to 'dry-out'. Old mate always made sure that he had a carton of beer stashed under the building there in case he got thirsty.

VD was rife and I confess I was naïve about somethings. Goldsworthy was 100km from Port Hedland and reached by driving about 50km towards Broome and then turning off the main road to the town and mine site. Ted, an Englishman, nurse and Boy Scout Master, had taken a patient into Hedland in the ambulance and on his way home picked up two young women hitch-hikers. When he reached the turn off he stopped to let them out to continue their journey to Broome. They then made it very obvious that one would drive and the other entertain Ted in the back and maybe swap around. Ted was gobsmacked and so was I when he told me that they had actually offered, 'A ride for a ride', apparently standard operating procedure.

Apart from any other consideration a nasty, penicillin resistant strain of gonorrhoea called 'Vietnam Rose' was circulating. I was telling Ian and Lyn about this one day and as Ian was running Bell Brothers large camp with many single men we swapped some stories. Before he was married he had a single room in a hut and next door lived one of the few females on site. She had her boyfriend visit most nights and Ian found it very difficult to sleep and it was against camp rules. The bloke and she kept denying it. The next time he heard the preliminaries he grabbed a bag of flour he had from the kitchen and scattered on the steps outside her room and to the exit door. Next day he confronted them both with the evidence. Problem solved. The poor bloke was killed in a truck accident not long after. Ian told me at the time of writing, March 2021, that he sees the lady in question every year or so but has never remembered to remind her about those days.

An erect penis is said to have no fear and no conscience and it stupid to think otherwise. Ian and I did get serious and thought that we should give his staff some information and advice. The big ones of course were gonorrhoea and syphilis but chlamydia was taking off and becoming a big problem for women as if may not produce symptoms but could cause sterility and other troubles.

We organised some educational sessions just hoping people would practise safe sex (I don't think we used that phrase then) i.e. to use condoms as VD was so rife. A few weeks later Ian told me he knew a female traveller from Europe had spent the night in the quarters with one of his staff, a bloke he regarded highly. He tore strips off the bloke as his boss for breaking company rules and then, as his friend, reminded him of the risks of shagging one of these travelling time bombs. He replied, 'I am sorry boss. It won't happen again. But I am ok with the germ stuff because I took her outside, undressed her and squirted her all over with the fire hose and I used a condom.'

Ian adds another story. 'I remember when Bell's came up with a mechanised (hoppers and hydraulic conveyors) way of loading manganese instead of using kibbles (200 litre buckets) that would halve the time to load a ship as less labour was needed from the wharf gangs. We were trialling this and the wharfies realised they were going to lose a lot of lucrative shifts.

When we started using the trucks to haul bulk ore to tip into the hoppers the wharfies all lay down on the road in front of the trucks at the entrance to the wharf to stop them entering. No mobiles then so we had to get the police. Two came down to the wharf including a large, no bullshit sergeant and Geoff the Harbour Master appeared as well.

There was some toing and froing between Bell's, the police and wharfies and not going anywhere. The police sergeant was getting seriously pissed off at all this and asked, 'Who is the driver of that first truck in the line being held up by the wharfies lying in front of it?' It happened to be Alf Pianta who was an even bigger bloke than the sergeant who said to Alf, 'There's only one way to sort this out so if you are prepared to get in your truck and drive over those idiots we can all get back to our jobs.'

The look on Harbour Master Geoff Monk's face told it all. He was sure the wharfies were going to be run over and I am as sure as I can be that Alf would have run over them. The wharfies thought the same and as soon as Alf started the engine, only feet from them, they bolted and we got on with the trial ship loading. Eventually it was sorted.

Geoff was a Master Mariner of great experience and started at Port Hedland in 1965 and oversaw a sleepy Port of Sunset become a global leader in the industry and at the time of writing in early 2021 it is processing 300 million tons of iron from BHP alone of the 830 million tons from all sources in Australia, 90% of which is from Western Australia.

Captain Marks OBE was a revered man and lived until he was 90. His obituary in WA News was typed and sent to me is one and a half A4 pages and mentions the quality of the man in helping his "flock. ' Ian certainly regarded him highly as did his peers as he was inducted into the Maritime Hall of Fame. I find two excerpts from this obituary give an insight into great and good man. *'The ships he dealt with were enormous but points such as the welfare of the crews, and the need for sobriety in captains whose ships were departing were important.'* (That last bit is nice to know). The other was, *'No storm, industrial, social or meteorological deflected Geoff Monks.'* A wonderful man.

I have not thought of this next little anecdote for decades. Many people know that surgeons in a hospital environment are referred to as Mister. This dates back to their origins as Barber Surgeons and like any other trade when they finished their apprenticeships were called Master that became Mister with time and so with surgeons. Physicians on the other hand studied at Universities and were and still are called Doctor.

Something else I learned in Port Hedland was the meaning of 'Wharfinger'-The keeper of a wharf. Sort of a foreman I suppose. I knew the Wharfinger at Port Hedland, an inexpressive chap but friendly enough.

We had a new surgeon turn up and for some reason I took him down to the wharf and introduced him to the Wharfinger and deliberately, as I would do with any surgeon outside hospital, called him Doctor. As they shook hands he said, 'Actually I am Mr so and so.' The Wharfinger let go of his hand, mouthed WTF looked at me, shook his head and walked away.

We enjoyed a lot of our time in Port Hedland but tired of the heat, dust and dirt and 2 ½ years away from our families with a precious new baby, they hadn't seen, we headed back east to Adelaide on holidays. On the flight I was reading a paper and saw a job for a GP /Commonwealth Medical Officer at Woomera. Leonore was dozing and I gently elbowed her and asked, 'Are you awake?' 'YSSS' was her reply. "Would you like to go and work at Woomera?'

'Yes that would be a nice change from Port Hedland' well that was my interpretation of what she said. And we did!

Ian worked for Bell Brothers, Robert Holmes a'Court and Boral for 30 years in WA and also Queensland. Ian then had 5 years with BLG Contracting as General Manager and was then instrumental in establishing Alliance Contracting, a civil and mining contracting company that became very successful.

It has not all been Ian of course. Lyn has been a tower of strength in the family as a wife and mother and as a Registered Nurse with exemplary clinical and management skills as a Director of Nursing. It was tough for Ian in the early days of establishing Alliance Contracting and they had to sell their beach house. Ian worked from home and was a house husband (and has always been very good at that even before the formal title) while Lyn worked full time

Ian and Lyn have stuck together through significant trials

and tribulations that would have felled many but they triumphed together. We admire them and their family very much and value the wonderful friendship we have had with them.

MY MATE OSCAR; OUR DADS' CARS, A STOLEN CAR AND A GUN

By Peter Morton

I have had a friend who I have called Oscar since we were in grade four at St Leonards School, Glenelg in Adelaide and have had all sorts of experiences together over the years.

One day at Glenelg, driving our fathers' cars Oscar was following me north along Tapley's Hill road when I turned left into Newhaven Street. Helen, a friend of Oscar's sister, who we both knew, lived on the corner and waved to me. I drove a little further and parked the car to go and say hello.

I looked in the mirror to see Oscar with his usual beaming smile looking to the left and waving to her with his left hand and heard the car accelerate. It was all in slow motion. He turned to look where he was going. His face froze with mouth and eyes open. Inevitably he ran into me. No one was hurt. That was in 1960.

The next venture was in the early seventies. In the years that had passed I became very careful with firearms. I had a friend who was killed when he used a double barrel shotgun as a golf club to hit a bush on his father's farm.

Another time I was quite scared when spotlighting in the South East of South Australia when a drunken shearer, accidentally I hope, poked me in the back of the head with a loaded rifle he was waving around inside the car instead of pointing it out the car window.

and tribulations that would have felled many but they triumphed together. We admire them and their family very much and value the wonderful friendship we have had with them.

MY MATE OSCAR; OUR DADS' CARS, A STOLEN CAR AND A GUN

By Peter Morton

I have had a friend who I have called Oscar since we were in grade four at St Leonards School, Glenelg in Adelaide and have had all sorts of experiences together over the years.

One day at Glenelg, driving our fathers' cars Oscar was following me north along Tapley's Hill road when I turned left into Newhaven Street. Helen, a friend of Oscar's sister, who we both knew, lived on the corner and waved to me. I drove a little further and parked the car to go and say hello.

I looked in the mirror to see Oscar with his usual beaming smile looking to the left and waving to her with his left hand and heard the car accelerate. It was all in slow motion. He turned to look where he was going. His face froze with mouth and eyes open. Inevitably he ran into me. No one was hurt. That was in 1960.

The next venture was in the early seventies. In the years that had passed I became very careful with firearms. I had a friend who was killed when he used a double barrel shotgun as a golf club to hit a bush on his father's farm.

Another time I was quite scared when spotlighting in the South East of South Australia when a drunken shearer, accidentally I hope, poked me in the back of the head with a loaded rifle he was waving around inside the car instead of pointing it out the car window.

Oscar's sister had marital problems and had fled to Adelaide in her soon to be ex- husband's new car. Oscar, being the caring brother that he was, swapped his car for the one she was driving in the hope that friends/relatives of her husband would not know where to nick it.

We had planned a weekend fishing near Mannum and duly headed off through the Adelaide Hills on what was a narrow winding road. Oscar kept drifting near or onto the double lines. It made me nervous and several times I suggested he drive on the left-hand side of the lane not the right. We arrived safely.

That night we went spotlighting for rabbits and he drove. I had his pump action .22 rifle. The magazine was a long tube under the barrel. We were unsuccessful. I did not want to unload the rifle in the car because it was so awkward to get the bullets out. I fired a shot into the ground, therefore leaving an empty cartridge case in the breech of the rifle and laid the rifle on the back seat.

Off we went on the dirt road. I thought he was going a bit fast but felt guilty for hectoring him through the hills and said nothing. There was a right-angled turn to the left coming up that he turned without slowing down. The car rolled and came to rest on its four wheels.

Oscar added a phrase to the 'Famous last words book. It was: 'But I was only doing 30 miles an hour' (50kph.) I said something like, 'Quite so old chap, you should have been able to go around a right-angled bend on a dirt road at that speed. It must have been the fairies that tipped us over.'

When we got back to where we were staying the first thing I did was grab the rifle, still on the back seat as I recall. I cannot remember thinking that the roll-over could have activated the pump action, ejecting the empty shell and putting a new one into the breech. Maybe I did, because I pointed the rifle at the ground and pulled the trigger and the rifle fired.

That experience needed about half a bottle of Oscar's favourite Cutty Sark Scotch, each, to settle our frazzled nerves.

Next day we went fishing and caught some red fin. One thing he can do, Oscar, is catch fish, any where, any time!

Part XI

UNIQUE TALES

JOHN VERSTEEG'S COMPENDIUM

With Introduction by Peter Morton

Ed: In the mid-1990s I met John as a patient in Port Lincoln and as the owner of a restaurant at Coffin Bay where we both had holiday homes. We and our wives, Ria and Leonore, became good friends over the years. Our friendship developed to the point that we cruised with them on their boat on the River Loire in France and a year or two later they joined us on an extensive, three weeks or more, camping trip from Port Lincoln to the Kimberley in Western Australia, the Gulf country in Queensland and places in between.

Naturally we had many conversations, and I was fascinated by John's experiences as a young boy in Holland towards the end of World War 2. My father served in that war and did not see me until I was two, so I have always had an interest in those times and John lived in them and on our various trips told us many stories. At one point in his story, he refers to being sent to a farm to be fed as there was no food in Amsterdam but he made the most of it and later when the war ended describes how it didn't take long to forget it. Many people my age (born in 1943) will remember many books about the brutality of the Germans, and for us Australians the Japanese, the suffering of the Jewish people. I remember reading *The Diary of Anne Frank*, a story about a Jewish girl who hid for years in a house in Amsterdam and a raft of war books like *The Great Escape, A Bridge Too Far* and many more. He was there and came though it and later prospered in Australia.

John's family moved to Australia soon after the war and his story was that of many migrants and I had some knowledge of that. We lived on Tapleys Hill Road in Adelaide about halfway between Anzac Highway and a migrant hostel on the south-west corner of the Adelaide Airport near the Glenelg Golf Club.

It was a familiar sight to see and hear migrant people passing by our house with their different languages and dress and there were some at the same school as me. No doubt they had similar experiences to those John describes about the time his family was at a similar facility at Finsbury. At the time of writing this John told me that his wife Ria was probably one of those folks who would have walked past our place in the late 1950s. The half-built houses were what John called 'back-enders' and they were very familiar to me where we lived, whether built by Australians or immigrants. John mentioned his countrymen, particularly relatives, helping each other erect walls, lay cement and so on when building their homes but that was also an Australian practice.

I found his story interesting, particularly how he and his family got on with things. There was sadness for sure, but courage a plenty, and John developed a determination to survive and succeed in life that nourished him throughout his career as an accountant and businessman.

I hope others enjoy his account of those times during the war, something that we in Australia have never had to suffer.

My dad used to say, 'Be careful what you wish for son. You

might get it!' I pestered John to write a short story of those times and when he did he was like a dog with a bone and has generously and kindly written an autobiography.

John has a long CV, eleven years studying, including two years post graduate work at Flinders University, a Fellowship of the Australian Society of Accountants, a Company Secretary. Years in Adelaide working up the career ladder and broadening the scope of his career, the same in Sydney, seven years in Europe and then back to my world building and running a restaurant in Coffin Bay.

We are very different but get on well. See John's response to buying his schoolmate's guitar. This says it all ---perhaps

John and I had a discussion in the Simpson Desert one night a few years ago and I told him how often people had told me, 'When I first met you I thought you were rude/arrogant/a smart arse---etc.' Those comments were then followed later by, 'Now I know you and you are really a nice person.'--

John replied, 'People always like me when we meet but when they get to know me, they say, 'I used to like you but you have changed. You are a real bastard' and Peter my friend they are dead right.'

To John's story.

A SPECIAL DAY THAT CHANGED MY LIFE

It was a beautiful September summer day in Amsterdam in 1943. Holland was under the yoke of the German occupation, but our local Catholic school had organised a special children's mass at St Rita's Church that was filled with children in the front, boys to the left and girls to the right. The

Nuns, who were also our teachers, were at the rear. That seating was official Catholic policy at the time.

I was six-years-old and hungry as we had fasted before communion. The officiating priest slowly worked his way through the Offertorium and the Consecration. Communion was yet to come.

The time was 9.30 am when we heard the moans of the air raid sirens and Allied aircraft heading towards the nearby Fokker aircraft factory, or so we thought. Many of the congregation started crying and some fled the church. Minutes later the bombs started falling. People sheltered where they could. Most, like me, hid under pews. At 9.35 that morning one bomb hit the rear of St Rita's instantly killing all the nuns. The scene was utter chaos with children screaming, many seriously injured and others crying in pain.

My injuries were minor. I was pinned under the pew, which although painful had given me all the protection I had needed. Strong hands lifted the pew off me. After checking that I was alright I was left to find my way out of the chaos of dust and fallen roof tiles. It was difficult to see and I found myself at the front of the church at the altar and realised that I had gone in the wrong direction. I worked my way along the sides of the church and the confessionals and finally saw the daylight. I was shepherded around the eleven-metre-wide crater where the nuns were killed and went into the street.

The walk and run home took about ten minutes. My mother and many others were waiting in Nachtegaal Street behind a barricade as no one was allowed near the scene of devastation. Her relief was incredible of course. We held each other and both cried.

Dad was at work that day and was home shortly afterwards. His place of work was the Fokker factory. It was unscathed.

That day changed our lives as Mum refused to live so close to the bombing targets. Within a week we had moved away. It is sad to reflect that many homes were available during those war years as the German occupiers had removed most of the Jewish citizens of Amsterdam to concentration camps in Poland.

THE END OF WORLD WAR 2 IN HOLLAND

In 1944, during the last six months of World War 2, food had become so scarce in Amsterdam that every day dead people were found in the streets and Europe was about to face one of the coldest winters in history. There was no fuel for fires and no food, a recipe for a human disaster.

Only the fittest survived. It was everyone for themselves. The food kitchens, when they were open, supplied only a disgusting mash of sugar beet that would not support life, particularly of the elderly.

Fortunately, Dad was a fit and healthy 30-year-old as he had a wife, three girls, and me to feed. Food could be found at some places in the countryside. This meant you needed to beg, borrow, barter or steal whatever you could lay your hands on. Many farmers were generous and ready to help, but others would not let anyone on their property as there were so many city people scrounging that everyone's generosity was tested.

At one stage Dad gave our Uncle Piet, a kind elderly man, a small sack of potatoes for him and his wife but Uncle Piet collapsed and died on the way home. His wife, Tante Jos, survived the war, that horrible winter and the arrival of peace but only lived for another month.

Dad was able to walk the long distances to find food but carrying it home was difficult, so he decided to make a hand cart. It could only be built at night-time down in an undercover storage area that was deserted by the Germans. Dad and a trusted neighbour made it there at night, something that they did not advertise as the police or Germans would likely confiscate it. They made a box from scrap timber and metal and the last thing that was needed to finish the cart was a pair of wheels and for that Dad had to sacrifice his own pushbike.

The handcart played a vital role in our survival. It had a drawbar so Dad could pull it by hand and return home with, mainly potatoes, but sometimes other vegetables that were shared with our aunties, uncles and our neighbour who helped make the lifesaving cart. Food was not the only shortage towards the end of the war. Shoes and clothing as well as rubber tyres for the bicycles that were the essential form of transport in Holland, became impossible to buy. To go to school, we needed footwear of some sort. Dad made us wooden kleppers, a pair of small wooden soles with leather straps over the top. They made a lot of noise, walking on them, hence the name. Mum repaired and altered clothing to fit and so we made it through.

In the middle of that terrible winter, known to everyone as the ' hunger winter ' the food situation in the cities became so desperate that thousands of young kids, including my sister Anne and myself were sent to farms in the country to be fattened up so to speak and that was where we saw out the end of the war.

We remember so well the days of celebration that followed. The war was soon forgotten!

MY POST WAR EXPERIENCE IN HOLLAND

When the euphoria of the post-war celebrations had ended Holland settled down to the hum-drum ways of more normal times.

Schools opened. Those who had a job, went back to work. Displaced people went back to their home countries and families reunited. Within a few weeks, and now aged eight, I was back at school with new teachers and other kids. Normal foods reappeared in the shops and we could drink milk for the first time in a long while. For the first time I tasted a banana. I loved the taste and still do.

We lived on one of Amsterdam's biggest and busiest canals. Inland freighters were common, bringing goods for Amsterdam or transhipments for export. They also loaded goods for distribution upriver. Those boats were often moored across the street from our house, so not only was there the ever-changing river traffic, but there were kids to play with.

Some of the moored boats were family homes as well the means of making a living. I spent countless hours playing on these boats and thinking how great it would be to cruise up and down the rivers, never having people tell you what to do and just having fun. As I look back on my life, I am sure those days and dreams influenced my love of boats and travel especially near or on waterways.

As always for children good things end. My parents made

me change schools once or twice, before settling on a good catholic boys' school run by the local parish and their clergy, about a half hour walk from home. I always enjoyed my schooling with the exception perhaps, of my third year of high school. My main teacher was Mr. Van den Berg; He and I just did not get on and my educational performance suffered badly that year. He said he would pass me as he could not bear to have me in his classroom again. The next year I topped my class and I believe he had a breakdown of sorts.

I had always wanted a guitar and an opportunity came in a strange way. A classmate was a very heavy smoker and very afraid of his father who hated him smoking. He was frantic that he owed the cigar shop money and had been unable to buy the noxious sticks. He must have known I was keen about guitars because he offered to sell it to me, and I duly bought it. Soon after he and his very unhappy father came to our house and they explained how it had been as a special gift from his parents and could they buy it back. I refused. I have often thought about that refusal. Was it the beginning of a not so nice streak in me? I played that guitar for many years in Amsterdam and Australia and even in a small band in Adelaide night clubs.

I joined the Cubs and then the Scouts. It is good training for boys. The level of discipline and the camping adventures were wonderful and was another thing that influenced my later life. It is now safe to admit that the best thing about the Scouts was being away from my three sisters and Mum's protectiveness as Dad was often working away from home.

There was always pressure in our household to earn your own pocket money and when I was 14, I got my first after-school job which was my own newspaper round for the Times, a Catholic daily delivered in the evenings. This first round was a real eye opener for an innocent 14-year-old. It was in the heart of the famous Amsterdam red light district. As the night descended, I became aware of what business was carried on there, mainly with the American service men on R & R leave. I got to know the service suppliers over time. They knew exactly what day I was collecting the subs and I remember to this day the common invitation from the girls, 'Hey boy, you want to come inside for a cuppa?' Oh no, far too frightened and thank goodness as I was not worldly wise. At school I was always badgered to relate stories of all the extraordinary things that I was thought to have experienced in my evening work and since then I have been very good at embellishing stories!

By the time I was 16 my father, who was quite an adventurer, started talking about migrating somewhere. Anywhere would do. Mum was not keen, but the rest of our family were all for it. After attending several information sessions, we decide on Australia. Lots of sunshine and a land of opportunity.

I had just completed my high school studies and was the only person in our household that could speak English and, if we did not go to Australia, I would need to look for a job in Holland. Frankly, I had no idea what I was going to do, so why not go to Australia. It all came together and on the 1st October we said goodbye to family and friends and boarded the Johan Van Olden Barneveldt together with 1700 other Dutch hopefuls.

Dad had 10 Australian pounds in his pocket. I had 10 US

dollars in mine.

ARRIVING IN AUSTRALIA

The voyage on the mighty *Van Oldenbarneveld* took us through the Suez Canal and a short stopover in Aden. We were allowed off the ship for a few hours and whilst feasting our eyes on the wonderful sights that the Middle East had to offer, I received an unexpected but nasty blow to my head from a young man on a bicycle, who did not stop. It was not until many years later that I understood the anti-western/Christian feelings in Muslim countries that led to that action.

The rest of the voyage was uneventful except for a severe storm in the Indian Ocean. Sea sickness was rife and the dining room nearly empty for several days. Dad and I held our heads high having not missed a meal.

After four weeks land appeared, and it was Australia. The ship docked in Fremantle and we saw our first Australians. They were 'wharfies' unloading the ship. We, from the number one bicycling country in the world, laughed at their basic bicycles with handlebars back to front.

Shortly after arriving in Fremantle a call went out for workers to load carcasses of beef and pork onto the ship and into the freezer rooms. I was one of many young fellows, desperate for money, who volunteered and started work at six the following morning. It was much harder than I had anticipated and after six hours I was completely knackered but grateful for my first Australian wage. I slept, well satisfied, that night.

Next morning we set sail for Melbourne and arrived early

in the morning two days later after a pleasant voyage through some of the potentially roughest waters in Australia. We had not been told what would happen to us once we got to Melbourne, but we soon found out. We collected our belongings from the ship and walked to a large building, clad with iron, and went through the registration and other processing necessary to be admitted to Australia. We then caught a train for a six-hour trip to Albury–Wodonga about halfway between Melbourne and Sydney. We were picked up by buses and, at two am, entered Bonegilla, a migrant camp. Mum and the girls were so exhausted they could not have cared less if they had been dropped off in Moscow. No doubt the giant Snowy Mountain Scheme was meant to draw a flood of job applications from us, the new arrivals.

We were allocated our own hut until the breadwinners found employment and permanent housing. There were two bedrooms with bedding and other furniture and a communal ablution block with toilets and showers. We were quite used to that way of personal hygiene. In our old house we had no bathroom. My parents, the girls and I had our weekly bath/shower at the community baths about a kilometre from home. We did have a toilet though!

Next morning we liked what we saw. Blue skies, massive gum trees and the Hume Weir close to the camp with swimming and walking opportunities all around the place. We often hitched rides with locals to Albury and wandered around in amazement at what Australia had to offer. I clearly remember my first milkshake and my first and only hamburger and helping out in the communal kitchen.

Life was pretty good at Bonegilla except Dad had to leave

but soon found a permanent job as an electrician, in Adelaide with the South Australian Railways. We had been sent economy class tickets and we were on our way on an early train from Albury to Melbourne and then the overnight Overlander train to Adelaide from the Spencer Street station. We were ready and excited about the last leg of our journey from Amsterdam to Adelaide. I think all of us managed to doze off, except poor Mum who had many worrying thoughts about the family members she had left behind.

My sister Rietje reminded me today, August 24^{th,} 2020 that we saw a picture show that day in Melbourne.

THE FIRST TWO DAYS OF MY LIFE IN ADELAIDE

It was the 3rd of December 1953. We were all wide awake by 6 am and caught our first glimpse of the green Adelaide Hills. As the train made its way slowly through cuttings, I felt the hills were embracing our family and welcoming us. Soon the train made its way past the township of Belair and descended towards Adelaide. Suddenly we had a clear view of this beautiful city bathed in the brilliant light of the morning sunshine, framed by the deep blue of St Vincent's Gulf. Its beaches stretched from built up areas in the north to the cliffs rising out of the sea in the south.

I knew this place was going to be good for us. From that moment I knew it was home.

In December 2019, my wife, Ria and I made that same train trip for the first time since that day in 1953 and that same magic feeling that came over me when I was aged just 16, came back to me last December at age 83.

Dad met us at the Adelaide Railway Station. We asked a

million questions in the taxi as we drove to our new temporary accommodation at the Finsbury hostel. The conversation was all in Dutch of course, which must have been mind-numbing for the taxi driver. Within 20 minutes we got our first look at the clean units and very nice communal dining room that provided three meals a day. We particularly loved the breakfasts that offered choices, a luxury for us.

However, there was work to be done and the next day I presented myself at the SA Labour Office in Currie Street. I came home that day with a job starting the following morning. I presented myself to the personnel manager at Cravens, a department store in the city, and started work in the Toys Department to help with the Christmas rush.

It was my first real job. Being able to speak English that I learned at school opened that door and many others to come.

MY FIRST TWO JOBS IN ADELAIDE

And so, I started my working life that Tuesday as a shop assistant at the Adelaide Department store of Cravens that was then situated on the corner of Pulteney and Rundle Street. My wage was 4 pounds, 10 shillings ($9) a week and I had no trouble getting by on my somewhat limited English.

My sister Anne, who was younger than me and could not speak any English at all, had also started working at the nearby Brookers jam factory and she was earning more than me and that was not right so I would need to find a higher paying job. On the other hand, I was quite enjoying the environment at Cravens where there were lots of young ladies who were only too happy to befriend a nice young boy from Holland. I had my first date with a lass from the second floor, who took me home to her Mum and Dad for a Saturday lunch and afterwards we went to the pictures and saw the movie about that great basketball team, The Harlem Globe Trotters.

In those days the lifts at Department stores were 'manned 'by young ladies. While I was quite a shy 16-year-old, I soon found out that Australian girls were not. I had a particular fantasy that one of these vixens would stop between floors and have her way with me------and it did happen, well sort of, she stole a quick kiss and that was it. Well, it was for her but certain parts of me did not recover for some time!

After the Christmas rush the toy department slowed down and I was transferred to the linoleum department of the 4th floor and worked there for some months under a very nice boss called Max Buttery. Learned quite a lot there about flooring and the quaint imperial measuring system, which I was not used to, coming from a metric country.

Much as I enjoyed the whole experience, there was pressure on me to earn a higher wage. As we had come to Australia to better ourselves and, being aware of the massive sacrifice our parents had made for all of us, we had undertaken to help them get settled as soon as possible and both Anne and I gave our parents all our wages and had to be satisfied with a handout of pocket money. This was accepted by us for quite some time and it never did us any harm.

Meanwhile Mum and Dad had purchased a back-ender on a large suburban block at Royal Park. This was a part house that could be finished later when money was available. Our back ender had a large kitchen/dining room, one bedroom, a half-finished bathroom and a sleep-out, a small bedroom with louvre windows. The plan was to add two front rooms and a passageway to a front entrance, but it took a couple of years before we got around to that. Meantime Mum and Dad shared the bedroom with the three girls, and I had the sleep-out to myself.

I found a better job as a steward at the Commercial Travellers Association (CTA) Club on North Terrace. I was 17 by that time but gave my age as 19 so that I would earn more. In those days no one asked for proof of identity and I spoke like an Aussie by then. I could not work behind the bar as 21 was the adult age. I was a teetotaller until my 26th Birthday anyway. The stewards' job was both early morning shift and afternoon work and I enjoyed the CTA making many friends with both the members and my colleagues. Meals were included at night and I became good friends with the chef, a jolly well-built lady, who served trombone, a type of pumpkin, cooked every which way each dinnertime and this became one of my favourite vegetables. She answered my question as to what that orange-coloured vegetable was with, 'That is called sunshine my boy' and I called it that for many years.

My boss at the CTA was a gentleman called Teddy Price who invited me to his house for dinner one day and his wife cooked a great roast with loads of 'sunshine'.

But my time at the Club came to an end for a reason I cannot remember, and I started looking once again for a job with higher financial rewards.

Before I go on to my next story, I would like those of you who are reading these stories that I learnt much in those early jobs. I was made welcome in my new country by so many people and the main lesson was to treat others you meet if life and at work well and you will be treated the same.

And a big thanks to the lift girls at Cravens.

MORE CHALLENGES - BAR WORK AND CONCRETING

In those early years of my working life, I changed jobs many times, mostly to earn more money, so that I could have some of the finer things this country had to offer, a motorbike, then a bigger one and eventually a nice car and you never know, some savings for a place of my own.

One of the more memorable job was the work in the front bar of the Rosewater Hotel. The Rosey was a bar frequented by real working people. Bus drivers and wharfies were the locals and in those days the law said that no drinks were to be served after 6 pm. This led to the famous 6 o'clock swill, where our clientele would order up to three pints of beer one minute before closing time and would consume these in less than 30 minutes before they were locked out. Nothing like the gentility of the CTA of course.

The head barman, a nice guy called Johnny, had a word with me about the poor takings in my till. Each barman, there were six of us, had their own keg and tap and were responsible for their own money takings and mine was not making the minimum required of me. I did not even know the rules at that time, but I soon realised that the problem did not lie with me but with one of my colleagues, who during his lunch break would shout his friends a few beers from my tap.

Not helpful in allowing me to meet my commitments.

I decided to put a stop to that and wrote down every drink that was so generously dispensed. This led to a minor altercation. The chap in question threw a glass of beer in my face and when I retaliated, the happy bar crowd dragged both of us outside and into the carpark where they closed the gates so that we were not disturbed by nosey police. It was not my best experience, I had never been involved in the real thing before, especially not being cheered on by a mob of blood thirsty idiots. So, after incurring some damage, we decided that enough was enough and we both went home. Roy, the other guy was fired, and I decided that I could do better somewhere else.

My mode of transport in 1955 was a motorbike, an ex-police bike and I was very proud of it. In those days you could get a driving licence if you were 16 or over, and the licence allowed you to drive anything, bikes, cars buses and even trucks. No experience required, just sit for a written multiple-choice questionnaire and 7 out of 10 correct answers would get you over the line. I had never driven a car, but Dad had a 1927 Buick with a wooden steering wheel and a floor mounted gearshift. The wipers were hand operated and indicator lights were not even invented then, not for the Buick anyway. It was his pride and joy, well it was, until I crashed it much later.

There was an ad in the paper looking for a fit person to work in a concrete foundation gang. 'Must be able to drive and be a teetotaller', it said. Well, that is easy, I'll just get Dad to teach me in the Buick.

It turned out that a requirement of the job, apart from pouring concrete and digging trenches all day, was to be the appointed driver of an old Bedford truck complete with a concrete mixer attached as a trailer. I did not have to show my licence and was accepted on the spot and shown the truck, but upped my age by three years, again to get the higher award rate. That all seemed so easy, too easy I thought, until I found out that in this crew of Eastern European concreters, each one had lost his licence for D.U.I. Johnny Adamson, the boss, was of Latvian origin, the others were Polish, Estonian, and so on. Good blokes but hopeless when they were drunk, which happened every weekend after work.

Dad did indeed teach me to drive the Buick on that weekend and on Monday morning I drove the truck with five men on board who were s..t scared and rightly so. Somehow, I survived the experience for six months and became an accomplished truck driver in the bargain. During my time with the crew, ready mix concrete started to be used on building sites and Johnny went broke.

There has been a price to pay though. As the work was always outside, shirts not worn, and sunblock unheard of, like many others of that time I used to get sunburnt and I am still paying for that today.

EXPERIENCING RURAL SOUTH AUSTRALIA
AS A SEED GRADER

'How much do you know about Australian farms and about different grains produced here in South Australia?' The questioner was Stan Hopkins, interviewing me for a job at Alf Hannaford the seed grading company based in Woodville.

'Nothing Sir', was my answer and I wished very much I could say something more positive, as the work sounded really interesting.

'Well, young man, we will give you an induction course for a week and if you pass that you can start immediately.'

I did pass and I became a seed grader operator. I was given a truck with a grading and pickling machine driven by an R & T kerosene engine mounted on the tray. That was how I started one of the most interesting jobs I have ever held. I was away from home and solely responsible for the work I was doing in my allocated farming district. It was the first time I experienced Australia's rural world, something that has taught me so much about Australia and an experience of inestimable value in my later working life.

I was given a list of all the farms in that area with names, phone numbers etc. and it was my job to contact all farms on the list to make appointments for a grading operation over the next week. For those who don't know, what grading is all about, a short explanation.

Farmers do not normally sell all the grain they have harvested as they need to set aside a percentage of their harvest to be used as seed for the next sowing. And for that, only the best grain should be used, no broken grains, no weed seeds that may have found their way in and so on and that is where the seed-grader comes in. In those days, the whole harvest was stored and sold in hessian bags, weighing around 180 pounds each and so was the seed that was kept back. It was the operator's job to man the machine with help from the farm owner and friends and maintain the whole thing, screens, elevators, conveyors, the chemical dispensers etc. and of course the old truck. Most farms would have a seed stock between 100 and 250 bags and that meant that I would spend up to two days at some farms. I always cleaned out the unit at the end of each day and at the completion of the job.

An operator, like shearers, was fed, watered, and

accommodated by the client farmer.

I would arrive at a different farm most nights, dine with the family and hear their stories and met so many wonderful farming families it was a great period of enrichment and probably it was an interesting experience for the family as well, to hear about the way things were done in another country.

Another responsibility was to do the invoicing before you could say goodbye and to collect a cheque from the farm for the work done. The account copies and payments were to be forwarded to head office at Woodville by post and I would be paid based on the number of bags I had invoiced. I cannot say that I was a star at repairing the truck, or the Ronaldson Tippet engine, but there were always people to help, that's the way of the bush.

While I was away Dad had completed building their house at Durham Terrace, Royal Park and had made it substantially larger than was envisaged. I had helped when I could, particularly with any concrete or cement work, but I was always amazed how someone who had always lived in a city environment in Holland and who had always been an electrician could just start making his own steel framed windows and build a house as though it was the normal thing to do. The house looked very nice and we were all very proud of Dad. My job in the country meanwhile was providing me with a very good income and when Dad wanted to start his own business, I was able to help him financially.

I would return to my family about once a month and tell them all the things I had learned in my time away and was always able to bring back a manageable bag of damaged seed left over from the grading operation, which Dad would use for his chickens. I worked with Hannafords for two seasons, about one year in total, and had varied districts allocated to me. Later the districts were further and further away from Woodville as the firm learned to trust the work I was doing and the good reports from farmers I dealt with. My districts included areas of the Eyre Peninsula, such as Streaky Bay, Ceduna, Kimba and Poochera, after Port Wakefield, Port Broughton and so on.

When the grading season was over, I would have to find another job to tie me over and apart from turning my hand to some door to door selling, I had a few months of work at an old-fashioned grocery store on Marion Road assisting customers and doing delivery work.

BIG CHANGES – MARRIAGE AND CHILDREN

It was during the off season that I met Cathryn who I later married. We had met one Saturday night on the dance of the Goodwood Stadium and started going out together on the Sunday. She was a sunny character, always ready for a laugh and came from a good Aussie background. Her mum's family was Irish, and her dad Baden came from Oodnadatta.

It was not long before were 'going steady,' both working every day and going to the Prospect pictures on Saturday nights. Only once during our courtship did we escape the watchful eye of her strict Catholic mum and managed a weekend away together with my sister and her fiancée, Bill, a Dutch lad, who to this day is one of my best friends. Cath's mum read the riot act to me after we came home. Fortunately, I did not get Cath pregnant (no pill in those days) otherwise the 'riot act' would have been much worse and not only that, but my own parents would have added their bit as well.

All was going well and then Cath needed an arthroscopy due to a netball injury and she spent a few days in Parkwynd Hospital in Wakefield Street. On one of my evening visits to the hospital, in a moment of madness, (I was only 19), I suggested we should get married and Cath said 'Yes.'

After the visiting hours were over, I stood outside on the footpath before going home and thought OMG what have you done, you have no proper job and no future. Mind you, Cath's family thought that I would have a job in a grocery store for the rest of my life. Little did they know!

So, it was then and there on the footpath that I decided to start studying to get some qualifications that would make use of my Amsterdam high school diploma and would further my/our life.

The next morning I succeeded in getting an interview with the Director of Studies at the South Australian Institute of Technology, Professor Lyall Braddock, who assured me that if I could pass various tests such as English and Maths entrance examinations I could start a course to become a qualified accountant. And so started some 11 years of evening studies, lectures, tutorials, and two years of post-graduate work at Flinders University.

We got married on the 15th of November 1957, when I was 20 and because my time with Hannafords had given me a pretty good income, we were able to start building a new house on Lower North East Road at Highbury which was then a rural community. We moved in early in 1958. But just like my parents' humble beginnings, we only built a half house to start us off. We designed the house ourselves and had great assistance from our neighbour Bill North, who was the local building inspector and who advised me on the requirements of the council for soil tests and specifications. We also had many friends and relations who were willing to help with the pouring of the concrete footings and that was how things were done then by Dutch migrants, you helped each other.

We did much ourselves but engaged a builder to do the brickwork and carpentry. Dad was the electrician and Cath and I painted inside and outside. I laid my own sewer pipes, dug the septic system and built the tank, laid all the concrete paths and driveway and so on.

That half house, a true 'back-ender,' had full concrete foundations, a large lounge/bedroom, a kitchen, laundry with a built-in shower alcove and of course a toilet. Two years later when the first half had been paid for, we had the front half built with three bedrooms and a bathroom and a very nice front entrance and garage.

But, I am running ahead of myself. Our honeymoon was spent at Victor Harbour with a couple of short interruptions when I needed to go to Adelaide to sit for my first exams, which I passed.

We had three children during our marriage, unfortunately the first, a little girl, did not survive the birth, a great source of sadness to us both and it made us very anxious the next time. However, this time all went well and a healthy son, Stephen was born on 21st February 1963 followed some 15 months later, 23rd May 1964, by a gorgeous little girl Susan.

While all went well with the birth of Steve, there was still an hour of panic. The birth announced itself early that afternoon and I was then working in the city. Unfortunately, the 21st of February was also the very day that Queen Elizabeth, who was visiting Adelaide was due to attend a school-children's presentation at the Victoria Park racecourse. The entourage left Government House to travel by motorcade to the racecourse and the entire route was closed for two hours.

Those who know the map of Adelaide, will appreciate that the Queen's route was the exact route that I had to cross to rush home to Highbury to collect my wife for the trip to Calvary Hospital.

I informed the police on duty at various points of the route that this was an emergency, but they would not budge and let me through. My panic was aggravated very much by the memory of our first baby. In the end I had no choice but to phone home from a shop in Rundle street and Cath went to the hospital by taxi and even the taxi driver was not happy about it. A harrowing day altogether, but what a great ending when I was told; 'You have a healthy little boy.'

The plan hatched at that time on the footpath in Wakefield Street was obviously the right move and it did indeed start a completely new and interesting career path which not only brought substantial improvement in our financial situation but made my life much more interesting and rewarding in other ways.

Right through my study years I had a working life as well as studying and the 40-hour week became a thing of the past. The part time studies were difficult at times and weekends before exams were spent swotting away from Cath and the kids. My mother-in-law, Evelyn had forgiven me my earlier indiscretions by this time. She was always very supportive when we needed her, and I often used her house at nights and weekends to study. This was a great help as I had a full-time job where the hours worked every day were getting more and more demanding. Evelyn is long gone, and it is a pity she cannot read these words.

JOHN'S BUSINESS CAREER
By Peter Morton

In 1957, just before he was married, John got a job at Phillips, a large business in Hendon and he had to study part time. But he soon left when he had passed his first year of accounting studies and joined MTPA, debt collectors, later to become Dunn and Bradstreet. He then joined ASM a manufacturer of saucepans and assorted sheet metal objects. At their annual shindig at Yaldara winery in the Barossa Valley John experienced one of the significant events in his life. He had only just started drinking alcohol and that day he got stone motherless, drunk as a skunk, pissed as newt, full as a tick and whatever else. So much so that despite being a connoisseur of champagne and other wines he has never got seriously drunk again. A man of great character.

Next came Wunderlich in Adelaide, much exposure to asbestos and importantly passing his first accountancy degree to become a fully-fledged member of the Australian Society of Accountants and he was ready to take on the world as an accountant but that meant change again.

In 1964 he joined a large engineering firm, Mechanical Handling PL and became a Fellow of the Australian Society of Accountants and Company Secretaries.

After five years he was head hunted by a Dutch flooring company Forbo and in 1969 moved to Melbourne and then back to Adelaide to an office on Greenhill Road to implement a full costing and accounting system for the new Elizabeth plant. It was not long before John was asked to present himself at the head office in Zurich, something he always had in the back of his mind with this job.

Unfortunately, all that glitters is not gold and the distance and inability to make decisions in Australia about Australian tastes rendered the company inoperable in Australia and John had to sack everyone. Interestingly John referred to this as a fashion business which you could not say about engineering where a different philosophy applied.

In 1984 Forbo Zurich bought Nairn Ltd., a flooring and wallpaper concern, from Unilever and asked John to transfer their operation to Sydney.

In 1976 John and Cathy's marriage collapsed, brought on by an affair by John in Europe, who later married the lady in question but was divorced soon after.

But all was not lost. On the 24th July 1984 he met an Adelaide girl of Dutch origin, Ria, at his youngest sister Rietje's home. They fell in love and moved to Sydney and soon married and 35 years later they are still together. John's son later married Ria's daughter another interesting facet of life.

Their time in Sydney was interesting and they were in a fast social whirl and deeply immersed in the Sydney social and music scene particularly jazz and the Sydney Symphony Orchestra. They built a new house in West Pennant Hills that took two years to complete and soon after John left the Forbo company after 14 years and joined Swedish multinational

Tarkett. Under John they became by far the biggest commercial flooring company in Australia. John's personal status in the company was such that he was appointed in 1991 CEO of the Dutch offshoot Tarkett Netherlands.

He and Ria spent six years in the Netherlands and had a wonderful time travelling all over Europe to work and play. They returned to Australia in 1997 and it must have been soon after that when I and Leonore, my wife, met John and Ria. A wonderful friendship developed that I cannot credit that we have now been friends for more than 20 years. How time flies.

COFFIN BAY – RESTAURANT AND RETIREMENT

Many years ago, when living in Sydney, Ria and I had stumbled upon Coffin Bay on the Eyre Peninsula in South Australia almost by accident and immediately fell in love with it. It was a great place to relax, far from the hustle of city life, a place with wonderful beaches surrounding the tranquil waters of Coffin, Kelledie, Yangie and Dutton Bays with a Port Douglas thrown in.

With a population around 600 people, its only commercial activity was oyster farming and a home for some of the cray fishers that had worked from the Coffin Bay wharf for many years. Little did we know then that it would play such a large role in our life. In 1985 we were told by a very good friend of ours, who happened to be a real estate agent, that the house he had arranged for us to rent in Coffin Bay was for sale. Ria said, 'Buy it.' We did and we have never regretted it.

Ten years later when we returned to Australia from Europe, we decided that we would live in Adelaide for the comforts of city living and spend our summers in Coffin Bay to enjoy not only the boating, the fishing, and the rest of seaside environment, but also the friendships and hospitality that only country living can offer.

An even greater pleasure was to catch up with our children. Ria's elder daughter, Natalie, married my son Stephen in 1990 before we went overseas and they had children in 1998 and 2000, Hannah and Sophie respectively after we returned to Australia.

By that time Ria's younger daughter, Rebecca, already had a son Taliesin, born in 1995.

My daughter Susan has never married but had a steady relationship with David. So, three of our children lived in Coffin Bay or Port Lincoln, the exception being Rebecca who lives in Adelaide. Susan living in Coffin Bay improved our relationship more than I had ever dared to dream and that has been wonderful.

Coffin Bay attracted tourists and many of our friends. A number of friends we had made while we were in Europe came to visit us and as we always seemed to be entertaining friends with dinners and general hospitality. The thought often occurred to start doing that entertaining professionally as I did not feel I was ready to retire. I had been reenergised by this lovely place. In 2000 we bought a small, run down and unviable Chinese restaurant on the seafront and everyone who drove into Coffin Bay passed it. It had the three most important things a business needed, position, position, and position!

This would be the only café/restaurant in Coffin Bay but the pub, sporting club and the yacht club all provided excellent meals. What possessed us? A good question!

My good friend, Sam Coughran and I worked for four months together, with a number of tradesmen, electricians, bricklayers, floor tilers and carpenters, to completely rebuild the old building and turned it, plus the next-door craft shop, into a brand-new seafood restaurant. It was the talk of the town for 10 years until something supposedly better came along.

Our cuisine consisted mostly of seafood and, as one would expect, and we specialised in oysters. The new name was 'The Oysterbeds' and we served a choice of 12 different styles of oysters.

Needless to say, in a small town like Coffin Bay it was difficult to attract professional chefs and there were times when Ria had to jump in and keep the cooking going. My main job was that of sommelier and generally 'front of house'.

When not needed in the kitchen Ria managed the dining area and so many other things. Looking back on that period, it was hard work, 100 hours a week, and financially not really rewarding, but we kept our head above water and made so many good friends.

For many years after we had sold the business, we kept getting the same message from our old patrons, 'The Oysterbeds Restaurant has never been as good as when you two were running it.' Frankly, that is one of the highest accolades that anyone can receive.

The sale of the restaurant and eventually the sale of the buildings finally allowed us to fully appreciate all the delights of Coffin Bay, the sea, the fishing and above all the hospitality and friendship of the township and its people.

THE HEALTH OF SEAMEN IN THE ROYAL NAVY 1762

I am indebted to Captain Rob Cobban for this absolute jewel from the bowels of the Royal Navy about the treatment of persons suffering from immersion hypothermia. *Ed.*

"But let us turn our eyes to those in a state more justly demanding the Attention of Humanity; such as have been unfortunately to drowned. So soon as a person supposed to be drowned is taken out of the water, he ought not, as usual, to be held up long by the Heels; the continuance in such a posture is the most likely means to prevent him from coming to life. The head must be inclined in a position favourable to empty the stomach; mean while the utmost dispatch is used to remove all the cold, wet cloaths, by stripping the person quite naked, and immediately exposing the body to the heat of the warm sun, or fire, to prevent stiffness and cold; or, to regenerate heat, he may be put in a bed well warmed, where the belly, breast, and especially the pit of the stomach, must be well and constantly rubbed with warm clothes, keeping the Head and Face gently inclined forwards, as in a person under the operation of an Emetic. At the same time, the Limbs must be well chased with hard coarse clothes, made very warm, and the whole body often shook or rolled about. All possible attempts must be made from the beginning to bleed; and there in different Veins. The

temporal Artery may also be cut. Warm Bricks, Irons, or bottles of Hot Water must be applied to the Feet; volatile salts, and stimulating spirits to the Nostrils; and air, moderately heated by being near a fire, blown by means of a Bellows into the Anus and Lungs. Or, a person that chew Garlick may endeavour to blow into the Lungs with his Breath, keeping the Nostrils of the Patient shut for a few seconds of time to prevent its escape; meanwhile, another person, by a gentle alternate pressure and dilation of the Ribs with a corresponding alternate Compression of the contents of the belly upward, imitates as near as possible the Act of Respiration in a living Body. A Clyster of Tobacco smoke may also be given, and Tobacco moistened, or its Juice, may be put into the Mouth, from the stimulus of which in the throat and stomach, a Recovery and Vomiting has sometimes ensured.

Though these Means should not speedily produce the desired effect, yet the person is not to be relinquished. They must be repeated and continued for some Hours, keeping the Body all the while warm, or in a hot place, persevering in the Concussions and Rollings; and lastly, he may be immersed and kept for some Time in a Bath of luke warm water, after which, the former Means are to be again assayed."

THE CONTRIBUTORS
(In Order of Appearance)

Editor's Choice
We have four children, Kirstin, Sarah, Tim and Peter. Five stories have been written by our immediate family. They are Kirstin's son Jackson Croser aged 20, Sarah Holden, Tim's wife Lisa and, their 10-year-old daughter Laila and Michael Sullivan, Leonore's brother. I will let them talk for themselves.

Colin Gamble
We have become friendly with Colin and his American partner, Terri, through the Chicken and Chablis club. He is a larger-than-life character physically being involved for many years at a high level as a rugby player and surf lifesaver in Wollongong. He also worked there from a trainee in metallurgy in 1970 to Senior Supervisor BHP shipping Department in 2002. They then moved to Port Lincoln where Colin worked in the prison system as an escort officer, a JP and a mentor for students at the high school. He has a BSc, BA and several diplomas and certificates in a range of subjects. He is an experienced traveller as is Terri and there are few subjects where he cannot add something to the conversation.

Dick Matson
We met Dick and his wife Sheri, from Washington State USA,

on a sailing, walking holiday for a few days in Tasmania in 2019, both of us and wives celebrating or Golden Weddings. We got on well together and his stories revealed amazing experiences in the USA and elsewhere few adventurers could match. He also likes books and writing and had some military experience in an engineering unit in the US Army as I did in Australia so that was a good place to start and we have progressed from there. They plan on visiting next year. After reading his stories Australia seems rather humdrum!

I served as a part-time citizen soldier in the Oregon Army National Guard from 1969 until 1992. I graduated from Oregon Military Academy (the State's officer candidate school) in 1971 and was commissioned a Second Lieutenant. From then until my retirement in 1992 I served in various engineer units and one infantry unit (as engineer officer) throughout Oregon in positions of increasing responsibility. About a third of my time was in command positions at the unit and battalion levels and my last assignment was as commander of the 1249th Combat Engineer Battalion headquartered in Salem, Oregon which consisted of about 750 men and women in companies scattered across western Oregon. At the conclusion of that command, because of increasing demands from both my military and civilian employers, I chose that time to resign my commission and was honourably discharged at the rank of Lieutenant Colonel. Sheri and I made a lot of good friends during this chapter of our lives and still keep in touch with many of them. In fact, one of the highlights of our summer - at least before the pandemic struck - was to host an annual gathering at our home of those we bonded most closely with.

We were never mobilized for combat during my times of

service and the most action I ever saw was a bar fight in El Paso, Texas while on a pass during basic training at Fort Bliss.

Jacqui Bateman
Her story has been told largely in the book but she has been an amazing contributor to Australian Veterans who, with their families, are suffering illness and other problems due to their military service. This started in her home town of Robe and has been adopted in a smaller way in several towns in Australia including Port Lincoln.

Terry Holden
He is our daughter Sarah's father-in-law and a man again who has also had problems in his life that he has faced with great courage. He is blessed with a wonderful wife, Judy, who pushed the right buttons for Terry to write his story about Vietnam. His comments about the importance and lack of recognition of the less colourful and dramatic branches of the Australian Army was perceptive, interesting and true. I can't think of anyone I would sooner share grandchildren with! 'On ya Tez'

Bill 'Swampy' Marsh
One of Australia's best-known writers having written 25 books about Australiana and other subjects, a magician, song writer and singer. He inspired and guided me on my first literary voyage four years ago and has been a friend and guide again for my current efforts. I have learnt an immense amount from Bill about the world of writing in Australia—it is tough.

Henning 'Chook' Kath
He is the real deal in the Queensland outback. Rodeo rider, worked all over the place and spent 20 years managing Mount Leonard Station, a high-powered rifle shot from the Beetoota Hotel, 165 km due east of Birdsville. He and his wife Lorraine headed north last January.

They were very hospitable when we were researching a book about Leonore's family, who once were part owners in the Station, particularly when we occupied their guest quarters, as we were surrounded by floods for a week. Most people would laugh at Mr North East, but 'Chook' was kind. I hope one day I can nail down some more stories from him and, indeed, Lorraine.

Ian and Sue Bishop
We have known their son Chris and his wife Erinn (it is not misspelt – it's Canadian) for some years as they are friends of our son Tim and his wife Lisa. They had dinner with us on New Year's Eve 2020 we discussed this book and that led to Ian and Sue, who we had not met before, each writing a yarn. They were beautifully written, as Sue is a teacher and perfectionist, with very interesting subject matter. They are gifted and lovely people and obviously devoted to each other to a rare degree. Vale Ian. The short time I knew you was a privilege. I am sorry you left us before you saw the story in print.

Gavin Stevens
An ex-test cricketer who was very close to my parents and me and nearly died in India from hepatitis many years ago.

Paradoxically that can be seen, perhaps, as a good thing because he would have been unable to play first class cricket for a year or more or perhaps ever. He used the determination that is inherent in an opening batsman and became very successful in the retail food industry. He is nearing 90, a milestone his wife, Betty, has reached. They are both generous with their time and kindness, e.g. Betty has made 200 quilts for charity. Gavin's mind is sharp and he follows the Indian economy closely. I am sure he did not expect the ending I tacked onto his story!

Aileen Pluker
Ninety years young on 27 Feb 2021 she celebrated her birthday at the Boston Bay Winery in Port Lincoln. There were almost 100 people there from her church, choir, the Eyre Writers' group, her immediate family, Siam station where she had organised help with education for the children, teachers and others like me who she has helped. She is a teacher, a devoted catholic, a writer and a woman who has suffered the slings and arrows of outrageous fortune more than most. An amazing person.

Robert Cotton
I am indebted to Robert and family for allowing me to include this eulogy that was read at his father's funeral.

Malcolm Schluter
Malcolm was a South Australian Chief Inspector in Port Lincoln and very well regarded. He also made his mark in our community during and after his career as a leading

Freemason in Port Lincoln and South Australia, a Rotarian and caretaker of the Nyroca Scout Camp, near Coffin Bay. He also has had many challengers in life he has faced with pluck and a cheerful manner.

Jayde Shields
We are neighbours at nearby Coffin Bay and have only met once. The conversation we had led to him writing a wonderful story, 'Silence,' his first. He left school at 15 and for seven years was a 200-sheep-a-day shearer in Western Australia and since then he has worked on drilling rigs in Queensland. It may well be the best story in the book.

Peter Kennedy
Peter is a local product, their family owning Eyre Traders in Port Lincoln and he did his apprenticeship in Port Lincoln. As he tells in his story, this was only about the first few years of his overseas career that he has lasted close to 30 years. If anyone could and should write a book it is him! Covid has thrown up some strange meetings and his partner, Cindy, a Canadian has been stuck in Port Lincoln for some time. Not one to let the grass grow under her feet she became interested in Probus where Peter's mother is a member and my wife the President at the time. She took on the onerous task of Secretary and that was most appreciated.

Brian Mills
Brian has worked in the mid north, far west and Eyre Peninsula areas of South Australia with SA Water for decades and I had the privilege of working closely with him, doing

some consulting work, when he was Regional Manager in Port Lincoln in the 1990s. He is unfailingly polite, well mannered, loves quiz nights and the English language 'as she is wrote and talked' as do I. He is, 'The pedant's pedant.' And thank heavens for that. His wonderful yarn about Bill Whitty was dissected, cut and shut, argued about in content, context, accuracy and relevance between him, the writer and me, the editor, for 34 hours and 18 minutes.

It was great fun and I owe Brian a huge thanks for the proof reading of the four books I have written.

Capt. Rob Cobban
Rob has written an excellent and amazing biography. Like Brian Mills at SA Water I met Rob, the Port Lincoln Harbour Master, when doing some consulting work with the Marine and Harbours Department. I doubt I have seen anyone calmer or more self-reliant. The events he described are very interesting and as they say on TV, 'But wait there is more.' He has designed and built a mud brick house on Winter's Hill in Port Lincoln with bricks he made by hand years ago and planted an orchard of olives and Australian natives for the fresh flower market. He is a business man and entrepreneur and at the time of writing is building a 30-40m x 2m wall by hand around his house with materials he imported from Asia. He has a home in Thailand and for variation has a WW2 Jeep he restored. I am unsure if he works on his Porsche.

Years ago he told me he used to do star jumps on the decks of various ships plus other exercises. When we discussed his article I asked him whether he still did this stuff and he replied, 'Not really just a bit of this' and put his hands on the arms of the wooden chair where he was sitting and lifted his bottom about six inches off the seat!

Chris and Ann Watts
Teachers at La Grange Mission south of Broome where I used to visit and do clinics long, long ago and we have remained friends since. They even visited Port Lincoln from their home south of Geelong for the launch of my previous books, a terrific gesture. Sadly, Chris is not enjoying good health as I write this and I wish him well.

Neville Gregory, Terry Hill, Rod McLeod and Ron Potter
Almost the first story I received. Well written and amazing stuff. Personal details in the story.

Mary Gudzenovs
A very clever lady with computers, cameras and books with two degrees in History and Ancient History and has been the midwife for some 40 books. This book would not have happened without her. Leonore and I have enjoyed this journey and Mary's cheerful outlook and encouragement has a big part in that. Thanks a million Mary.

Dr Stephen Ballard
Steve and I worked at the Investigator Clinic for more than 12 years and he then moved to Port Augusta and worked for the Royal Flying Doctor service for 21 years and four years since as a GP anaesthetist and a Visiting Medical Officer with expertise in emergency medicine. What he can do and does, and the stories he tells me, makes me shake my head in

amazement.

He has an amazing mind and knowledge of languages, history, medicine and many other subjects far more than I can begin to pretend. The story he has written about Covid makes a difficult subject understandable.

Angela Moloney OP
Angela, a nun, came from Ireland to Adelaide many years ago as a postulant attached to Cabra Convent (now Cabra College) in Adelaide where my wife and sisters went to school. Leonore's elder sister, Susan, became a nun and is very much part of this story.

I met Leonore in 1968 and Susan was Sister Mary Fabian and likely to live a sheltered and restricted life in a convent seeing her family rarely.

I am a little rusty on the details but when we were married in 1969 she wore a habit but was only allowed to take part by guarding our wedding gifts in the family home wearing her habit. In early 1970 she joined us on a camping trip to the Flinders Ranges wearing extremely modest, shapeless clothes but not a habit. She lived in the convent at the time. Two years later she was attending University and sharing a cottage in the Cabra gardens and wearing normal modest dresses etc. Soon after that she was living in normal houses. Quite a change.

Graham Fleming
I am grateful for the honesty and courage of Graham in responding to my email.

Peter Hawke
I am pleased to call Peter a friend. From 1996 to 2002 I shared his Physiotherapy rooms with his lovely wife Mary the receptionist. I don't recall a cross word in all that time. His story about his beloved dad and uncle is well researched and written. It is a sad and no doubt has features of many stories from those times but the coincidence of those two young men meeting and what followed was the stuff of fairy tales both good and bad. How they lead successful lives and had loving families is heart-warming.

John Versteeg
His story has largely been told but he and Ria his wife, have become great friends of my wife Leonore and me. They have, in the book and in life, shown and told us about a world we knew nothing about from life in a world at war to travelling the waters of Europe in a house boat.

They also have had and still do have significant physical and personal challenges in their day to day lives that they approach with courage and good humour.

www.ingramcontent.com/pod-product-compliance
Lightning Source LLC
Chambersburg PA
CBHW071233290426
44108CB00013B/1397